Exposing Fraud

Exposing Fraud

Skills, Process and Practicalities

IAN ROSS

WILEY

Library of Congress Cataloging-in-Publication Data is available

A catalogue record for this book is available from the British Library.

ISBN 978-1-118-82369-9 (hbk) ISBN 978-1-118-82368-2 (ebk)
ISBN 978-1-118-82367-5 (ebk) ISBN 978-1-119-17749-4 (ebk)

Cover Design: Wiley
Cover Image: © Mega Pixel/Shutterstock

Set in 10/13pt PhotinaMTStd and UniversLTStd by Aptara, New Delhi, India
Printed in Great Britain by TJ International Ltd, Padstow, Cornwall, UK

To Neil

Contents

Preface

A consistent view across many investigators of fraud, including myself, is that fraud is, arguably, the creator of more criminals than any other area of crime. The temptations which reach and 'turn' people who last week either had no criminal history – or in any case had no notion to commit a crime of this kind of aggravated dishonesty – are too much to ignore. The numbers of fraud offenders swell at a frenetic rate in all manner of business or other opportunist situations and places. Fraud as both a crime and an entity also ranges from levels that perplex the work of both the investigation and prevention of it. Hence, as a crime, fraud brings a unique set of problems not usually present in other criminal scenarios.

The above statement is not to be confused or misunderstood to mean that corruption (or money laundering) is less serious than fraud. Nor is it the case that corruption is more serious than fraud, albeit that media reporting of corruption carries a higher emotive character of public and business community awareness. In fact, the reporting of fraud tends to be coded or sporadic. A high-profile fraud case will attract a news headline, but it needs to be exceptionally serious, whereas corruption is spread across national newspapers and TV news, and even splashed around social media sites openly by community members and non-professional people commenting on financially driven crime. There is no attempt made in this book to explain why this is so, but merely to highlight an irony, in that pitching and achieving 'fraud awareness' even to some professionals is a more arduous task than that of publicising or fostering understanding of corruption initiatives. In this context fraud plays second fiddle to corruption, yet *fraud* is as rampant as any other economic crime.

Therefore in writing this book, I convey the notion that investigating fraud is *the* ultimate challenge in investigating crime. That is if we *choose* to make the effort needed, and surmount the hurdles we must overcome in investigating fraud at any level or scenario.

Ian Ross

Foreword

Fighting fraud is hard work. I have been fighting fraud and crime for over 40 years. As I write this, I have just returned from the Association of Certified Fraud Examiners' global fraud conference. There were nearly 3,000 people there with a single purpose: to detect and prevent fraudulent conduct.

As I stood on the stage and looked at the sea of faces in the audience, I found myself wondering why someone would want to do this work. It is certainly not glamorous. Fraud examiners are not celebrities. The work is often tedious, and a complex case can take a year or more to investigate and present to prosecutors.

So why then do people want to do this for a living?

I can't speak for everyone, but I can say that for many people, it is the satisfaction that comes from the work. The types of fraud schemes are limited only by the human imagination – so there is always an opportunity to learn something new.

Likewise, each fraud case is different – different people, industries, amounts, methods. And although a good investigator follows a well-conceived plan, that plan is constantly changing as new facts and information are found.

But as complex as things get, as many late hours as you put in, you feel good at the end of the day because you have prevented someone from stealing the hard-earned assets of your client or organisation. Running a successful business is hard. No one can afford to lose money or assets to thieves and fraudsters. There is no greater reward than helping the good guys and punishing the bad guys.

If you are reading this book, then it means you have that innate drive to do the right thing and stop those who don't. It won't always be easy, and many times it will be frustrating. When it gets hard, remember this quote, believed to have originated from the philosopher Edmund Burke: 'The only thing necessary for the triumph of evil is for good men to do nothing.' Welcome to the group of us who refuse to do nothing.

James D. Ratley, CFE
President and CEO
Association of Certified Fraud Examiners
Austin, Texas

About the Author

Ian Ross MSc, CFE, CICA, IAiP

- Regional Director: GIF Consultora
- Associate Consultant: Intersol Global.
- Full Associate: International Academy of Investigative Psychology (IAiP)

A former United Kingdom (UK) police officer, since then Ian has undertaken fraud investigations in a range of international locations and contexts. Specific cases have involved high-end value insurance frauds, procurement and corporate fraud and money laundering.

Ian is recognised as a leading incisive, clinical and dynamic investigator.

Strategically, Ian is a fraud control advisory and investigations project lead, with oversight of enhanced business-critical due diligence operations. Implicit within Ian's experience is advising companies concerning corporate espionage.

A highly sought after global trainer, Ian has delivered fraud detection and prevention training programmes to a range of audiences across five continents, of police forces, the military, and corporate clients. Likewise, Ian has presented at numerous global events, including for the ACFE.

Ian has given numerous television and newspaper media interviews in Africa and the Middle East and has authored numerous articles on fraud and money laundering.

Acknowledgements

I would like to express my thanks to colleagues with whom I have had productive working relationships over thirty years of involvement with investigating fraud (some of whom would not have thought at the time that they would be thanked in the context of countering fraud at some later point).

To certain former colleagues in Greater Manchester Police (UK) who were *truly* in the battle against fraud, withstanding the internal tide and overriding institutional notions of fraud being a 'victimless' crime. Of course, it was then led by the most inspirational Chief Constable in English policing history, James Anderton. It was an honour Sir.

Post police service, I thank the following colleagues:

Anatoly Yakorev, Director at the Moscow Centre for Business Ethics & Compliance.

James Ratley, President of the Association of Certified Fraud Examiners (ACFE) for the foreword to this book.

Professor Eric Shepherd, a name of world renown in our area. Massively inspirational, and whose academic and vocational brilliance benefits so many. 'SE3R' and 'Conversation Management' are but two such hugely influential contributions ahead of their time, that have shaped so many investigative interviewing best practices in so many places. Professor Shepherd's kind permission to include these models is highly appreciated.

Suleiman Al Rawahi, Senior Auditor, Ministry of Defence, Sultanate of Oman.

Ehi Esoimeme, associate within Deji Sasegbon (SAN) Nigeria, author of so many excellent scholarly articles and an asset to the anti-money laundering cause overall.

Laurie Pieters-James, Forensic Criminologist at Expert Profiling, Johannesburg. CNN Commentator and renowned author. Supporting victims and the courts, Laurie does so with clinical precision to ensure integrity and justice in the most serious of criminal cases. Thank you for these excellent contributions, filling in gaps of informing behavioural aspects of fraud offending.

Pablo Colombres, GiF Consultora, Buenos Aires. The best and most highly skilled field investigator anyone could work with.

Dr Spyridon ('Spiro') Samonas, Virginia Commonwealth University, USA, and the London School of Economics. Senior lecturer. Cybercrime expert. Thanks for your great support.

John Hughes, Director of Interventions, Hertfordshire Probation Trust, (UK). A modest but inspirational man, who radiates trust and integrity. Communication, understanding and tolerance development learned from John has found a rightful place here. Thanks John.

DISCLAIMER (1)

All efforts have been made to ensure that this book is accurate and free from error.

The information provided herein should be regarded as guidance and not as a single source of reference.

The author and contributors to this publication do not purport that the publication ought to be used for the purposes of providing legal advice and shall neither have liability or responsibility to any person or entity concerning any loss, damage or injury caused or alleged to be caused directly or indirectly by any information contained within or deemed to be omitted from this book.

DISCLAIMER (2)

This book is not a guide on 'how to' commit fraud. Neither should it be assumed to be such.

Structure and Method of the Book

Welcome to *Exposing Fraud: Skills, Process and Practicalities,* which I hope you will find to be interesting and appropriate.

OPENING THOUGHTS …

The fact that you are reading this book has, I believe, triggered three essential points in your subconscious or nascent feelings towards fraud as a crime. These are, that fraud is a crime of deceit and dishonesty actively or silently practised. Next, that you are ready for the challenge of understanding the extent and nuances of how fraud is committed in a set of wide scenarios in either a course of study or a situational crime prevention role appropriate to you. Crucially also, why victims, including corporate-identity fraud victims, are reluctant, even dismissive when it comes to reporting being a victim of fraud. Thus a peculiar and slightly warped circle revolves, because already it is clear that as at the first point just made, the atrocious criminal behaviour to cheat someone out of something without any hesitation or remorse ought to be enough to make the whole matter of discussing and dealing with fraud straightforward. But it is not. Our circle becomes slightly misshaped when the conflicting terminologies and confusing dialogue appears. Likewise, we will encounter and clarify some varying meanings to what fraud is as a crime, with definitions in some countries and regions having side-effect meaning to definitions of fraud.

Then, we come to realise the fact that there are deeper victim reactions to fraud, more so than other crimes. To be a victim of fraud is to be made a fool of. Certainly in this regard also, the historical thinking amongst enforcement authorities and even the courts in many jurisdictions have demonstrated little sympathy for fraud victims. Fraud kills, and my offer to you in presenting *Exposing Fraud* means exactly this. After all, it is fraud that is the enemy – not each other.

Of crucial importance also is that this book will primarily deal with FRAUD. Money laundering is a vast area on its own. Likewise with corruption. Some overlaps are inevitable and comparisons will be made, but any overlaps and links will be kept to a minimum, selectively pulled out if the crime informs a larger fraud scenario (such as a bribe to another to forge something or accept something that is fraud itself and further that activity, or the laundering of proceeds of fraud) and will be used as linkage phrases or reference points.

Therefore, intended to be a working or resource book, *Exposing Fraud* has a key objective of providing a new focus on fraud investigations, with a refreshing departure from the conventional texts and awareness publications. This book is formed from the 'ground up' by first, instilling awareness, via definitions with added explanations to fuse these together, moving through to concepts of fraud and then through to newfound excellence in investigation and outcomes – and finally training.

 ## APPROACHING COUNTER-FRAUD WORK

To benefit from this book, you need not necessarily be planning a career in law enforcement, or as a 'crime-fighter' per se. Many professionals in many situations can benefit from this advancement of conceptual thought, and in fact many managers do benefit from such materials as this, to enhance their performances in their roles and industries. Much of what you will read is transferable in this regard. You can apply new thinking, problem-solving, and even reading body language effectively, added to IT, communication, study skills, risk assessment, project management skills.

At the same time, the approach to enforcement and awareness and like courses of action also needs to be stabilised – to stop this running off and following the fashionable hypotheses that fraud is 'complex' or so fully technical that it can only be addressed by technical resources, which is a ridiculous attitude. In fact, because fraud is the exploitation of human weakness and fallibility, it is really the case that IT and cyber methods to further fraud attacks are merely a means of leveraging misrepresentation and deceit. This is why the structure of this book is holistic and not merely strictly divided into simplistic or convenient separate parts. The three elements informing this book title form a running theme and thread together all elements and aspects within it.

 ## CHAPTER SPECIFICS

Chapter 1, 'Cutting through the Maze' does exactly this. I aim to codify and achieve succinct *understanding* of fraud as a clear explanation as opposed to wrestling with the bewildering number of self-made definitions of it on so many different fronts. I also present a clear pathway of the most sensible and logical way of viewing counter-fraud work: from awareness, to identification, to detection, to risk management and then to prevention. Definitions are purposely entwined with the law itself. The law is kept to a proportionate amount of content in the book, as I wish to avoid giving an over-chronicled exhaustive account of the law. Instead I give a clear account of the scheme and intention of the law, from overriding legislation into local jurisdictions. We examine the scheme of the law, in what that law was designed for and enacted to achieve. We also make a strong point of the need to understand and apply the concept that evidence is law itself.

Chapter 2, 'Concepts and Dynamics of Fraud Crime', gives indications of being set as categories of fraud, but this is purposely marginalised and builds up a running theme of skill and wider case scenarios, as opposed to mundane realisation of fraud 'types'. Scenarios build knowledge, and these range across finance, accounting, procurement and a range of topics. Costs of fraud are ever-evolving, and are referenced in this chapter.

In this chapter also we address cybercrime as combined with fraud. Many talk about the 'new age' of fraud and fraud IT and electronic *modus operandi* but already some aspects of cyber-fraud are well established and being overtaken by their own dynamics and 'developments'. Underpinning the visible results of cybercrime and 'e-washing', are the feeders of the problems: 'digital fraud', social networking, IT security lapses, and human fallibility.

Chapter 3 is a key focal point of risk: 'Beyond the definitions'. A strong legal backdrop and policy backdrop to your work. Risk assessing as opposed to investigation. Risk thinking is not just about policy setting, it informs better investigative thinking, and hence it is placed at this point in the order of the chapters.

Chapter 4. 'Exposing Fraud: Fraud Investigation at Work'. We step fearlessly into the realm of investigation. This chapter draws on topics that make up the composite professional profile of a fearless competent investigator. You must be exactly that, not brash, offensive, a pathological rule-bender, intimidating, an evidence fabricator – but fearless. This entails dismantling some so-called 'common sense' assumptions that create the myths and knock-on effects to the polarised problems in investigating fraud. Fundamentally, it is crucial that you engage in some self-appraisal of your whole approach to investigating fraud. Investigation is not massively complicated, but it takes clinical approaches, lateral thinking and character to do it well.

One strong inclusion (often missed by investigators) is the ability to perceive 'naturally occurring' evidence from one crime to another. One reason sometimes co-offenders are missed. Also, finding 'trigger points'. This chapter will exemplify this.

To this end also, this chapter has a brief but pertinent engagement with Investigative Interviewing. To conclude Chapter 4, we deal with outcomes reports. This is the culminating of the evidence gathering tasks in a format of showing which the best evidence is and why.

Chapter 5, 'Training and Education'. This chapter lands upon the issue of training. The question posed means exactly what it says concerning what counter-fraud training actually means to all people in all places. This chapter will also benefit the student at university following an academic programme.

This crucial chapter urges the reader to identify and to pull out the maximum benefit for themselves in finding the right training. I encourage that the investigator *insists* on this at whatever stage in her/his career.

 **FINALLY …**

In all, I have set out an ambitious, infilled but proportionate approach to *exposing* fraud. It has grown out of many years of experience between myself and colleagues with an application of strenuous study and investigation in many arenas of fraud activities.

'The only free cheese you will find, is in a rat's trap'
Russian Proverb

CHAPTER ONE

Cutting Through the Maze

Half the work that is done in this world is to make things appear what they are not.

—E. R. Beadle

 ## INTRODUCTION

'Cutting through the Maze.' This chapter attempts to codify and achieve a succinct *understanding* of fraud as a clear (but not over-simplified) explanation. Avoiding the incessant circular discussion around definitions saves time and gains more convictions. Moreover, a common output of this problem among others, being that professionals across investigations, risk and data analysis, audit, are often at odds with each other with the ever-present dilemma on agreeing what fraud actually is.

Risk management and prevention are alluded to but the main emphasis of this book is *investigation*, to introduce you to the issues and nuances of fraud awareness from a fresh perspective, with *practicalities* to combine with your skills, side-by-side.

The run of this first chapter commences with a fundamental engagement of fraud definitions, leading to more involved engagement with the theoretical perspectives and explanations, which are then closed in and combined with practical guidance to reassure you that the definitions are mostly in common with each other, to then lead to a chapter summary of accepted definitions. Therefore, this chapter does not purport or claim to 'reconcile' definitions (which cannot be done) but forms the fundamentals to counter-fraud work and places them into a workable practical perspective.

PLEASE NOTE

When I refer to a fraud 'player' in all chapters, the word **'offender'** is used, as opposed to the word **'accused'**. In *Exposing Fraud*, together we will deal with a range of examples of how cases are both investigated and disposed of. An 'offender' is identified when a case of fraud is established in any context. The 'accused' is normally the reference to a (fraud) criminal who is legally charged (or sued) to appear before a court. Hence, non-police or enforcement Investigators whose cases are addressed by HR policy as opposed to a case for indictment to court, differ in terms of the scale of the standard of proof. Fraud Investigators (not necessarily 'dedicated' Investigators) need to be clear on how far they need to go in 'proving' a case with this describing of a person involved in fraud, and to remove existing confusion.

The above benchmark is to be borne in mind and used as a running element when reading and working through this book.

1.1 WHAT IS FRAUD? THE MOST DEBATED QUESTION

This chapter hits upon one the most challenging aspects of fraud and its explanation: the differences and the argument about that amorphous area which is 'problematic' to some, being the difference between what is fraud and what is 'sharp practice.'

At this early stage in our working together, to help delve into this area, write down your first response to the scenario in the activity below.

Activity:

Please state *your own* understanding of what the word 'fraud' means.

This is not a trick question or a test. It is just to help discover your notions of fraud as an entity as well as a crime at this point.

....

....

....

....

....

Broken down further, and in connection with another which was once at least a burning question, was looking at the 'mis-selling' of financial products by UK banks. Source evidence was gathered which included sales pitches such as, '*Your mortgage application will be viewed "more favourably" if you take out the mortgage protection insurance' – or, 'the credit card insurance is compulsory'.*

So are these two examples fraud? To me, the short answer is yes, as this is over and above and (dishonestly) extraneous to a bona fide business transaction because there is a blatant misrepresentation of fact, actual gain for the offender and actual loss to the parties. Banks in the UK were guilty of systemic and institutional fraud when the staff were given open licence to sell financial products that were needless to a customer by any means. Sales 'techniques' with 'patter' and half-truths were prima facie fraud (and hence why billions of pounds were set aside in compensation in the wake of it). But the practicalities of outcomes are different. Cases of fraud do not always get prosecuted, as we know. No one from the banks went to jail. So this early engagement with definitions and live practicalities is to set out our way forward.

Next, is a fraud case which is an extended example from the above, and we can make use of a case study involving United Airlines in February 2015.

CASE **STUDY**

A currency exchange-rate error in third-party software supplied to United Airlines affected several thousand bookings on United's Denmark-facing website. The technical fault temporarily caused flights originating in the United Kingdom and denominated in Danish Kroners, to be presented at only a fraction of their intended prices.

Because tickets became available at unusually low prices they were instantly 'snapped up' because of the technical errors.

Customers booking the flights (mostly in the US) identified 'Denmark' as their country, in, other words, where their billing statements are received when entering billing information at the completion of the purchase process, and were able, online, to complete their purchase at the mistaken fare levels.

News of these obviously wrong fares spread like wildfire online. 'Bloggers' boasted about buying multiple tickets, hoping that when the mistake was discovered, they would use the consumer authorities to bully United Airlines into honouring the cheaper fares.

Please state if you think this case contains 'fraud' and why. Or, if not, then why not?

....
....
....
....
....
....

The above activity is not a 'test'. It is a platform to engage early and deal with the 'ethical versus fraud' dilemma. Please return to this page and case after the next section, so you can review your account above and re-appraise and sharpen up your approach to fraud as a crime.

Perceptions and representations of fraud

Many academic, legal and vocational disciplines lack definitions to work with, but a polite though honest point made in this chapter (and in furtherance of the good of countering fraud) is that in the world of counter-fraud work there are too many. Academic definitions vary widely and become more and more disparate the more authors become involved and colour the meaning of fraud with their own hypotheses.

As with most serious crimes, many notions of what fraud actually is miss the point of how fraud should be understood, and as such are often fragmented from each other. Moreover, problems persist and lie within inconsistent fraud definitions, political influences, corporate terminology and policy classifications of fraud and inconsistent legislation across jurisdictions.

Therefore, new meanings 'seep in' and germinate as definitions. This cluster of influences sidewind actual fraud definitions as a result of certain policies effectively watering down the law and other fraud investigations and even enforcement, in different ways.

Hence, with the growth of 'fraud awareness', ironically the complexity has increased in understanding what fraud actually is. It has, in some ways, grown out of proportion. The saying goes that 'a little knowledge can be dangerous' and whilst the intentions of the various contributors and injudicious investigators with their definitions are well-meant, they can be collectively and exclusively problematic.

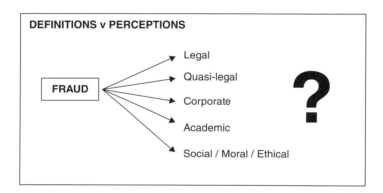

Explanatory Notes

Legal: The issue of definitive requirements in *law* to establish a fraud case MUST be your working 'anchor' (not to interfere with of course multi-jurisdictional fraud cases, which are the ones often left unchallenged) and also will raise the debate if fraud is actually present. For example in US law, a financial gain for the offender and loss for the victim must be present. However, in UK law this is not so because the offence of fraud is now 'offender' focused, and a 'risk' of loss to the victim will substantiate a case of fraud to answer – legally.

Quasi Legal: Not to be underestimated or viewed here as dumbing down the legal, but referring mainly to auditing standards and such mainstream organisations which operate them, such as the 'Big 4' who naturally herald the highest standards in the countering fraud cause. But there is a practicality that appears in that, unlike corporate entities, the courts are not customer-led. Again, it is emphasised that an organisation dealing with auditing and/or investigation of fraud must, and does, work to the legal backdrop, but financial parameters creep in. If, for example, in the event of the discovery of internal fraud, would the audit mandate state the amount concerned should be over a certain value for it to be *fraud*? This is often the case. Hence, the legal and the corporate entities branch away from each other.

Added to the above exemplar is business-related operational services, such as due diligence. A more detailed comparison of the practicalities and overlaps with investigations is made in Chapter 4. If we take the standard definition of due diligence to mean an investigation of a business or person prior to signing a contract or other risk-based project, or an act with a certain standard of care, I trust this gives a brief summary of it. The word 'investigation' throws the understanding slightly, as it invites a myriad of corporate business formalities and practicalities.

Corporate: This refers to the huge inconsistency regarding definitions of fraud. Far too often a discussion of fraud is pulled into different directions in the boardroom. Equally, even in the IT industry, or in corporate settings, it is often the case that definitions are made up to suit, to give a formal analysis of notions of fraud but often in a singular context. For example, key words such as 'specification' and 'verification' of 'normative systems', 'detection and prevention' and 'trade procedures design'. These often represent a fraud possibility as opposed to a fraud definition.

Academic: Fraud definitions are revealed to have a long history (longer than one would expect) and developed since the 15th century. Arguably, not a great deal has changed, because even then, the term 'fraud' included behaviours such as a breach of position of trust.

Newburn (2007) made the most excellent argument that definitions of fraud have been caught up in modern trends and types, and as such the definitions have been narrowed by the contextual attachment of fraud to so-called 'white-collar' crime. But this to my mind creates yet another dimension: that of a vacuum of 'white-collar' crime whereby the meaning has become so frivolous in many quarters, that it now has little useful substance as a definition.

What has happened also is that the academic approach to defining fraud has realised a cross-over with 'categories' which include corruption, theft at work (which will of course align with the US fiduciary breach), 'employment offences' and consumer offences (one which attacks the moral wrongdoing against an innocent consumer at all levels of business to business or to a related business-to-consumer transaction).

Social and Moral: This refers to representations of fraud at street level or media-based terminology, including associated words such as 'scam', 'con', 'swindle', 'extortion', 'double-cross', 'hoax', 'cheat', 'ploy', 'ruse', 'hoodwink', and 'confidence trick'.

Equally, when a case arises which brings in emotional influences (such as a pensioner being conned out of his life savings, or theft from a children's charity) if the element of misrepresentation is present, then the presence of fraud is established with it.

But as in the case of the United Airlines ticket shambles we saw in the case study, the sheer welter of opinion of 'defining fraud' diversified to a massive extent. It even reached the point whereby many publicly blogged online, defying the airline and even trying to allegedly bully the airline by way of the United States Department of Transportation (DOT), a federal department of the US government governing transportation. The point being that the seemingly social acceptance of this was the airline's own fault, so 'tough luck' completely overrode the notion of any kind of wrongdoing at all, let alone fraud.

One commentator wrote a lengthy article denouncing the actions of the 'chancers' and exploiters who took advantage of a golden opportunity to them to secure the most ludicrously cheap transatlantic flight tickets. What was presented is indicative as being one of *the* most talked about points in the field and generated further debate between both active professional consumers of fraud issues and passive recipients alike. Words such as 'lack of character' seeped into the article. The content then transformed into cybercrime with the repeated use of the word 'hacking' (which it wasn't, in any form, because customers simply went onto a website which was promulgated by in-house IT efficiency lapses and paid the prices on display) but certainly the word 'misrepresentation' was rightly used, as customers lied about their localities.

Many responders kept saying over again 'it must be wrong' or 'it's unethical' but then many also concluded 'so therefore it "must" be fraud'. Of course it is 'wrong' to do what these passengers did and this is not so much to be scathing or unsupportive of United Airlines, but this reference is merely to point out the type of debate it presents. You, as a professional or student of the subject, need to be able to unravel the debate and apply a clear, reasoned answer to it (there are extended 'problem solving' scenarios and assessments for you in the investigations chapter).

Definitions, key distinctions and informing elements

The point must be stressed most clearly that this section is intended to establish a baseline standard of knowledge and understanding of what fraud is and what needs to be proved when both investigating and seeking to prevent fraud (including by way of governance and policy).

Therefore as opposed to jumping straight to definitions, I trust the preceding pages served as a platform and build-up to lead us where we are now: the definitions themselves. These now follow with their integral points.

The mens rea *of fraud*

Irrespective of your legal and geographical jurisdiction, the following essential elements must be present before an actual finding of fraud will occur:

- **Misrepresentation** of a fact – a false representation. This gives a connotation of an 'active' false utterance or statement of fraud, such as lying or forging; however, a misrepresentation can also be withholding, concealment and/or non-disclosure.
- Thus the evidence of misrepresentation can be established (causing the victim to act or not act and suffer loss as a result) by standard items of percipient evidence to prove 'lie-based' conduct, such as forged documents, or documents which contain partially

falsified content (such as misrepresentation of the price of an order, or the quantity or quality of imports or exports). Items (forming exhibits) include fake websites, etc.

- A blatant verbal lie can constitute misrepresentation in fraud, but it must have a significant weight of percipient evidence to substantiate it as such.
- The offender *must know* that the statement is untrue. A statement of intended fact that is simply mistaken is not fraud. To be fraudulent, a false statement must be made with intent to deceive the victim. This is usually a straightforward element to prove, once falsity and materiality are established, as most material false statements are designed to mislead.
- The victim's reliance on the false statement must be reasonable. Reliance on an absurdly false statement will not generally give rise to fraud. However, people who are especially gullible or superstitious, for example, or who are illiterate may have a cause of action in fraud if the offender both knew of and took advantage of their condition.
- Finally, the false statement must cause the victim some injury that leaves the victim in a worse position than she or he was in before the fraud.

Misrepresentation. Practicalities

Whether the fraud is committed by an *individual* or by a *corporate identity*, the same standards are applied. It is merely the practicalities that differ in investigations and legal outcomes.

- To inform the above, it must be established that the offender:
  - had *clear* knowledge of the falsity;
  - had *intent* to deceive, to induce the victim to act or give over something in a context that the victim would not have done if the true intention(s) of the offender were known;
  - sought actual reliance on the misrepresentation; and
  - intended to gain from that (mis)representation, or resulted in loss or risk of loss.
- For example, if you interview a 'suspected' fraudster do you think you ought to push the issue until you hear in your own estimation, a clear and total, and unequivocal account or utterance of 'knowledge' or confession of the falsity or practised deception?
- Or, in parallel, if appraising other evidence (documentation, data, footage, 'e-discovery' evidence) what level and kind of detail or perceived clarity do you work towards obtaining?
- Equally, and in the alternative to a direct misrepresentation, a breach of a fiduciary duty. This will be dealt with in this and later chapters as we thread together these issues and questions they raise.

Conveying the misrepresentation

Another critical point to prove is that the misrepresentation of fact was conveyed directly from offender to victim. For example, employees of a company may sell products or offer a service but without *personal* knowledge of any kind of wrongdoing. A sales officer who sells a completely fraudulent insurance policy on behalf of a dishonest company would not have known the policy was bogus at the time of the sale. Hence, in order to prove fraud, the prosecution or investigating authority (if in-house) must not merely demonstrate, but present beyond doubt that the (employee) offender in this example had prior knowledge *and* willingly misrepresented *and* conveyed facts both legally-orientated and in effect, hijacking the entity of a binding contract.

Summary: Misrepresentation

Lie = achieving false insurance claim = but to prove fraud will need authenticity in writing from the insurer

Lie = offering fictitious investments = affirmation by the investigator that the scheme does not exist

Lie = so-called 'phishing' emails = percipient evidence of a scam per se, (production of the email)

Lie = falsifying invoices for personal gain = tracing through an audit trail and engage with auditors

Lie = creating fake website = hacking law firm database, stealing customer IDs = emailing for additional fees or 'disbursements = asking client to pay via bank transfer or on line process on fake website which is identical to the law firm's = fake website then closed down so cannot be tracked.

Lie = forging references = equals lying = fabrication = fraud

Lie = using certain words = misleads = but not a fraud

Definition of fiduciary duty

Definition of 'Fiduciary' (as defined and confirmed by the cases of Svanoe v. Jurgens, 144 111.507, 33 N. E. 955; Stoll v. King, 8 How. Prac. (N. Y.) 299):

- A 'fiduciary duty' is a legal duty to act solely in another party's interests. Parties owing this duty are called *fiduciaries*. The individuals to whom they owe a duty are called principals. Fiduciaries may not profit from their relationship with their principals unless they have the principals' express informed consent. They also have a duty to avoid any conflicts of interest between themselves and their principals or between their principals and the fiduciaries' other clients.
- A fiduciary duty is the strictest duty of care recognised by the US legal system. Hence, albeit the fiduciary duty is governed by the law of the United States, it does cross practically with other jurisdictions. As does the term misrepresentation.
- Moreover, aside to a misrepresentation of fact, fraud is most likely to occur where one party exploits a position of trust and confidence, being a fiduciary relationship. Fiduciary relationships prominently include those between doctors and their

patients, lawyers and clients, financial advisors and clients, and the executives and partners of a corporation and their shareholders.

■ Taking this into another practical aspect, an example of a breach of a fiduciary relationship could be where an employee steals items from the office whilst in a position of trust. (That trust could have been formalised by a contract of employment with HR policy about codes of conduct inbuilt into it.) If the employee conceals the items and removes them, there has been no misrepresentation, but there has been a clear breach of a fiduciary duty. The matter would not, therefore, be a theft but instead a (more serious) matter of fraud by way of the aggravating features of breaching this enhanced standard of trust.

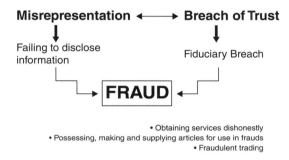

SUMMARY **POINT:**

Repeated is the point that to be a victim of fraud is to be made a fool of. So as harsh as this may seem, it is at the root of ALL fraud investigation cases that you clearly establish fraud in a case. Even if emotional dialogue raging about 'ethics' and right and wrong and insouciantly applied dishonesty is brought in by one of the parties to the case, if there is no misrepresentation of fact for gain or requisite breach of trust you will have a scenario of dishonesty in its basic sense, but you will not have fraud.

 ## 1.2 OTHER DISTINCTIONS

Intent

This means intent to do the harm that was actually done, or recklessness as to whether harm would be done. For example, if A represents something to B and B relies on the representation and the undeniable result of that misrepresentation is loss to the victim (or mere risk of loss in some jurisdictions) and the victim would not have followed an action or paid something had [he] known the offender's true intentions, or the offender is reckless about the loss (such as the scale of amount of money lost), then this will constitute fraud.

The difference between 'misrepresentation' and a hoax

A hoax is a separate action that involves deception but without the intention of gain or of causing loss to the victim. If, of course, the offender 'cons' or misrepresents to the victim as a means of 'poking fun' at the victim but the representation contains such substance of deceit as to cause loss to the victim (incidentally or as 'fall-out') then a *material fact* of fraud could be established. But the misrepresentation must go to a material fact and not merely result in an insignificant issue.

If a sales agent makes a representation to a customer which causes the customer no monetary or any other type of harm, the customer would have a very difficult task to show that this was 'material' and a *fraudulent* statement. An agent, for instance, could misrepresent something which would be of little significance, even though the representation was untrue.

1.3 LYING, FRAUD AND THE STATE OF THE MIND

The trust of the innocent is the liar's most useful tool

—Stephen King

In his book, *Born Liars,* Ian Leslie argues that far from being a 'bug' in the human software, lying is central to who we are; we cannot understand ourselves without first understanding the dynamics of deceit. Using a vivid, panoramic style, Leslie explored the role of deception and self-deception in our childhoods, our careers, and our health, and the part played by lies.

He describes so-called spin doctoring, which is a method, for example, of providing a favourable slant to an item of news, such as potentially unpopular policy, especially on behalf of a personality or party; in short ... the politically acceptable method of lying. One sure example and comparison is when the 'consultation period' leading to the implementation of the UK Bribery Act (and afterward) saw very petulant responses from business leaders against (legally) being made to stop bribery in their own organisations. The dialogue ranged from complaining about costs, to a rather uneasy plateau with directors effectively arguing to be allowed to write their own rules and set up formal business arrangements to effectively allow themselves to act in a corrupt manner. To a point they got their way with help from political meddling and watering down of the Act. Nothing much changes. Setting up the lie to set up the fraud.

The UK Fraud Act of 2006 was enacted to modify the law to deal with fraud as an acquisitive crime (not just to be fooled, as was enshrined in the law before it) but certain lawyers argued that the Act criminalised lying for the sake of it. The four-part definition of fraud as an offence presented a transformation from what was a 'result' crime to a 'conduct' crime (see summary of statutes in this Chapter).

Equally the (legal) need to have a confirmed monetary loss was removed also, with risk of loss being sufficient to set out a case to answer in fraud. The 'catch-all' scheme of the law, the tightening up of the clarity, or better put, simplifying of the *mens rea* ('guilty mind') to be proved made an offence of fraud prima facie easier to prove than before. Easier that is, in terms of lowering the barrier of the standard and burden of proof that favoured the offender instead of the victim. It also showed a break away from the traditional neoconservative way of thinking and the very unhelpful precedent set by Lord Chief Justice Holt circa 1700, in his judgment speech: '*Shall we indict one man for making a fool of another?*'

Hence, one of the most justice-balanced, enforcement-friendly Acts (and ethically so) ever to come from parliament is not used to its full potential by any means. It bridges this gap from the dubious to the legally-proven dishonest.

Does the reliance on a statement or representation or act put someone at risk of loss? Is that utterance or representation firm enough to have no other meaning as to rely on its content, implication or form of 'guidance'? Fraud?

Definitional work in any vocationally-driven profession is crucial, and whilst Chapter 2 will increase the meanings and understanding of this point, it is important even at this stage that we partially expand the explanation of key points to prove, in order to go beyond the basic or literal or dictionary meaning of words like 'lies' and 'misrepresentation'.

A critical pathway in seeing the 'right v wrong v fraud' debate in such a case.

Lying and the problem with words

Fraud cases can involve complicated financial transactions conducted by (to reluctantly quote the vernacular) 'white collar criminals', and professionals with specialised knowledge, underpinned by criminal intent. An unscrupulous investment broker may present clients with an opportunity to purchase shares in precious metals, for example. Status as a professional investor gives credibility, which can lead to a justified belief among potential clients. Those who believe the opportunity to be legitimate contribute substantial amounts of cash and receive seemingly authentic bonds in return, which of course are totally fraudulent.

This example is used as it alludes to lies with a sphere of mostly 'business' dialogue, often thick with tactics. But pulling out the fraud indicators from the semantics can be done, with the right training and application (and 'knowing your business' in Chapter 2).

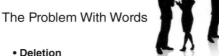

The Problem With Words

- **Deletion**
Language is selective to the experience

- **Distortion**
We simplify what we say. But over-simplification inevitably leads to distortion

- **Generalisation**
We generalise in order avoid spelling out every condition and exception.

For example, the phrase 'mistakes were made' is a statement that is commonly used as a rhetorical expedient, whereby the speaker (really) acknowledges that a situation was badly managed or failed because of low-quality or inappropriate handling of a situation: the speaker seeks to evade any direct acceptance of responsibility by not naming the person who made the mistakes. The acknowledgement of a mistake is often framed in an intellectually uplifted sense. But a 'non-evasive evasive' response might be, 'yes I made the mistake' or 'the buck stops with me'. That speaker neither accepts personal responsibility nor accuses anyone else. The word 'mistakes' also holds an intention to dumb down an admission of liability – especially in fraud. UK politicians caught up in the so-called expenses scandal often used the words, 'errors' and 'omissions'. When we reach Chapter 4 (investigations) I will provide some insight on how to dismantle 'the rules are not clear' type rhetoric which has extended from politicians to corporate fraud offenders.

Activity:

What would you make of the following statement?

In the UK, large positive net errors and omissions likely represent unrecorded financial inflows. As well as cyclical, these inflows are linked to the UK's status as a refuge for international capital flight. For the first time we confirm through balance of payments data the popular belief that Russian money has flooded into the UK in recent years. Indeed, there is strong evidence that a good chunk of the UK's GBP 133bn of hidden capital inflows is related to Russia. Hidden inflows have been marginally supportive of GBP in recent years, and are another factor behind the UK's large current account deficit.

(*Source*: Dark matter: the hidden capital flows that drive G10 exchange rates. Deutsche Bank Market Research Report, 2015)

You could relate such an article to a 'problem with words' as opposed to 'lies' as one cannot help but detect a political agenda by the authors in the above statement. It is not suggested that the writers of the statement are being dishonest. When you encounter a phrase such as *'a refuge for international capital flight'* you will learn, when we deal with 'knowing your business' in the next chapter, that terms such as 'capital flight' are used when money and assets are hastily moved out of a country for any manner of reasons, usually economic collapse. But capital flight often also goes hand in hand with international money laundering.

Therefore, a reasoned response or restatement of that extract could be:

The UK is the money laundering capital of the world, with laughably weak money laundering controls, the ones responsible for controls and regulation being too ready to avert their eyes to billions in illicit revenues pouring into the country, so long as it pours into the country. Ably indulged by non-interested UK enforcement authorities, the point is suitably demonstrated by sporadic enforcement against money laundering that is too disconnected from the law itself.

In fact, what I have done with the statement is a mere extraction of the indicative content and turning the wording and eccentric phraseology back on itself. If you see the issue as *both* an intellectual problem *and* an investigative one, you expose the raw material of the scenario, and you are left with a definite presence of illicit monetary practices and movement in one form or another. You then see which direction money flows come from, then you can work out why, and then move to your analytics and colleagues to trace finer and particular lines of monetary movement as necessary, expose identities and spot relationships and tack these in. The case is now created. Then you address jurisdictional protocols.

Ensure you deal with quality and credible resources if you are a professional who investigates cross-border money laundering and even asset tracing. Appraisal of these kinds of reports is something you really ought to include in your work. From an *investigation of fraud* perspective, seeing evidence of fraud is often only possible (really) when you make yourself clearly aware of what these kinds of terms are and what informs them. Think of known examples of this happening. For myself, take Argentina in early 2000, up to 2002 when the economy collapsed there also, and every bit as it did in Russia (but without the enlarged media and other publicity). I was working there at the time and one gentleman in banking made the point that the country had been 'looted'.

Ethnicity misunderstood: the chasm between belief and actual criminal deception

In the field of investigative psychology, a study took place about word usage differences between truths and lies. Most of the existing research involves an examination of truths and lies in 'low stakes' situations, written statements or interviews (not both) and native speakers of a single language. In handling definitions of fraud, the defining of lying is very open.

Matsumoto and Wang (2014) examined differences in word usage between truth tellers and liars in a moderately high stakes, real-life scenario (mock crime) involving participants from four cultural, ethnic groups: European-Americans, Chinese, Hispanic and from the Middle East. Each participant produced a written statement and participated in an investigative interview; word usage in both was analysed. Word usage differentiated truths from lies in both the written statement and the interview, and the effect sizes associated with these findings were substantial. For the written statement, word usage predicted truths from lies at 68.90% classification accuracy; for the investigative interview, word usage predicted truths from lies at 71.10% accuracy. Ethnicity did not moderate these effects. These findings are discussed in terms of their implications to cross-cultural applicability of the psychological demands placed on liars and in terms of their practical field utility. (Published by Wiley, 2014.)

Following on from the above, compulsive liars are easily spoken about and conjured into conversation, but are not so prevalent in reality in line with lies turning into provable fraud. Lies often go hand in hand with rhetoric. It matters not just to show a lie or lies were told in a fraud case, but that the lie misrepresented a fact sufficiently to the legal standard to make it a criminalised lie, breaking away from the sticking point of the lie being an immoral or unethical one.

 1.4 CUTTING THROUGH THE MAZE

At this point, this model may be useful to proceed with as a workable tool, both to take away the worry of being hung-up on definitions, and to handle a new case (but not to oversimplify it).

'The Three Cs'

The Three Cs

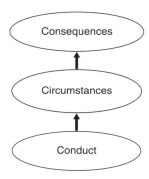

Conduct: Look at the overall conduct, and how the 'players' appear and act in it. Avoid 'relevance filtering' in your reading of the facts. Evidence of fraud will sometimes leap out immediately, but this is not about 'gathering evidence' at this point. It is a brisk and effective appraisal of the case that arrives with you.

Circumstances: The circumstances in which the conduct took place. It may be that this part will lead you to investigate underlying causes and effects of a fraud offender, and related items of evidence to look for in such circumstances of a fraud, such as a corporate fraud, and evidence will (but not exhaustively) include:
   ▦ Manipulated contracts.
   ▦ Fraudulent/forged financial statements.
   ▦ Fraudulent conveyancing.
   ▦ Conflicts of interest.

Consequences The consequences of the conduct in those circumstances. Monetary loss to the victim? Risk? Deferment of debt, to delay, to eventual full evasion by fraud?

Remember also that the **Three Cs** application is a first-point screening process. Your findings from this will then inform a full investigation and how you will prioritise and resource it.

CASE **STUDY**

Using the Three Cs model, review the following case study.

T is the managing director of a security company. He secures government funding by application and subsequent contract for training of his staff (over 2,000 personnel). But T, instead of using the funding for training, uses the money for 'other purposes' in the business (to cover other debts). The company accounts show the funding recorded as 'liquid assets' (assets which can be easily converted to cash).

The following is to be extracted from the scenario:

Conduct: Notes, 'accountancy lies' – fiduciary breach? – accepted government monies specifically released for training and compliance purposes for 'other purposes'?

Circumstances: Notes, unethical practices, informing evidence of fraud appearing in the misrepresentation of how the monies are accounted for in formal company records, recorded as liquid assets is 'red flag' of preparedness for fraud. But is this fraud, because the funding is actually accounted for?

Consequences: Notes, T secured money he would not otherwise have had, which is an 'end-result' gain by continuing to accept the funding and misusing, misreporting and misrepresenting it. Misrepresentation of the application that the undertaking would be that the funding would be used for training.

Result: One count of fraud against the government agency by misrepresentation (will take investigation to establish intent at the point of application); alternatively, a clear fiduciary breach of trust directly amounting to fraud. Abuse of position of trust. Fraudulent conveyance if the accounts were presented in that state to pass an audit.

Fraud victim is government (and also an offence of money laundering in disguising assets from (his own) crime).

Even at this stage, it is important you realise that by applying a model such as this, you can quickly appraise all the information, apply the tests of fraud, and be assured that fraud is not complicated or 'complex'. It would just remain for you to decide which element of the fraud behaviour would prioritise your case (see Chapter 4) and what evidence from this point you will secure and how (statements, contract, funding application form and follow on accounting statements to compare and thus to offset and expose fraud).

Activity (1)

Using the Three C's model, review the following case study.

This time apply your own reasoning of the case. Don't look at the suggested response overleaf until you have appraised this case on your own.

L is a Company Director with the responsibility of running an extended cleaning contract at strategic level. Staff from her company clean a large number of offices in London, and

(Continued)

because of the scale of the operations and service delivery there are 200 staff engaged, many part-time, working various shifts. L has also appointed a number of managers and supervisors that report to her, to run the service for corporate clients.

The staff are made up of wide range of nationalities, for whom English is their second language. L is running over budget each month, and the CEO has put L on notice that the matter must be turned around. In response L understates the working hours of the cleaning staff by 10% from approximately half of the staff, and enters the falsified figures on the spreadsheet to the Head Office finance office. This she does over the next 3 months. Consequently those staff are underpaid each of those months by at least 10% in line with the stated hours.

L made no personal gain. She saw this as a 'cost cutting exercise.'

Conduct: Notes ....

Circumstances: Notes ....

Consequences: Notes ....

Result:

Activity (2)

How does your response compare?

Conduct: Notes, definite 'misrep' – by falsifying workers' hours – material fact, loss to victims, but gain? Who has gained? Fiduciary breach?

Circumstances: Notes, senior level position of trust, client management, contract financials, budget holder, taking advantage of workers, many of whom cannot speak English very well, won't question the discrepancies on their timesheets, not all will keep a record themselves, clear reporting lines, no allocation of staff pay returns to Head Office.

Consequences: Notes, probably not a fiduciary breach, but definitely a continuing misrep, by misrepresenting the pay returns, which clearly results in the staff each having incurred a loss, and by volume across all workers. The quantum will be substantial (need to confirm amount).

A slightly unusual twist is the losses to fraud of the staff victims, having been deprived by fraud of monies owed to them. A type of evasion of payment by fraud, a kind of rough parallel with tax fraud, but against her own staff. Company not liable criminally (L is personally) but company could be sued if civil recovery was the option pursued.

Result: Fraud clearly established. Confirmed financial injury/loss, notwithstanding L did not take the money for herself (this being a UK case – if in another country then proof of loss would be necessary).

Question the facts against fraud definition points as per the above cases. Do not just follow an ongoing theme to guilt; you will notice in the case studies above that effective use of the Three Cs will entail asking yourself short questions of what you find. This helps settle your appraisal of the scenario, ready for the investigation plan.

Never skip the 'circumstances' stage.

The Three Cs is a good way to place the whole scenario in context and then, clinically, the facts. It may be that evidence indicated then has to be gathered, but the above is a good starting point.

If you cannot identify and pull out evidence (not necessarily 'conclusive' at first sight) in a case such as this then the case will *not* be fraud. The worst unethical or even dishonest behaviour will not always equate to the fraud standards required to prove or substantiate a case. A step down to the HR disciplinary process could be the best option for this type of disreputable behaviour.

1.5 DISTINGUISHING AND OVERLAPPING: FRAUD AND MONEY LAUNDERING

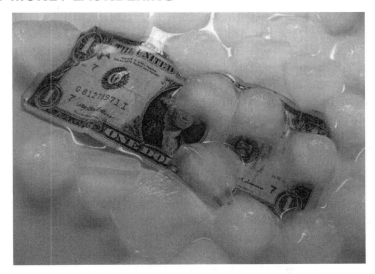

Many books have been written about money laundering, but here we tactically narrow the scope and essentially refer to the inevitability in economic acquisitive crime of there being overlaps between fraud, corruption and money laundering (along with what are called 'second tier' offences such as 'false accounting' and forgery or a related 'predicate' offences, meaning the application of one offence to support another). It is now often the case that these offences form part of the prosecution evidence to inform the fraud, such as a fake contract or invoice. This section will therefore address money laundering succinctly and make connections with fraud (as the underpinning crime).

For example, an ex-MEP for a British political party was jailed for two years for expenses fraud. The prosecution had sought to charge him not only with false accounting but also with 'using criminal property'. His lawyers argued for dismissal of this second charge on the grounds that it would merely complicate the case for the jury, which required the prosecution to prove the offence of false accounting anyway.

The predicate offence was a matter of factual evidence, which it would be necessary to prove in order to show use of criminal property, that is, money laundering. If the prosecution was unable to prove the predicate, there could be no criminal property, so rendering the second count pointless. The judge agreed with this reasoning; the money laundering charge would only 'obscure the Crown's pure case' against the defendant, which was one of 'unvarnished dishonesty'.

Interestingly, the money laundering offence was punishable by a maximum of 14 years' imprisonment, whereas the maximum term for false accounting is seven years. Although the money laundering legislation is drafted sufficiently widely to embrace the activities of the predicate criminal holding the proceeds of his crime, the defendant in this case was doing no more than 'enjoying the fruits' of his crime.

What is interesting in this case example is the interplay between fraud and money laundering (aside from the unfortunate misapplication of the law by the prosecution, who seemingly wanted to charge the defendant with money laundering to aggravate the case before the court, but oddly without the evidence for it).

If we return to our case study, the key difference is that the offender in that case actually disguised criminal proceeds to make them appear legitimate. The stolen money came from an outside source and was concealed as something else after it was misappropriated (the lynchpin point to make it 'criminal proceeds') and that is money laundering in itself. So based on that distinction, the British politician-turned-fraudster (among many others) 'cooked the books' and committed fraud purely for greed and self-gain with no discernible attempt to commit money laundering, whilst our other case with the crooked company director demonstrated a pattern of one financial crime being complemented with another: that being fraud working alongside money laundering.

Offences including tax evasion and terms such as 'embezzlement' remain in some jurisdictions, but have largely been swallowed up by modern fraud definitions. This also demonstrates a change in the way of legal thinking by aligning traditional crimes with relatively modern money laundering activities. However, money laundering is defined in such a sporadic way regionally, and many jurisdictions have a focal point of terrorism implicit in their definition of money laundering.

Money Laundering is therefore essentially best explained as an example:

- **Whereby the criminal disguises the existence, nature, source, ownership, location and disposition of property derived from criminal activity.**

With specific reference to money laundering affecting financial institutions and financial movements and management generally, the basic money laundering process has three steps:

- Placement.
- Layering.
- Integration.

NOTE: Whilst competent, the 3-point definition of money laundering falls short of connecting with more intricate or elaborate money laundering operations. This is a common criticism, and notwithstanding that the banks for example will be targeted and in line with their banking procedures, the discussion of money laundering mostly is over-simplified and lacks scope and detail for more sophisticated or involved money laundering schemes. Not all laundered money goes into the financial systems.

Training in this area is unfortunately also akin to assembling a piece of flat-pack furniture. (One highly possible reason why so much money laundering goes undetected.)

Please note:

- Money need *not* actually 'move' to be laundered (but moving the money can be if movement or transfer of it is established as an attempt to disguise it).
- The disguising of the criminal proceeds by any means is sufficient.
- The above (3) stages of money laundering need not occur in that order, and not all of these stages actually need to happen.

Also note, that the 'proceeds' of crime to entail money laundering ('dirty money') can be from any crime. Likewise, it is important to note that the investigator and prosecutor need not actually prove or, better put, precisely identify the originating crime and *those* offenders. It has to be established reasonably and on balance that the criminal proceeds are from crime of some kind. But we will confine this reference point to the proceeds of fraud. We will also look at how fraud acts as a perverse funding mechanism for money laundering and vice-versa.

'**Money**' in money laundering can include other tradable commodities. For example, a United Nations team was able to expose that gold mined in north-eastern Congo was shipped to Uganda and then Switzerland to be processed into ingots so its origins would be concealed.

Money laundering: the *mens rea*

Money laundering as a criminal offence traditionally had a 'dark twin', a predicate offence which generates the funds to be laundered. Cases decided on the law require proof that such criminal conduct has in fact generated the money being laundered.

There are two ways to confirm the 'property' is criminal property:

(a) By showing that it derives from conduct of a particular kind or kinds and that conduct of that kind or those kinds is unlawful; or

(b) By evidence of the circumstances in which the property is handled, which is such as to give rise to no other inference that it can only be derived from crime.

(c) Money laundering is an offence in its own right. It criminalises an arrangement which facilitates the 'acquisition' of criminal property. (Note, it facilitates *acquisition* of criminal property, not the creation of it; however, in the majority of acquisitive economic criminal cases (especially fraud), in practice 'criminal property' only becomes such at the moment it is 'acquired'.)

In other cases criminal property is created before it is acquired by the criminal, such as when a transfer goes awry or is stopped by the bank or by agency intervention. Nonetheless, the degree of overlap between the predicate offence (fraud, conspiracy to defraud) and the 'laundering' offence (an arrangement which 'facilitates ... acquisitions ... of criminal property') is all but complete.

For example, where a credit card fraudster makes a payment using stolen credit card details, he is both committing an offence of fraud and, arguably, laundering his criminal property by transferring it. A fraud offender who alters the payee and amount details on a cheque in order to divert funds fraudulently to him is both committing an offence of fraud and simultaneously laundering the proceeds of that fraud.

The following examples incorporate both fraud and money laundering.

Example 1
▦ A commits fraud. Buys a car with the proceeds. Then A sells the car to B.
▦ A deposits the money into a savings account.
▦ B uses the car as a taxi for a year, and makes a good turnover in the business. He had a 'good idea' where the money came from and its source.

Example 2
▦ A steals mobile phones and laptops from the office and sells them to a local shopkeeper B.
▦ B sells the items to C and D. B promises A a 'bonus' if she brings more items to sell.
▦ C and D do not know A but know B sells stolen gear as a matter of habit.
▦ B deposits the cash and then transfers it via a cash transfer service to a relative's account.

Reference to other crimes which inform money laundering cases (such as drugs trafficking) are for direct comparative purposes and not subject of further exploration in this book.

To further this, the next illustration, a case example, shows how fraud layers up more funding for money laundering, as an evolving criminal funding in process. The example used is a case of car smuggling.

CASE **STUDY**

Car Smuggling

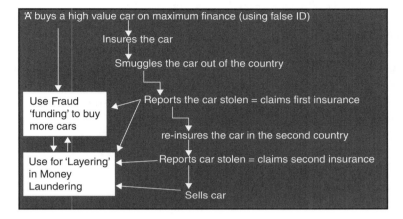

▪ Try to pinpoint the elements where fraud takes place and how.

What we have in effect is a 'continuing' offence of fraud. At each element of contact between the parties there is a misrepresentation. Avoid thinking of fraud in separate elements and types in a prolonged financial crime scenario like this. Think through the scenario.

▪ I investigated a case similar to this. So here is my quick assessment of the case:

Offender buys car on finance obtained by fraud (misrepresentation of facts of loan, what it will be for, possibly online, or the adulteration of an application, informed by fake references).

Offender smuggles car out of the country (money laundering – by both disguising and movement the proceeds of the loan obtained by fraud).

Offender reports car stolen. Claims insurance (straightforward insurance fraud).

Offender reinsures car (again money laundering – by disguising the proceeds of the fraud in the preceding act in the chain. *And* fraud again, by misrepresentation to obtain insurance – the car is not his to insure).

Offender reports car stolen (2). Claims insurance (straightforward insurance fraud, and another wave of money laundering).

Offender sells car? (Fraud, the new owner will be lied to, to the extent of being led to believe the car is owned by the offender).

Offender uses proceeds for 'layering' back into money laundering.

Additional Issues: If you scan back over the scenario, what should leap out at you is the high likelihood of more than one offender being involved. Staging points, physical movement of the stolen items, and the accompanying money transfers that combine with it.

- If you train yourself in problem-solving activity like this, some excellent productive thought processes will come to you instinctively and instantly. You will have implanted the definitions into your subconscious 'vault' and thereafter, your investigation plan will hook in information such as co-accomplices. It will also hint your thinking towards protocols and evidence-gathering formalities (such as the bureaucracies of getting statements from insurance companies, and cross-border protocols and data sharing).
- **Please note also:** Evidence of dishonesty in one claim does not necessarily constitute evidence of dishonesty in another. It may be intelligence but not evidence. Of course insurance companies reserve the right not to pay or pay out on a claim on an informed business decision, but when it comes to investigating fraud this is an important point.

Now:
- How would you prioritise the evidence?
- What offence would you cite and lead your case with?

These will be your next steps once you are in a position to present your case (after you have secured the physical and other evidence on each of these points to justify the naming of the offender/s). We will deal with these ensuing *skills*, *process* and *practicalities* in Chapter 4.

'Politically Exposed Persons' – a reference

Politically Exposed Persons, known as PEPs, is a term used as a benchmark of those professionals (mostly) who are often main targets to assist money launderers. For example, lawyers, agents and investment managers: those who handle clients' money professionally. Of course, some in those professions have been convicted of laundering the money of criminal clients (such as Umberto J. Aguilar, who features in Chapter 2).

But the term, 'politically exposed person' has its critics, who say the term is a textbook cliché that has found its way into law. Moreover, the term merely restricts the understanding and awareness of certain money launderers – namely PEPs themselves – and I agree.

Practicality: The long and laborious arrival of the 4th EU Directive extended the definition of PEPs and thus directly represents an over-simplified 'strategic' approach to countering money laundering. It does this by inventing terms and constructs that are neatly theoretical and operationally convenient. The problem is, however, that the investigative eye goes off the ball. Enforcement authorities, fixated with modelling money laundering cases around text book terminology, miss massive amounts of money laundering going on all around. They are too busy, or too programmed to terms like 'placement' and 'layering' and 'PEPs' of course – and if it doesn't fit into those tick boxes then there is no money laundering. A lack of sophistication leads to avoidance of more sophisticated money laundering schemes. Equally, enforcement policy blindly follows.

One could wager also that many lawyers for example do not like being labeled up-front as at least 'potential' money launderers ('so look out for them') by what has become a convention of enforcement bias, just to suit the accolades of those who sit behind desks and come up with clichéd models that cover only a smear of the global money laundering problem.

This is on a par with the incessant impersonating of who actually constitutes who and what in 'organised crime' – i.e., ones of a certain category. It goes circular. It takes little more creativity or operational know-how to know what a money launderer is, or who is money laundering in a given case.

Trade-based money laundering

Methods of money laundering continue to evolve. When authorities constrain certain types of money laundering, perpetrators migrate to other methods and law enforcement has focused its efforts on two methods:

1. The movement of value through the financial system using cheques and wire transfers; and
2. The physical movement of banknotes via cash couriers and bulk cash smuggling.

Now a third method called 'trade-based' money laundering is growing in popularity.

CASE **STUDY**

'iTunes' being used for money laundering.

Five men in the UK were jailed after using stolen credit card numbers. They bought £750,000 in vouchers, then sold them at cheaper prices over eBay (the originating crime being fraud committed with the stolen card numbers).

Therefore, on a par with our examples in procurement fraud, so-called trade-based money laundering presents the same business modelling and schema, but this time extracting the points of the money laundering implicit within a scenario.

Trade-based money laundering is defined by the Financial Action Task Force (FATF) as 'the process of disguising the proceeds of crime and moving value through the use of trade transactions in an attempt to legitimise their illicit origins' (which as you may notice created yet another definition).

Disguising funds as goods is now the way a significant portion of laundered money is moved illicitly. If Y can move $100 million from New York to Columbia via Venezuela, Y is not going to smuggle cash there when Y can move it through trade-based money laundering.

The newly revised Bank Secrecy Act (see law chapter) contains an expanded section on trade-based money laundering. These operations are necessary to aid the detecting of complex relationships between trading operations, operators, and money movements.

But two key barriers are present and in the way of detecting trade-based money laundering:

1. The high volume of trade makes it easy to hide individual transactions.
2. The complexity that is often involved in multiple foreign exchange transactions.

Arguably, the volume of trade means that highly scalable *automated* methods are needed, as the complexity of sifting through multiple transactions and finding hidden connections is beyond the capabilities of normal methods. But fixation on this can lead to problems.

Indeed, as trade between the Middle East and the rest of the world continues to grow, trade-based money laundering increases with it. Many countries in the Middle East depend on trade to grow their economies. This growth is highly dependent on a transparent and predictable process that importers and exporters can rely on. According to the World Bank, the United Arab Emirates' percentage of merchandise trade as a share of GDP rose from 136% in 2010 to 157% in 2014. Dubai in particular has seen the growth of its gold trade from $6 billion in 2003 to $75 billion in 2014, accounting for 40% of global trade; a sure indicator of the increasing reliance on trade as an engine of growth. Money laundering can and does disrupt this growth.

When moving illicit money, offenders see trade as an opportunity. The main method by which criminals launder money is through value transfer of goods traded. For example, if drug traffickers in Mexico want to launder money, they would consider entering a trade transaction by raising a letter of credit. They could set up a fictitious import company in the United States or other jurisdiction that would 'buy' goods from an exporter in Mexico and pay higher than normal prices. The trade documents would reflect the value of the goods being shipped. The importer would pay for the inflated goods through a bank to the seller in Mexico. This seller could also be a 'front' company based in Mexico. The seller in Mexico would then receive the funds through a local bank. From the bank's perspective, the transaction would be proper, since relevant documents were used. However the value of the goods was misrepresented, resulting in transfer of money through the trade. In this example, the buyer in the United States would pay $100 per unit for a pen typically valued at $1. The seller in Mexico would mark up the invoice to $100 per pen and ship the goods. Once the seller receives payment from the buyer for $100 per pen, $99 has been transferred from the United States to Mexico due to overvaluation of the goods. There are occurrences of these trades happening globally.

This is an area of economic crime not to be underestimated, and its connections with fraud cannot allow this area to be separated from the discourse. Mis-invoicing goods distorts the true value of goods in an economy, causing unpredictable patterns of trade. So-called dirty money can be directed to consumption or investment activities that benefit the money launderers, potentially at the expense of the region's economic development.

In terms of fraud and security, we get back to the same problem: poor due diligence checking and standards. Banks have a role to play in minimising the impact of trade-based money laundering but fall very short of determining the legitimacy of trades. Regulators should be more focused on ensuring that banks actually identify where the goods are being shipped to, and even what transportation is used; and whether the goods are potentially used for dual use purposes.

 ## 1.6 NOW ADDING CORRUPTION ... LINKING TO FRAUD

Key distinctions (between fraud and corruption)

Corruption is mostly a crime of influencing as opposed to misrepresenting. Therefore there are distinctions from fraud, but equally there are overlaps or facilitating episodes of both offences within a financial crime scenario.

The main distinctions from fraud are the giving, offering, or receiving of bribes and exploiting conflicts of interests.

Bribery is also the inappropriate offering or use of favours in exchange for gain of some kind. No-one has been deceived, just tempted. There are also kickbacks. This is the most common form of corruption (as we will see in the Sainsbury's case later) but on a grand scale it is in parallel with fraud and money laundering.

Types of favours are diverse and are not just money. They can include gifts, sexual favours, company shares, lavish entertainment, employment and political benefits. We have shown examples which connect with these.

Equally, corrupt behaviour involves behaviour such as nepotism, favouritism, and covering up. Internal politics also have an influence in regard to allowing it to go on unchallenged (and hence the UK saw fit to place reporting measures into the law, albeit it took the UK nearly 100 years to do so).

It also demonstrates for pure learning purposes in this chapter concerning handling definitions and perceptions of fraud and corruption etc., that to some people in business, perceptions and explanations of financial crime are appeased with the application of corporate spin. A bribe is suddenly a 'preferred supplier payment' but to the more discerning is a direct and in-house systemic practice of receiving bribes.

Another phrase for this kind of scenario is 'reciprocity' or as is often the case as I have worked in the Middle East, in Arabic, where 'bakshish' really means: 'redistribution of wealth' (not another form of corruption as it is so often and mistakenly referred to).

Each and every time I run a training course on fraud corruption, the subject of whistleblowing combined with fraud and corrupt practices comes up – every time, without exception. I infer from experience now that these so-called 'cultural' or nationalistic differences in this particular context are mythical really. Of course some things work differently in different places, but those who choose to put spin on the word BRIBE such as 'customer support' or 'part of our continuing customer relations' or 'recognition' or – the best one I heard – 'our gift as part of a platinum introductory package for special customers'.

This topic, however, demonstrates clearly the gulf in terms of attitudes and assertions in how to win business. It is not a complicated subject really, but many choose to make it so, and even amongst fraud and corruption professionals this point of discussion brings in many different perceptions and opinions of what is 'OK' in business in terms of both offering or accepting gifts, incentives, or 'guarantees' (yes, that is another interesting one).

Key Distinction:

Fraud has a central legal element of dishonesty, whilst corruption is a deliberate act of inducement to gain favours or financial advantage or commercial favour.

As asserted by Duperouzel:

A discussion about corruption must start with some theory about fraud, as the phenomena are interlinked. However, they are not the same; rather they are like two circles that overlap in some areas but are separate in others. *Fraud can occur, but without corruption; corruption can occur without fraud.* Yet where fraud is, corruption often is too.

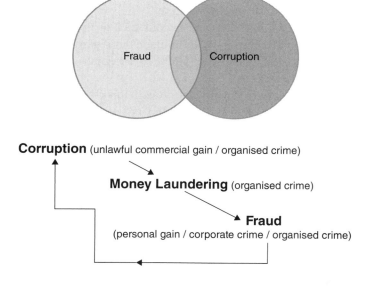

Threads running through fraud to money laundering are:

Coercive practices

'Coercive practice' is impairing or harming, or threatening to impair or harm directly or indirectly, any party or the property of the party, to influence improperly the actions of a party:

- ▪ A kind of 'aggravated' bribery likened to blackmail. This distinction is in the definition, as there is no demand 'with menaces'.
- ▪ Coercive practices are actions undertaken for the purpose of bid rigging or in connection with public procurement or government contracting or in furtherance of a corrupt practice or a fraudulent practice.
- ▪ Coercive practices are not intended to cover 'hard bargaining', the exercise of legal or contractual remedies or litigation.

Collusive practices

'Collusive practice' means an arrangement between two or more parties designed to achieve an improper purpose, including influencing improperly the actions of another party.

 ## 1.7 LEGISLATION SUMMARY

A comparative study of the laws alone is a demanding and particular task in its own right. This is directly due to a lack of direct or precise legislation, which has been a problem in combating fraud, corruption and money laundering.

Therefore, reconciliation of these globally is impossible, but if the core elements of misrepresentation and breaches of (enhanced) trust are followed, you need not be unduly worried about achieving this. What is important is that you have a clear grasp of the law you are likely to be working with, as well as an ability to state its purpose and constituents simply and without hesitation. You then apply more overreaching legislation with international jurisdiction (when appropriate and necessary).

Of course, there are differences in law across jurisdictions, but keeping in step with the modernisation of global laws and the evolving new definitions they bring, this book takes the standpoint that misrepresentation has now overtaken the term 'deception'. The focus on the act of fraud should be, and very wisely is, about the behaviour and intentions of the offender, as opposed to the historical view of the victim having to be fooled and having to have incurred loss before anything is either done, or even formally considered to be actual fraud.

Indeed, in relation to international perspectives, across international jurisdictions, fraud (and money laundering) definitions are often addressed by category.

The necessity, however, for actual monetary (or other) loss to have occurred is a requirement still present in some jurisdictions. In US law, there is a legal requirement for the accuser or prosecution to establish there was 'injury' to the alleged victim as a result.

This is in complete contrast with the UK Fraud Act, for example, which is a broad-ranging Act to capture offending activity by fraud. (See below.)

What is important is to distinguish the substantive law from the procedural law. Likewise, the purpose and 'scheme of the law'. Criminal Law is designed to prohibit something, compel you to do something, or both. Incorporating the above points, this is broadly divided into four main areas:

Definitions: comparatives

Africa – Middle East – Malaysia – South Africa

There follows a summary of legal definitions of fraud and procedural statutes across strategic jurisdictions. These are not exhaustive and many jurisdictions will apply these.

For practical purposes, I have condensed this section into a workable and enabling element so as to track to your indigenous legal jurisdiction. But again, the point is emphasised that whilst 'the laws are different' across countries and regions, these are effectively labelling and terminology differences (such as 'embezzlement', which is still used in certain places) and the purpose of addressing misrepresentation and loss (and risk) is mostly consistent.

As a means of added support, we make the point that in many jurisdictions the law is structured to address individual or silos of fraud activity by 'type'.

Africa   **Example**: the Penal Code of Kenya creates the substantive law to combat fraud and corruption.

Individual laws therefore tend to go with individual offences and specific fraud contexts.

For example:

▦ Bank fraud.
▦ Credit fraud.
▦ Insurance fraud.
▦ Marriage fraud.
▦ Investment fraud.

Middle East   **Equally, for example in the United Arab Emirates, where the UAE Government passed Law No. 24/2006.**

An example is the regime in the United Arab Emirates against damages posed by defective industrial products, unfair business practices and misleading advertising, unfair and deceptive practices such as the selling of defective or substandard goods, the charging of ridiculous prices, misrepresentation of the efficacy or usefulness of goods, and negligence as to safety standards. This is not to be confused with the principles of Sharia law (see below) and that of the coverall legislation of the UK.

The sheer volumes of these issues go to an 'extreme' level, which informed the new legislation in the UAE. Two examples are:

- A Ministry of Health report on energy drinks and a fraudulent and illegal service charge levied by some restaurants in the UAE to cash in on the craze of this. Fines were imposed on offenders and as a result 95 to 98% of restaurants and cafes in the UAE implemented the removal of this charge.
- The UAE Government also presented a report concerning car dealers and the widespread problem of manufacturing defects in cars, which were withheld from consumers.

South Africa   The wording is subtle, but the structure and definitional reach is similar to the UK Fraud Act. According to C.R. Snyman 2002 (520) 'Fraud consists of the unlawful intentional making of a misrepresentation which causes actual prejudice or which is potentially prejudicial to another.'

Malaysia   Financial fraud is the focal area. Fraud can be broadly defined as an intentional act of deception involving financial transactions for purpose of personal gain. Fraud is a crime, and is also a civil law violation. Many fraud cases involve complicated financial transactions.

An unscrupulous investment broker may present clients with an opportunity to purchase shares in precious metal repositories, for example. His status as a professional investor gives him credibility, which can lead to justified credibility among potential clients. Those who believe the opportunity to be legitimate contribute substantial amounts of cash and receive authentic-looking bond documentation in return. If the investment broker is fully aware that no such repositories exist and still receives payments for worthless bonds, then victims may sue him for fraud.

Hence, we identify another aspect in relation to the enactment of new law to address a worrying trend or increase in certain fraud contexts (and unfortunately also how slow some governments are to react and how fraud is still marginalised in the way of thinking for officialdom).

Sharia law

In recent years, the Islamic financial market has become increasingly global. Financial contributors from many jurisdictions are taking the opportunity to pool their resources and form alliances to jointly participate in the global business. Therefore, and given that the cornerstone of Islamic finance transactions is the application of Sharia principles, such principles are being adapted into the wider non-Islamic legal environment. Attempts are made to implement Islamic finance transactions in jurisdictions which are not bound to give effect to Islamic principles.

Sharia law is divided into two main sections. The part which is relevant to our work is applicable to, amongst other issues, human interaction, or al-mu'amalat, which includes financial transactions, and judicial matters (and forms of evidence).

Islamic financial transactions pose a challenge to the choice of law and the parties will mostly want to opt for Islamic law as the governing law of the finance documents. Sharia is not a national system of law and there is not a standard codified Islamic law to be used as guidance and reference to deal with fraud. Parties cannot merely adopt Islamic law as the governing law without reference to the law of a particular jurisdiction.

In contrast to other countries who have adopted either their common laws, or civil law system, there is a lack of a comprehensive legal system to support the application of Islamic principles in specific Islamic finance transaction documents, and hence against fraud. Even if market participants agree to use contracts based on Sharia principles, most Islamic laws and their courts lack the sufficient specific legal backdrop, infrastructure, and resources to interpret and enforce the transaction documents. Criminal cases of fraud, especially at less serious monetary levels or 'day-to-day' scenarios, are mostly disposed of by an alternative means (such as deportation, if the offender is a foreigner, or the suspension of work permits, or some other kind of sanction which is more of a convenience in punitive terms as opposed to proportionate sentences to fraud activity).

Sharia law does not contain a definition of fraud; however, this is not to be misunderstood that economic crime is not heeded. The 'corruption trials' in the Sultanate of Oman in 2013 and 2014 saw the handing down of hefty sentences.

A main issue that arises as a result of the increasing participation of financial institutions and other market players from multiple jurisdictions is about the choice of governing law which will govern the Islamic finance transaction documents and the extent to which Islamic law principles are applied within the chosen governing law framework.

The role of Sharia principles regarding the choice of governing law

The choice of governing law can be a point of confusion, especially for cross-border finance transactions involving parties from multiple jurisdictions. For a conventional cross-border financial arrangement, there is less complication as there is no requirement to consider the application of Islamic principles. Instead, the issues revolve around the applicability of the choice of law in the jurisdiction itself where a fraud case, for example, envisages a legal action in another jurisdiction, and the enforcement of a (foreign) judgment in the jurisdiction where the obligor resides and/or where the assets of the obligor are located.

A scenario of that nature gives rise to the question as to the extent of applicability of Sharia principles in the law of a selected jurisdiction. In practice for example, English law is mainly chosen as the governing law of Islamic cross-border finance transactions, which may give rise to financial fraud within them or arising from them.

This overcomes another practicality in that judicial system. Parties who follow the Sharia principles as the law of a specific domestic jurisdiction, often discover in litigation that the courts lack the expertise or resources to implement the Sharia rules. There have been a large number of cases litigated in the English courts in civil cases involving Islamic finance agreements, where the courts examined the issue of the governing law in such agreements.

One case, *Shamil Bank of Bahrain* v. *Beximco Pharmaceuticals*, presents this point very well. This set a noticeable judicial precedent because for the first time, questions of the validity, interpretation and scope of the English law against Islamic principles were measured by a secular court.

The judge in the first instance held that English law was the governing law and there was no scope for the Sharia law to apply as there could not be two separate law systems governing a transaction. Further, it would be highly impossible that an English secular court would apply religious principles in making the determination of a dispute. The appeal by Beximco against the decision of the first instance judge was dismissed along the same arguments. The judge in the English Court of Appeal case further argued that the general reference of the Sharia law in the agreement did not identify any specific Sharia principles to be applied and further ruled that the reference to Sharia law is repugnant to English law.

This above case illustrates two challenges:

1. The reluctance of a secular court to admit the application of Sharia principles; and
2. The clear scope for potential abuse by fraud and by defaulting parties using debt as cover for earlier fraud intentions to use Sharia invalidity arguments to avoid making payments under the Islamic documents.

Insurance and the law: a special mention

This section is not so much about investigating fraud but in keeping with this chapter, makes reference to the unique legal derivatives from an insurance fraud case up in the theatre of the law. In insurance cases the courts have a large element of their work assigned to post-conviction settlements and hence there are hearings within hearings. Recoveries and claims hearings represent a point in the proceedings which have left the investigation part of the case well behind. Moreover, disposal of criminal cases in insurance fraud often presents a different type of closure to other crimes. If an offender steals, or commits an assault for example, the conclusions and case disposal are straightforward. But in insurance cases, much emphasis is put on recovery and the legal arguments arising therefrom.

Civil cases brought after alleged breaches of contract often form the main body of cases, certainly at corporate levels, whereby highly financial penalties and contracts are at stake. One main point on this is that the higher courts face uncertainty on the position in a case where fraud is not alleged in the original proceedings. Equally, it is not possible to rescind settlement agreements fraud where that very fraud is alleged in the original proceedings.

Practically, for the investigator of insurance fraud it means thinking a little differently. It is crucial that the exposer of fraud in insurance cases stays outside of the rights and wrongs of what should happen to an offender. Very often insurance companies are obliged to pay out in cases where fraud is suspected. The traditional term 'beyond reasonable doubt' in criminal law across the world is propagated more so in insurance cases than in any other area of fraud investigation work.

In an English Court of Appeal case, *Hayward v. Zurich [2015]*, it was held that a person can only be said to have relied on a false statement for the purposes of the law of deceit and fraudulent misrepresentation insofar as that person believed that the statement was true.

The point here is that in insurance cases a person who has settled previous litigation may seek to use the doctrine of fraudulent misrepresentation to rescind a settlement agreement and obtain repayment of money paid under it.

In this case, an insurance claimant brought a claim against his employer for a back injury sustained at work. It was exposed by investigation that at first instance he had fraudulently and hugely exaggerated the nature and extent of his injuries. He claimed over £420,000 in damages; but if the claimant had told the truth, he would have recovered just £14,000.

Video surveillance footage was produced as evidence of the fraud, which undermined his credibility, in that he had recovered not long after the accident.

On the basis of this new information, the insurance company brought a claim of deceit against the claimant for rescission of the original settlement agreement, and a repayment of the difference between what it paid under the settlement and what the claimant (fraudster) would have been entitled to be paid on the basis of his injuries as they really were.

The claimant appealed to the Appeal Court on the basis that the judge had used the wrong test for determining whether there had been reliance by the insurance company. Lawyers argued that the judge was wrong to treat the authorities referring to a person being 'influenced' by a misrepresentation as 'including anything other than being influenced by believing that it was true'.

It was decided that a person entering a compromise agreement in an insurance claim where fraud is alleged should not be able to escape from that agreement later (which, by necessary implication, compromised the allegation of fraud) on the basis of the very fraud that was compromised.

The leading judgement in this case was as follows:

> In my opinion the true principle is that the equitable remedy of rescission answers the affront to conscience occasioned by holding to a contract a party who has been influenced into making it by being misled or, worse still, defrauded by his counterparty. Thus, once he discovers the truth, he must elect whether to rescind or to proceed with the contract. It must follow that, if he already knows or perceives the truth by the time of the contract, he elects to proceed by entering into it, and cannot later seek rescission merely because he later obtains better evidence of that which he already believed, still less if

he merely repents of it. This seems to me to be *a fortiori* the case where, as here, the misrepresentation consists of a disputed claim in litigation, and the contract settles that claim.

This is about the misrepresentation in documents and statements.

Many are unsettled by this judgment. The reasoning to a degree is understood, as it is about a settlement that was agreed, based on dishonesty – a direct lie to the court in the first place. The fact that it was not sworn testimony but submitted as part of the legal process, does not make it any less of a false representation (in my view). When evidence is later discovered that proves the falsehood, one cannot see how the court can reasonably find in favour of the dishonest party. It sets a peculiar legal precedent which is clearly unhelpful to those engaged in combating fraud. Certainly from an *investigative* viewpoint.

One senior London lawyer even went so far to say, that '... no cases in which fraud was alleged could ever realistically be settled, which would be the result if a settlement agreement could be rescinded for the very fraud that it was purporting to compromise.'

In surface court cases, the problem goes circular, because most insurance companies rightly do not pursue cases in the criminal courts because the criminal courts do not consider compensation to the value of the settlement in such a case. Yet enforcement against fraud does not occur because the only real possibility of criminal liability is by a long and winding road of using the civil courts to have people committed for contempt of court instead of fraud.

Hence the belief that criminal courts should be used more in cases like this is a very valid one, but unfortunately the police do not often specialise in fraud prosecutions (other than 'low hanging fruit' cases, which invariably involves a police-corporate partnership) and neither do many prosecution authorities.

One final ingredient for the mix is that recovery of funds is distinct from compensation. The criminal courts can make compensation orders or confiscation orders upon conviction, but there is no separate concept of 'recovery of funds' (and this is totally different to asset tracing in money laundering cases).

In all, the proceeds of an insurance fraud are quantified on how they are informed in the courts and are thus viewed differently in that regard to other fraud cases in other scenarios.

Concluding note:
- Insurance fraud investigation has a high standard of proof.
- Insurance fraud cases can invite different influences (and frustrations).
- Court cases regarding insurance fraud can continue beyond the limitations of other crimes.

The United Kingdom Fraud Act 2006

Structured in a four-part definition:

Fraud by false representation, to make a gain for self – contrary to section 2.

Fraud by false representation –
(1) A person is in breach of this section if he—
   (a) dishonestly makes a false representation, and (b) intends, by making the representation—
      (i)   to make a gain for himself or another, or
      (ii) to cause loss to another or to expose another to a risk of loss.
(2) A representation is false if—
   (a) it is untrue or misleading, and
   (b) the person making it knows that it is, or might be, untrue or misleading.
(3) 'Representation' means any representation as to fact or law, including a representation as to the state of mind of—
   (a) the person making the representation, or
   (b) any other person.

A person is in breach of this section if he—
   (a) dishonestly fails to disclose to another person information which he is under a legal duty to disclose, and
   (b) intends, by failing to disclose the information—
      (i)   to make a gain for himself or another, or
      (ii) to cause loss to another or to expose another to a risk of loss.

Fraud by failing to disclose information, contrary to section 3
Fraud by abuse of position, contrary to section 4.

▦ In addition, the UK Fraud Act addresses categories concerning the fraudulent behaviour of companies, covered by section 10 – and a new offence of participating in fraudulent business carried on by a sole trader was established by section 9.

▦ Section 12 of the Act provides that where an offence against the Act was committed by a body corporate, but was carried out with the 'consent or connivance' of any director, manager, secretary or officer of the body — or any person purporting to be such – then that person, as well as the body itself, is liable.

▦ The key difference between the Fraud Act and the Theft Act is that Fraud Act offences do not require there to have been a victim as was the case with the Theft Act.

Bribery Act 2010 (UK)

It took the UK almost 100 years to pass a new (and much needed) law to deal with bribery and corruption. It is referenced here to conclude with our comparing and identifying where fraud and corruption cases connect. The dominant legislation will apply in such a case.

The Act has a near-universal jurisdiction, allowing for the prosecution of an individual or company with links to the United Kingdom, regardless of where the crime occurred. As the title of the Act indicates, it is to address and criminalise the giving and taking of bribes, but also adds a punitive element of placing a legal obligation on organisations and businesses to ensure both adequate corruption (bribery) controls and reporting procedures.

United States – definition of fraud

A false representation of a matter of fact – whether by words or by conduct, by false or misleading allegations, or by concealment of what should have been disclosed – that deceives and is intended to deceive another so that the individual will act upon it to her or his legal injury.

Fraud must be proved by showing that the defendant's actions involved five separate elements:

1. A false statement of a material fact;
2. Knowledge on the part of the defendant that the statement is untrue;
3. Intent on the part of the offender to deceive the alleged victim;
4. Justifiable reliance by the alleged victim on the statement; and
5. Injury to the alleged victim as a result.

The (18) U.S. Code Chapter 47 – FRAUD AND FALSE STATEMENTS sets out a lengthy schedule of definitions and contexts:

- 1001. Statements or entries generally.
- 1002. Possession of false papers to defraud United States.
- 1003. Demands against the United States.
- 1004. Certification of checks/cheques.
- 1005. Bank entries, reports and transactions.
- 1006. Federal credit institution entries, reports and transactions.
- 1007. Federal Deposit Insurance Corporation transactions.
- 1008, 1009. [Repealed.]
- 1010. Department of Housing and Urban Development and Federal Housing Administration transactions.
- 1011. Federal land bank mortgage transactions.
- 1012. Department of Housing and Urban Development transactions.
- 1013. Farm loan bonds and credit bank debentures.
- 1014. Loan and credit applications generally; renewals and discounts; crop insurance.
- 1015. Naturalization, citizenship or alien registry.
- 1016. Acknowledgment of appearance or oath.
- 1017. Government seals wrongfully used and instruments wrongfully sealed.
- 1018. Official certificates or writings.
- 1019. Certificates by consular officers.
- 1020. Highway projects.
- 1021. Title records.
- 1022. Delivery of certificate, voucher, receipt for military or naval property.

- 1023. Insufficient delivery of money or property for military or naval service.
- 1024. Purchase or receipt of military, naval, or veteran's facilities property.
- 1025. False pretences on high seas and other waters.
- 1026. Compromise, adjustment, or cancellation of farm indebtedness.
- 1027. False statements and concealment of facts in relation to documents required by the Employee Retirement Income Security Act of 1974.
- 1028. Fraud and related activity in connection with identification documents, authentication features, and information.
- 1028 A. Aggravated identity theft.
- 1029. Fraud and related activity in connection with access devices.
- 1030. Fraud and related activity in connection with computers.
- 1031. Major fraud against the United States.
- 1032. Concealment of assets from conservator, receiver, or liquidating agent.
- 1033. Crimes by or affecting persons engaged in the business of insurance whose activities affect interstate commerce.
- 1034. Civil penalties and injunctions for violations of section 1033.
- 1035. False statements relating to health care matters.
- 1036. Entry by false pretences to any real property, vessel, or aircraft of the United States or secure area of any airport or seaport.
- 1037. Fraud and related activity in connection with electronic mail.
- 1038. False information and hoaxes.
- 1039. Fraud and related activity in connection with obtaining confidential phone records information of a covered entity.
- 1040. Fraud in connection with major disaster or emergency benefits.

Foreign Corrupt Practices Act 1977 (FCPA)

A United States federal law with two main provisions:

1. Addressing accounting transparency requirements re: the Securities Exchange Act 1934.
2. Concerning the bribery of foreign officials.

Sarbanes–Oxley Act (USA)

Enacted July 2002, also known as the 'Public Company Accounting Reform and Investor Protection Act' (in the Senate) and the 'Corporate and Auditing Accountability and Responsibility Act' – a federal law which set new or enhanced standards for all US public company boards, management and public accounting firms.

The Act was a reaction to a number of major corporate and accounting scandals including those affecting Enron, Adelphia, Peregrine Systems and WorldCom.

Dodd–Frank (USA)

The *Dodd–Frank Wall Street Reform and Consumer Protection Act* (referred to as 'Dodd–Frank') was signed into federal law by President Barack Obama on July 21, 2010.

Dodd–Frank brought the most significant changes to financial regulation in the United States since the regulatory reform that followed the Great Depression in the 1930s. Being regulatory-dominant, it made changes in the American financial regulatory environment that affect all federal financial regulatory agencies and almost every part of the nation's financial services industry.

But controversially also, in 2010 the Dodd–Frank Act enabled the SEC whistle-blower reward program. Both US citizens and foreign nationals may file whistle-blower claims and receive rewards.

Other fraud related legislation

1. The Financial Action Task Force (FATF) initiatives (explained further in later chapters).
2. BASEL customer due diligence and Know Your Customer (KYC) principles. Essentially to support the banking industry, but is a good guidance tool in procurement fraud prevention.
3. Wolfsberg anti-money laundering (AML) Principles for private and correspondent banking. Enacted concerning the financing of terrorism, and monitoring and screening for suspicious financial activity.
4. EU Directives on Money Laundering (the 4th Directive being continually updated and added to, the latest released addendum in relation to online gambling was released in January 2015).

 ## 1.8 EVIDENCE

Armageddon wipes out the good as well as the evil…

—Anon

Evidence – law in itself. Not a 'free for all' game to ensure prosecution

In Chapter 4, we will have a *practical* handling of evidence in fraud cases: extracting evidence from information, weighing, prioritising and presenting.

At this point, however, it is important to stress that evidence and its issues can form a huge pit behind you, ready to fall into if you either fabricate evidence or try to circumvent the rules of evidence. The 'Armageddon Effect' certainly appears at such instances that form it. Far too many cases have been lost simply because of an ego-centric approach to 'rubbing it in' on an offender or defendant by grafting layers of superficial legality onto the case evidence. That is with either macho rule-bending or management investigations gamesmanship. Worse yet, is the full-on malpractice some of which is relevantly chronicled in this book. Training also has some involvement in this whereby many average trainers unflinchingly follow an aims and objectives format, and directly encourage investigators to embellish what they can do, and fail to point out pitfalls and poor practices in handling evidence, and exercising powers generally.

The Regulation of Investigatory Powers Act 2000 (RIPA), an Act of the Parliament of the United Kingdom is supposed to regulate the powers of public bodies to carry out surveillance and investigation, and covering the interception of communications. However, this is open to abuse, for example by local authorities, who use the powers to enforce minor by-laws and thus impose fines at random to instigate and gather revenues on the shakiest legal grounds. Also used to hound whistle-blowers in the UK (HMRC and the NHS).

All of the above inform crucial points of evidence and attitudes to the issue.

Basic principles of evidence for fraud investigators

Format

This section will begin with an outline of:

▦ Evidential sources, classification and practicalities.
▦ Perceiving 'naturally occurring' evidence.
▦ 'Beyond Red Flags' – specific evidence of fraud.

It will then summarise evidence by category and the rules of admissibility. This will lead into the next section about expert witnesses.

Evidential sources, classification and practicalities

Evidence (definition)

Evidence is information given to a court or other authority to help them decide if a crime has been committed or not, and tends to prove the truth or probability of truth about a fact or facts put before it. Evidence is based on *facts* upon which a case is eventually decided.

The two main distinctions in law (in any jurisdiction) are: **Civil and Criminal**.

Fraud investigations can and do involve either or both of these.

'Proof beyond reasonable doubt does not mean proof beyond a shadow of a doubt. The law would fail to protect the community if it permitted fanciful possibilities to deflect the course of justice. If the evidence is so strong against a man as to leave only a remote possibility in his favour which can be dismissed with the sentence "Of course it is possible but not in the least probable", the case is proved beyond reasonable doubt; nothing short will suffice.'

Denning J. **Miller** v **Minister of Pensions** [1947] 2 All ER 372

The above judgement by Lord Denning in the *Miller Pensions* case has been over-reached by later precedents such as the jury 'being sure'(?) but for me and many others, this still forms the best standard of proving a (fraud) case that there is. The judgment set a standard and the clearest of legal principles and is deemed to be the best possible guide for every case, even though the case may not end up in a court.

The statement bridges the civil and criminal areas of evidence at this point.

Civil cases (being a lesser standard of proof) are to be addressed with equal importance and verve as criminal but it is not normally for you as an investigator to decide or overly concern yourself with the 'civil or criminal' question. Although your experience and role will obviously contain this awareness for you. The key point is that you *effectively investigate*, and do not work to an injudicious legal agenda. Furthermore, some investigators have made the mistake of taking their foot off the pedal when quoting 'it's only a civil case' and the like. The civil standard of proof needs as much expertise and acumen as the criminal, and our lawyers are highly competent to engage with and apply these matters in cases they either defend or prosecute, or mediate outside of the courts.

- ■ What matters is what can be admitted.
- ■ If an element of evidence or testimony cannot be tested then it is not admissible.
- ■ Evidence will not be admissible if its prejudicial effect outweighs its probative value.
- ■ **Hence, each time you go into ANY fraud case, think of yourself as being in court.**

Burden of proof: criminal

'He who accuses must prove'

In criminal procedure, the burden of proof (in all jurisdictions globally) is on the prosecution.

Albeit the following legal term is enshrined in English law, and taking into account that some prosecution jurisdictions are *adversarial* as opposed to *inquisitive*, it also holds good in all legal provinces in all places about being innocent until proven guilty:

Ei incumbit probatio qui dicit, non qui negat – *'The presumption of innocence'*.

You will always be obliged by law to co-operate with those you accuse, in respect of their right to probe the veracity of the allegations that they face as a serious predicament.

The main classifications of Criminal evidence are:

- ■ Direct.
- ■ Primary and secondary.
- ■ Circumstantial.
- ■ Hearsay.
- ■ Forensic.
- ■ (Expert).

    (The above quoted in brackets applies in civil cases also.)

Other cross-jurisdictional applicable terms are *prima facie* (at first sight) and 'probable cause'.

Burden of proof: civil

The unheeding burden of proof is on the party asserting a claim, since the default position is generally one of neutrality or unbelief. Each party in a case will carry the burden
of proof for any assertion they make in accusation, although some assertions may be
accepted by the other party without further evidence. If the case is set up as a mediation
or resolution the burden of proof is on the side supporting the resolution.

In practical terms, the US system of *clear and convincing proof* means that the evidence
presented during trial must be *highly and substantially more probable to be true than not*. In
this standard, a higher degree of believability must be met than the 'on balance' standard
of proof in civil actions, which only requires the facts as a reference point to be 'more
likely than not' to prove the issue for which they are asserted.

This aspect is also termed as the 'clear, convincing, and satisfactory evidence'; 'clear,
cognisant, and convincing evidence'; and 'clear, unequivocal, satisfactory, and convincing evidence', and is applied in cases or situations involving an equitable remedy or where
a presumptive civil liberty interest exists.

Criminal evidence

Direct

Direct evidence is evidence that is known personally to the witness because this is based
on what they

- ▧ Saw.
- ▧ Heard.
- ▧ Touched.

Direct evidence (mostly) demonstrates proof beyond reasonable doubt that an individual or co-offenders committed fraud.

If the direct evidence that is submitted at trial is true, the charge against the accused
is substantiated and established. A claim that the accused committed the crime charged
with can be proved by direct evidence alone.

Interestingly, in the United States, the law shows no distinction between circumstantial and direct evidence in terms of which has more weight or importance. Both types of
evidence may be enough to establish the defendant's guilt, depending on how the jury
finds the facts of the case. (This effectively affirms the point that circumstantial evidence
is capable of being very 'good' evidence.)

- ▧ Direct evidence can have varying degrees of weight depending on the witnesses who
      deliver the testimony. The testimony of an upstanding and trustworthy source will have
      a stronger influence on the jury than the testimony from a shady and unreliable witness.
- ▧ Direct evidence is obviously helpful (to make it easier) for a court or other author-
      ity, because it lessens the degree to which they infer that the fraud was committed.
- ▧ Direct evidence is totally based on fact, and not coincidences.

Primary and secondary

Primary evidence is:

- An original document; or
- A statement about its contents.
  (Primary evidence is usually required to prove the contents of a document.)

Secondary evidence is:

- A copy of a document; or
- Verbal evidence (testimony) about its contents.

Circumstantial

Circumstantial evidence is based on supporting facts in a case. It *implies* truth to an allegation. Circumstantial (and direct evidence) exists in many forms including: testimony, documentary, physical, digital, exculpatory, scientific, and genetic.

- Please be aware that circumstantial evidence can be very good evidence. If there is sufficient volume or capacity of it in a case, it is the closure on the detail in the circumstances that eliminates doubt.

The reliance on circumstantial evidence itself can be sufficient in the civil standard of proof. In criminal cases, circumstantial evidence mostly needs supporting with other evidence but not always. Each element of evidence, although it will belong in a classification, needs to be appraised within the case itself, and not horizontally regarded as always being the same in all cases.

- A confession (much) later after a (fraud) crime which is made under controlled legal conditions (such as being under oath or caution) is an exception to the hearsay rule.

Circumstantial evidence allows a conclusion to be drawn from a set of circumstances or information. For example:

- The offender is accused of fraud by forging an invoice to make it appear it had arrived from an external source and have it paid to one of his own bank accounts, and a witness in the office saw the offender writing on an invoice form which had the same false letterhead as the item concerned.

What the witness saw is direct evidence. The conclusion that the defendant committed the fraud based on what the witness saw is circumstantial evidence.

Hence, circumstantial evidence is not necessarily weaker than direct evidence if there are number of circumstances that together can lead the court or a jury to a guilty verdict. One English legal maxim that:

> One strand of a cord might be insufficient to sustain the weight, but three stranded together may be quite sufficient of strength. Thus, it may be circumstantial evidence – there may be a combination of circumstances no one of which would raise a reasonable conviction, or more than a mere suspicion; but the whole, taken together, may create a strong conclusion of guilty, that is, with as much certainty as human affairs can require or admit of.

This means that, even though you may only have circumstantial evidence, if there is enough of it, then altogether, it may be enough to prove guilt.

Hearsay

Hearsay is 'a statement not made in oral proceedings'. This means a statement that has not been given in court, hence, it is effectively second-hand evidence, for example something:

▓ You have overheard;
▓ Someone has told you; or
▓ Someone has written.

In hearsay you are asking the court to believe:

▓ You are telling the truth; and
▓ The person who told you or whom you overheard was also telling the truth.
▓ It is the second assumption which mostly means that hearsay evidence is generally not admissible in court.

Forensic

In some fraud cases you may need to request forensic tests to be done on pieces of evidence, for example:

▓ Data analysis.
▓ Facial mapping (if the case demands it to prove a situational point in the case of locations).
▓ Handwriting.

Or procedures, such as forensic audit.

Forensic audit:
▓ Is carried out by forensic experts.
▓ The expert can give the results as evidence in a court.
▓ This evidence is subject to the same standards of admissibility as for any other class of evidence.

Digital forensics and evidence

Digital forensics (sometimes known as digital forensic science) is a branch of forensic science encompassing the recovery and investigation of material found in digital devices, often in relation to computer crime.

Digital forensics investigations have a variety of applications. The most common is to support or refute a hypothesis before criminal or civil (as part of the electronic discovery process) courts. Forensics may also feature in the private sector, such as during internal corporate investigations or intrusion investigation (a specialist probe into the nature and extent of an unauthorised network intrusion).

The technical aspect of an investigation is divided into several sub-branches, relating to the type of digital devices involved: computer forensics, network forensics, forensic data analysis and mobile device forensics. The typical forensic process encompasses the seizure, forensic imaging (acquisition) and analysis of digital media and the production of a report into collected evidence.

As well as identifying direct evidence of a crime, digital forensics can be used to attribute evidence to specific suspects, identify sources (for example, in copyright cases), or authenticate documents.

Investigations are much broader in scope than other areas of forensic analysis (where the usual aim is to provide answers to a series of simpler questions) often involving complex timelines or hypotheses.

- emails,
- digital photographs
- ATM transaction logs
- word processing documents
- instant message histories
- accounting programmes
- spreadsheets
- internet browser
- histories, databases
- contents of computer memory,
- computer backups,
- computer printouts,
- Global Positioning System tracks, logs from a hotel's electronic door locks,
- digital video or audio files

Never write on *original* items of evidence.

Perceiving 'naturally occurring' evidence
'Naturally occurring' evidential phenomena in ANY criminal offence are:

KNOWLEDGE DETAIL	EVENT DETAIL	EPISODES AND CONTINUOUS STATES
– Identities	– Actions	– Simple everyday episodes
– Locations	– Interactions	
– Objects	– Reactions or Responses	
– Relationships	– Utterances	
– Routines	– Verbal Exchanges	
– Rituals		
– Plans & Intentions		

Then, 'Beyond Red Flags' – specific evidence and evidential phenomena of fraud

STATIC ACTIONS	UTTERANCES	'MOVING'
– 'Bid rigging'	– Supporting a formality, such as a signed declaration	– Multiple frauds
– Manipulated Contracts		– Money movement
– Documentation		– Email harvesting
– Overstating Revenue		– Mass credit card cloning
– Forgery		– Systemic normal activity to cover a 'single-hit' fraud
– Misrepresentation		

The above are addressed in Chapter 4 (investigations) with a practical approach with actual scenarios and content in regard to prioritising and handling evidence.

Most criminal cases, including frauds usually get decided on a small number of key facts. Evidence to support those facts is provided as a consequence of human activity.

Other fraud-relevant incidental evidence

Electronic (digital) evidence

(1)'Information stored or transmitted in (2) binary form that (3) may be relied on in court.'

Those three steps are especially complicated today. With all the different 'smart' devices, evidence is everywhere, and capturing evidence from a smartphone, for instance, requires a different process than harvesting data from a computer or even a smart refrigerator.

'Volatile' data

One area of special focus is 'volatile' data.

It is worrying when those in authority in an organisation or company, whereby upon learning there is something seriously wrong (after an audit for example) order 'suspect devices' to be shut down to prevent any further damage.

Although it is accepted that management could stop criminal activity, it is also, however, problematic in that they could be destroying crucial data evidence and thereby directly hindering an investigation of the problems for the company. This will at least inhibit possible 'E-Discovery' or data recovery.

Witness testimony

Witness: *a person who sees an event, or otherwise can provide information in relation to an event.*

■ Witness testimony can form part of other evidence.

Examples of this are as follows:

■ When a witness produces a report derived from large amounts of data for data analysis in order to support a particular evidential purpose in a case. This will be direct evidence; namely, what a person did. (The witness providing this evidence may also in some instances be an 'expert witness'– depending on the context.)

■ When a witness is party to an event, a conversation and discusses it later. This will be hearsay. If a recording is made of a conversation (such as a police interview), the tape will be primary evidence, and the production of it will be direct. If a copy is passed to a colleague it will be direct. Copies of the tape and any written summary of it will be secondary.

■ An important note also is about **Independent Witnesses**. Most expert witnesses are independent, but non-expert independent witnesses are not and, moreover, often fall in with some formal policy matters. For example, (and outside the box for a moment) some enforcement authorities will not accept evidence or an account from a witness who is not independent. If the allegation of crime is between family members for example an 'independent' witness such as a neighbour will be sought.

■ The above account tends to go with eye-witness accounts to incidents such as assaults, to ensure as much objectivity as possible and to remove the emotive substance from it.

■ In fraud cases, documents and documentary items forming primary or secondary evidence need to be authenticated legally and independently in some instances. In other instances the mere production of an item or document is acceptable. It depends on the purpose of its submission.

Eyewitness testimony is a precise context of what evidence a witness will give.

∎ Even in the modern era of fraud investigations with all the technical advancement and focus, we must anchor ourselves to the point that fraud is a human crime. Witness testimony is, and always will be, the introducer of most evidence in most cases.

Massive amounts of research in cognitive psychology and human memory are done to analyse the effectiveness of eyewitness testimony, because juries especially tend to pay close attention to eyewitness testimony and generally find it a reliable source of information.

However, research into this area has found that eyewitness testimony can be affected by many psychological factors: stress, anxiety, bias, duress (has a witness been led or coerced?).

Naturally also, there is the distinct possibility that the witness is lying. If we refer back to the 'problem with words' and lies and liars, this issue appears prominently in the area of witness testimony.

A link here with our previous reference to memory, is *Reconstructive Memory*.

Bartlett's theory of reconstructive memory is crucial to an understanding of the reliability of eyewitness testimony as he suggested that recall is subject to personal interpretation dependent on our learnt or cultural norms and values, and the way we make sense of our world. With fraud cases this can be key, given certain social and religious concerns about fraud (and corruption).

Likewise, it is a feature of human memory that we do not store information exactly as it is presented to us. Rather, people extract from information the gist, or underlying meaning. In other words, people store information in the way that makes the most sense to them. We make sense of information by trying to fit it into 'schemas' which are a way of organising information.

Schemas are mental 'units' of knowledge that correspond to frequently encountered people, objects or situations. They allow us to make sense of what we encounter in order that we can predict what is going to happen and what we should do in any given situation. These schemas may, in part, be determined by social values and therefore prejudice.

Schemas are therefore capable of distorting unfamiliar or unconsciously 'unacceptable' information in order to 'fit in' with our existing knowledge or schemas. This can, therefore, result in unreliable eyewitness testimony.

SAMPLE WITNESS STATEMENT FROM FRAUD VICTIM

NAME OF INVESTIGATOR

Address:

Phone:

Date of fraud incident or first date if several dates involved:

Amount lost: $10,000.

Offender: XXX

Address:

Occupation:

1. My wife, J and I live on a fixed income of $_____ from investments and pension funds. We are both retired.

2. On **Monday, September 30th**, we attended a dinner sponsored by our charity club. Drinks were served at 7 pm. J and I arrived around 7.30 pm, had one cocktail and chatted with our friends.

3. At 8 pm, a friend of ours from church, introduced me to his friend XXX. Our friend told me that XXX is an investment advisor, and that he had made good profits by investing with him. We shook hands and XXX gave me his business card. (Exhibit 1) I am always interested in making more money to boost our retirement fund.

4. XXX told me about his investment portfolio. He told me he runs an exclusive investment club, and that by using a secret system known only to a very select group, his club has been able to realise profits of up to 300% per year. He said that our friend is a trusted member, and that he, XXX, would trust anyone our friend recommended. XXX began to elaborate a bit about currency exchanges and bank guarantees when the dinner bell rang. We agreed to meet for lunch on **October 2nd**.

5. The following morning, **Tuesday, October 1st**, I received a call from XXX. This must have been at 10 am because I was just getting ready to take the dog for a walk, which I do at the same time every day. XXX was very polite, and apologised for calling at an inconvenient time, and said he wanted to confirm the luncheon meeting scheduled for the following day. He asked me if a certain restaurant would be okay, and asked if I would be his guest.

6. I met XXX at the restaurant at 11.15 am. We had cocktails and were joined by his friend. XXX introduced his friend as the pastor of a church in the neighbouring town. XXX stated that members of his congregation had already invested in the opportunity.

7. Foolishly in hindsight, I wired XXX $10,000 to an account XXX provided. He disappeared. I could not contact him by phone or mail.

Practical Exercise: extracting witness knowledge from information   As an example of how crucial it is to handle eye witness testimony as any other element. From this case I dealt with, please read the following account. Read it with a purpose.

- First, separate the eye-witness account data from other information.
- Identify the key points which can *lead to* being direct evidence.
- Which other points are useful but need to be verified and why?

Witness Statement

My name is Miss D. I am the new CFO at XYZ Loans Company.

I am concerned about the behaviour of one manager. I don't know his name, but I know him from a previous company. I have now received what I think is a fake invoice. It has come from his office. I know this because I went to his office and found the invoice pad there. He always had a reputation for being a little 'suspect' with his expenses. He was always joking about it. It was always when he was with his friends. I have been informed that Mr. X found some auditing irregularities last week. The invoice pad has turned up in this manager's office. The fake invoice is from it.

I was stopped in the corridor by someone who wouldn't give his name but stated that this manager is regularly overcharging clients for admin fees for loans and pocketing the difference.

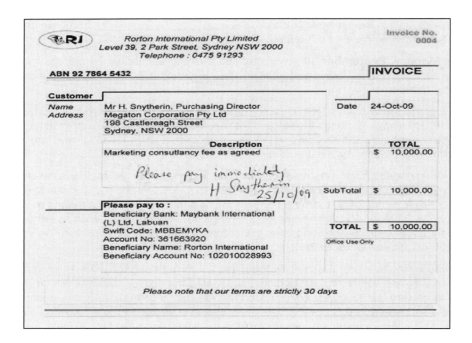

Investigator Response

Witness Statement

My name is Miss D. I am the new CFO at XYZ Loans Company.

I am concerned about the behaviour of one manager. I don't know his name, but I know him from a previous company. I have now received what I think is a fake invoice. It has come from his office. I know this because I went to his office and found *the* (?) invoice pad there. He always had a reputation for being a little 'suspect' with his expenses. He was always joking about it. It was always when he was with his friends. I have been informed that Mr. X found some auditing irregularities last week. The invoice pad has turned up in this manager's office. The fake invoice is from it.

I was stopped in the corridor by someone who wouldn't give his name but stated that this manager is regularly overcharging clients for admin fees for loans and pocketing the difference.

- Knowledge: I think it reasonable to suggest that Miss D knows her own name.
    - Miss D, in her position as CFO, with her qualifications, competence and experience is likely to know a fake invoice when she sees one. Direct and opinion evidence (but subject to cross examination).
    - The first point of the misrepresentation is when the invoice is submitted to the company. It needs to be established who has first received it and then reported it, how it came to be forwarded to Miss D (crucial to the chain of custody).

- Knowledge: yes, but more opinion than anything else. It needs to be verified.
  - When you see comments like 'I know' or 'I know for a fact' it usually means they don't.
  - Likewise when a witness says 'I am sure'. Sure means you are not.
  - The invoice itself may or may not be from the invoice pad found. However a simple check of the process will establish if it was submitted through the normal accounting system. If not, the invoice is a complete forgery. If it has then the invoice is still fraud. It is a key point to establish the misrepresentation to nullify any reliance on a mistake.

- ***Information as Knowledge***: We must locate those with knowledge of the crime and manage the transfer of the information. Using the skill set we demonstrate an ability to receive knowledge – and then <u>classify</u> it.
- ***Information as Evidence***: the extraction of evidence from that information.

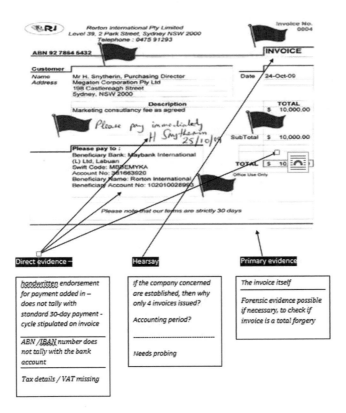

A slick and efficient handling and appraising of information will also help in terms of the evidence falling into place. You need not concern yourself with looking for types of evidence yourself at first instance. But if you reason out where in the information evidence of fraud exists, you will establish fraud immediately and plan an investigation effectively.

Whistle-blowing – witnesses nonetheless

Personally speaking, the term 'whistle-blower' is one of the most pointless and most dangerous pieces of jargon ever. It demeans people. Another cliché, like 'mugging' and others, has found its way into a myriad of settings. But the growth of the meaning of this label has become so warped and out of control that many have simply lost sight of what the concept and ideal of someone exposing serious criminal wrongdoing (such as fraud and corruption) actually is.

In the UK, if you are being approached by a whistle-blower, then consideration has to be given to the Public Information Disclosure Act (PIDA) or is the person happy to disclose the information openly? Has the informant brought any information to reinforce their allegation? This is a basic safeguard to investigation in any case.

Other points are that, in the corporate world, whistle-blowers are regarded as 'snitches' and informants, just like in the criminal underworld. But this could attract the wrong kind of volunteer. This presents fraud risk itself. It also presents a problem about the authenticity of witness testimony in some cases (they could be in it for the money, human nature being what it is).

Whistle-blower retaliation and criminal charges

Sometimes a company uses criminal charges as a form of retaliation. If successful, the company gets rid of the whistle-blower and discredits them, thereby minimising the possibility that they will file some kind of claim. If that isn't enough of an incentive, the tactic has a ripple effect throughout the entire company. Employees soon learn that if you make waves, the company can make your life miserable.

Thankfully, tactics like this rarely work. Smart, ethical businesses know that nothing encourages whistle-blowing more than retaliating against concerned employees who first try to bring concerns to the attention of management. While setting up an employee for failure and prosecution might scare some people away, companies that choose this extreme tactic run the real risk that the whistle-blower will have nothing to lose. Then the risks for the company are much higher, as many falsely accused employees will take their concerns to the media or the government.

Expert witnesses. Who are they?

Expert Witnesses carry out a major role in the judicial system of your country, by providing *opinion* evidence to assist courts in reaching decisions.

Such witnesses are commonly thought of as doctors or forensic scientists, criminal profilers, psychiatrists, and handwriting experts, but the remit of the expert witness can be an HR Director, or an IT expert with specialist knowledge of a given system or, as one witness in a case I encountered, an expert and CEO of a company in Kenya making industrial pesticides. Inside fraud was taking place whereby some employees were stealing some chemicals and adding other substitute chemicals and then selling these in the name of the company and keeping the money themselves.

Expert Witnesses may be asked to write a report or statement and be called to give evidence in a range of legal forums including civil and criminal, but also in tribunals, arbitration cases, and inquiries and professional conduct hearings, such as in health care.

International standards vary, and some countries have Associations and hold databases of experts who can attend court and give expert testimony. Qualifications are often set as a requirement, and a number of years professional, industrial or vocational experience. Equally, a requirement may be to have up-to-date training and accreditation (as pilots, or safety engineers).

But the 'E' word is one which has become so easily (ab)used in so many vocational contexts that it has become mundane and the true expert status cheapened across a range of professional benchmarks. In our area alone we have 'experts' in fraud who have never been anywhere near a fraud investigation.

Technical advancement creates experts but who are aligned to something else, and not necessarily with what the 'material cause' is (my polite way of saying that some 'experts' slide in from other vocations and pronounce themselves as 'experts' in fraud).

Another favourite word bandied around with equal effrontery is the word 'forensic'. (True) experts are often little-known 'doers' who create standards – not the opportunists who pretend to be.

Another twist to the tale is the warning to lawyers not to 'doctor' the reports of expert witnesses, as reforms are argued to be causing conflict between expert witness services and instructing lawyers.

Deadlines have affected turnaround and referred work. Expert witnesses are increasingly pressurised by deadlines to produce documents and reports.

One issue is the removal of dates for expert reports. Our way of practice is to put into an appendix the reports we've relied on with their dates. But we are asked to remove the date of the report.

Lawyers are found to have taken the dates out before serving the reports, without asking the expert witness who provided it, which is not particularly good practice.

'Subconscious analysis' is another aspect of controversy in this context.

Experts are often asked to remove a report from our list relied on for a case. The assumption is that if you have read something, then consciously or subconsciously, it's in your mind and may well affect your analysis. This a questionable assertion. The expert knows best.

What is clear, in any case, is that the expert's report must be authored by the expert. Whilst it is acceptable for a lawyer to make *suggestions* to the expert about changes to the report, it is unacceptable for a lawyer to 'doctor' an expert's report.

Accreditation and representation

Forensic expert witnesses should be accredited. The ones who matter say this, namely judges.

A former South African police officer in one case I was involved with was torn to pieces in court by a judge who pronounced that the individual was not a forensic expert of any kind. The one concerned had agreed to appear as a defence witness claiming to have carried out a forensic audit on the records and client files of a business acquaintance. He had no qualifications or even professional external auditing experience. He sounded, and was made to look, ridiculous.

In one famous UK case, a criminal profiler was described by one outraged judge as a 'puppet master', who had led the police along entirely the wrong path from beginning to end in a very lengthy (and costly) investigation. The police had failed to carry out any kind of due diligence on the profiler and alignment with that type of case. The whole reinvestigation was based on misconception and the police blindly followed it.

◼ **The above two examples are factual cases, one of which I observed first-hand, so please do not shoot the messenger. My aim is to support you.**

The dangers of this credibility void are obvious; theoretically, anyone with any sort of background and sufficient personal confidence, perhaps less politely described as having the nerve, or who was sufficiently misguided, could set themselves up as a forensic science expert and produce evidence that, at best, is unhelpful and, at worst, positively misleading; nobody would necessarily be any the wiser.

A Council for the Registration of Forensic Practitioners (CRFP) was established with UK Home Office support in 1997 as an independent regulatory body to promote public confidence in forensic practice, but it later ceased to operate due to lack of government funding. CRFP accreditation was based on peer review only of forensic practitioners. Therefore, experts (rightly) had to obtain separate accreditation for each field of expertise in which they wished to give evidence, and had to specify precisely what they were accredited in.

Ironically the demise of the CFRP is a step backwards, as this is precisely the sort of regulation and accreditation which is now lacking.

SUMMARY **POINTS:**

- A common criticism is that some expert witnesses step outside the bounds of their expertise. In fairness of course, some lawyers insist on asking the wrong questions of witnesses in this context and actually invite an opinion that they ought not to be asking for at all. For example, a criminal profiler who is assessing a fraud offender pre-sentence can give opinion evidence of personality traits but cannot *diagnose* an offender's personality and propensity to commit fraud in the future.
- People find it tempting and as easy to exaggerate their professional status as a witness as they do with their CVs and resumes.
- As for all witnesses, the witness box can be a very lonely place if you are in any way trying to bluff your status. It is therefore inevitable that your evidence will be flawed as well.
- Politely put, if you want to be regarded and classified as an expert or 'forensic' witness, then please ensure you are accredited to be one. Judges have more than picked up on this and do not hold back when it comes to stating problems of this misrepresentation of professional status. In fact judges have been at their most outraged and outspoken in tearing into expert witnesses publicly, more so than the defendant on trial. Beware.

CHAPTER SUMMARY

- Fraud is not the same as money laundering, but fraud can be the originating crime (or will form the 'criminal proceeds') for money laundering.
- Money laundering usually includes a fraud somewhere along the way.
- Fraud is not the same as corruption. No one has to be actually deceived in a corruption case (down to 'wheeling and dealing') but for fraud the misrepresentation and/or breach of fiduciary trust must be present.
- Lies do not necessarily equate to 'fraud'.

These first references already point to the fact that the level of guilty knowledge the offender must have to have a case to answer in fraud is a matter of subjective assessment.

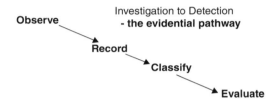

Remember also that you are working towards *exposing* fraud to a tangible level of establishing the presence of fraud in a scenario to a legal standard *per se* (and ideally to incorporate accepting of guilt by the offender) and the case being capable of being understood and legally acted upon by an objective third party to whom you present the case. This can be a court or tribunal, or HR department or senior decision maker.

But do not make the mistake of assuming that if the case is not being heard by a court and is 'in-house,' that the quality of the investigation and the evidence acquisition and handling of it can become casual or reduced to a lesser professional standard. The best rule of thumb is to assume that your case will end up in court one way or another – which includes the prospect of the offender suing you later for investigative malpractice, or there has been an abuse of process.

Casual thinking leads to adverse professional outcomes.

CHAPTER TWO

Concepts and Dynamics of Fraud

I find that the harder I work, the more luck I seem to have.

—*Thomas Jefferson*

 INTRODUCTION

Having engaged with definitions and made reasonable discourse on certain key points (misrepresentation, for example) we now begin to deal with fraud contexts and scenarios in earnest.

In the main, in fraud there is no 'scene of crime' and often there are no mistakes to follow. This is a major reason why there have been such enormous hurdles in tackling the problem. But these hurdles are in effect man-made. That is still a true entity and the existing state of the norm in investigating crime even when fraud activity took a new turn, when fraud visibly and palpably was worked into alignment with cybercrime.

A recent development also covered in this chapter is the speed and rapidity of frauds in contexts of finance and credit cards, with the unenviable task of reconciling security against fraud with the insatiable need to have the business edge against other banks and hence leading a strategy for 'Faster Payments.'

Exposing Fraud must, if it is to be taken to its full value, also bring out the short-comings and wanton political hurdles by some in enforcement, and those with formal responsibilities to investigate, but who habitually or culturally by organisation fail to do so, and by conclusive fact, fail the victim of fraud. This is not to be critical for the sake of it. It is a simple fact that victims of fraud are not interested in hubristic politicised boasting by enforcement authorities. Instead they want action. Therefore this is to inform some simple needs for attitude adjustment to the public as opposed to promoting empires that produce little. Often also with the ever-present excuses of either 'lack of funding' or oddly constructed priorities in crime enforcement policy, or simply refusing to do what they claim to do.

Incidentally, this chapter also may help you to decide which counter-fraud industry to work in (insurance, finance, the banks, legal, main-stream industry) and you MUST 'know your business'.

2.1 COSTS OF FRAUD – INCLUDING THE HIDDEN ONES WE DON'T LIKE TO MENTION

I will be brief but pertinent at this point. I will also spare you from another dry repetition of pitching statistics with hackneyed statements of fraud losses which will be of no use by next week, and most of which evade the more inherent hidden issues of fraud 'losses'.

There are excellent resources (which pitch some scary realities) in regard to the cost of fraud. The Association of Certified Fraud Examiners (ACFE) publish their annual *Report to the Nations* and base their research findings on very comprehensive qualitative terms of reference. It is accepted as the foremost report of its kind. Again, the point is made that this book focuses on fraud and, whilst there are publications to report corruption levels, these are not of the same construct. Likewise, measurement of money laundering is not and in fact cannot be measured in the same way as fraud.

But the failure to learn from or even think about previous fraud occurrences is a major part of the reason why, despite more technological advances and armies of risk experts, there is more fraud and money laundering in the world than ever before. The costs never lessen. Also, it is true to say that corporations actually refuse to address previous fraud incidents to inform new counter-fraud policy planning because of reputational risk, for one reason. A brief repetition of an earlier comment will do no harm: that to be a victim of fraud is to be made a fool of. This point applies to a corporate identity as well as the individual. Too many businesses view fraud losses as mere business losses instead of criminal losses, and hence do not think in terms of crime prevention (which is not so complicated if one chooses to) and prefer to spend massive amounts on marketing to gain more revenues yet are prepared to stand by and watch some of these revenues fall to fraud. Incredibly, though, we insist in maintaining this 'pool' of availability for fraudsters, or a swamp of business loss and that swamp is endlessly refilled and replenished – we fail to TRULY learn from past mistakes, because FRAUD is embarrassing and something we don't want others to know about. Internally we just want to move on. But there is an absolute duty to know why it happened!

Hence online and corporate fraud remain a serious concern for global business. But part of the problem in tackling the ever-evolving nature of fraud often comes from the very techniques but more importantly, lacklustre approaches used to prevent it.

The global market research and survey company, Frost & Sullivan, estimates that there are 2.28 million information security professionals worldwide. This figure is expected to increase to nearly 4.2 million by the end of 2015. Consequently therefore, the information security industry is going through an exponential growth rate. Current worldwide growth rate is billed at 21%. The information security industry is currently over $100B ($60B in US, $20B UK, $4.5B Japan, over $1.5B in India).

So acknowledgement and 'credit' where it is due, must go the financial institutions for the marked increase in fraud prevention controls over the past 3 years, especially formulated to grow with the surge in popularity of social media, e-commerce, and mobile services. E-finance is proof of the benefits consumers are enjoying from information and communication technologies. But there is also the creation of a worthless fraud prevention sub-market of its own; the creature 'solutions' based IT resources being a means of leeching off the need for security and fraud prevention; namely a fixation on selling as opposed to securing.

Conversely, these same technologies can create harm, when personal consumer information is stolen by way of fraud and identity theft. Or is it purely down to the 'technologies'? Studies show that information systems workers, as expert as they are in matters technical and analytical, lack basic security knowledge. Proof? Since 2005, an estimated 543 million records have been lost globally from over 2,800 data breaches, and identity theft caused $13.3 billion in consumer financial loss in 2011 (BJS, 2011). That is a cost of fraud as well.

Thus it is a major challenge for policy makers whose job is to keep on the right side of the law while trying not to lose the business, by balancing ex-ante regulation with ex-post litigation to protect both consumer and commercial interests.

Furthermore, a survey among lawyers in the USA, UK and Europe shows a serious concern about cloud computing services (using software as a service: users rent use of servers; cloud providers manage the infrastructure and platforms on which the applications run). Lawyers clearly state that data in the cloud is a 'business risk'. Yes that is so, but when we look beyond the business risk, there emanates a conflict, which in turn equals risk of loss to fraud and puts companies at risk of massive penalties because of 'naturally occurring' data protection transgressions. Legal experts contacted by *Future Intelligence* (independent IT expert analysts) say that in its current state, the cloud technology system (worth £14.4 billion globally to the technology companies promoting it), puts companies trusting personal data in breach of data protection legislation.

But the legal experts have also uncovered the potential for corporate fraud. The natural cross-over opens a can of worms which squirm off in different directions: data fraud, breaches of auditing standards (which could constitute an offence of fraud in its own right by failing to disclose information if cover-up attempts were made) financial statement fraud, 'skimming' or understated sale or debtor payments.

Therefore, getting behind enemy lines, as opposed to following never ending saleslines may warrant some thought. This is so because the battle plans drawn up by fraudsters vary as much as the countries in which they operate, some with single-cause fraud motives, or those who attack with a scatter of scams, cyber-attacks, and multi-layered, organised and systemically networked financial crime activity.

A TRILLION-DOLLAR WAR

Is there an inescapable link to fraud in order to fund drug habits? Afraid so. Many criminals have gone beyond shoplifting to do this and say 'ID theft is the way to go'.

By some estimates, the war on drugs just in the USA has cost close to a trillion dollars. What has that vast expenditure bought? Very little. According to the government's 'Survey on Drug Use and Health', more than 22 million Americans – nearly 9 % of the U.S. population – used illegal drugs in 2012.

And laundering drug money is often done online and by social networks. Hence, the amounts of money involved are de facto immeasurable, staggering figures (that fraud institutions and the 'Big 4' auditing companies are reluctant to admit to).

So where are the systems and 'controls' etc., which control this?

Answer 1: The financial institutions cannot even agree on what fraud is half the time. The whole concept of fraud falls down when it gets to the measurement of fraud, with private sector regulators insisting upon creating their own definitions and wildly inconsistent financial fraud measurement parameters (per Chapter 1).

Answer 2: We spend far too long 'developing' and indulging the same recycled initiatives. There is the Financial Action Task Force (FATF) which rolls out initiatives and recommendations which is its role (and they are not helped by some governments taking over 2 years to implement the recommendations, if at all) and there is an array of anti-corruption conferences and summits such as, for example, the G20 summit talks, whereby the participatory agenda is thick with tactics from all parties and plied with personal agendas.

To illustrate this last point: KPMG – Global Anti-Money Laundering Survey 2014:

The top 3 areas where bank AML budgets are invested were:

- ▦ Transaction Monitoring Systems.
- ▦ Know Your Customer (KYC) reviews, up-dates, maintenance.
- ▦ Recruitment.

These figures represent the *investment* the banks make in countering money laundering.

Fraud: The total annual global loss to fraud in 2014 was above $3.5 trillion

'The Global Cyber Black Market' is confirmed to be more profitable than the global illegal drugs trade. Just in South Africa alone, the total loss to fraud in 2014 was 5.8 billion South Africa Rand (19% of online banking users have fallen victim to online fraud that has increased by 10% from a year ago). Hence this context of fraud with such massive losses is not merely a means of relaying statistics, it provides evidence that fraud is such an amorphous entity of a crime. Fraud can be categorised, but not *truly* measured.

Finally on this point, for those who still regard fraud as a 'victimless crime' or regard fraud victims as second-class victims of crime, the effects of fraud, namely loss of business, insurance problems, stress, etc., do not provide justification to remove the need to support victims of fraud, and de-categorise economic crime.

In summary, losses and the resulting costs of fraud involve not just the losses to fraudsters; they are also directly attributable to inept fraud prevention controls or even behind that, some matters of reporting the issues.

- A development in economic crime measurement has been introduced in Russia in 2015, whereby Russia launched its own corruption index, to replace what they call the 'biased' Transparency International 'Corruption Perception Index'.

Indeed a Russian government institute has developed a sophisticated programme for evaluating the level of corruption, which its authors say is superior to the widely advertised, but subjective and widely criticised Transparency International Corruption Perception Index (CPI). They argue that the CPI is merely a representation of how a particular society is concerned about corruption. It lacks objectivity, is politically motivated and indulged as such by high-paying corporate 'donors'.

The new report will be presented by the Institute of Law and Comparative Jurisprudence at the Eurasian Anti-Corruption Forum. It is called the International Corruption Monitoring Program, or MONKOR. The new index is based on criminal statistics, economic data, opinion polls and analysis of national legislation, one of its authors, Artyom Tsyrin confirmed. This makes the analysis and findings wholly different from the Corruption Perception Index, prepared annually by Transparency International.

 ## 2.2 IT IS NOT ENOUGH TO KNOW 'WHAT FRAUD IS' – KNOW YOUR BUSINESS!

The main challenge you have is combining your fraud knowledge and skills with the situational case or business context in which you find yourself.

A fact that must never be overlooked is that, to the majority of people, the word 'fraud' is a very serious and negative word. Flinging the fraud word around casually is an unforgiveable sin for a counter-fraud professional. Not only will such foolish and wantonly unprofessional behaviour help destroy your reputation, the ever lurking legal implications hover overhead – and will not go away easily.

If the figures quoted in the last section concerning the losses to fraud do not concern you then they ought to. Quoting segments of an annual study of 'occupational fraud' (ACFE) and fraud hitting the banking industry shows that no matter how effective the reporting of costs is, we really do not know the true figures. In fact it is even argued that Money Laundering is 'de-facto' immeasurable and out of control (FATF Report 2010).

Therefore, if you refer to our quote above by Thomas Jefferson, a former US president, it gives quite a rallying message, and you as a counter-fraud professional, or aspiring one, MUST be ready and willing for some hard work. Hastening to add, that you need to be realistic about how the work you put in should be aligned with your 'forte in fraud'. What I mean by that is, will your area of counter-fraud work be in insurance, or in finance, or as an IT professional aligning the reduction of cyber-crime initiatives with economic crime? You will not be able to do it all. But the ground work you commit to at this stage (which really ought to be re-visited with continuing professional development, as it does no harm to return to basics sometimes, as well as keeping up, as it were) will give you that backdrop of certainty and confidence.

- One worthwhile exercise the fraud investigator can indulge, is to locate and watch well-chosen TV interviews with suspected and/or convicted fraudsters. To pitch you into the deep end here, or even if you are an experienced fraud investigator, look at an interview with Lynn Tilton on CNBC news channel. The self-proclaimed 'turnaround queen' Lynn Tilton is, at the time of this publication in 2015, suing the U.S. Securities and Exchange Commission (SEC) after being investigated by them for alleged securities fraud, an investigation which was dragged out for over 5 years. The private equity executive and her New York-based Patriarch Partners funds are suing the federal regulator on constitutional grounds, after the SEC accused them of fraud and improperly collecting nearly $200 million in 'undeserved' fees.
- Lynn Tilton has one of the most brilliant business minds in the world. She has a grand comfort and ease in which she articulates legalities when she accounts the breach of her constitutional rights. 'Unleashed subpoena power' and 'one-sided testimony' gives the clear stance of someone at the pinnacle of business achievement with an aura of both the business person and the 'warrior fighting for truth' as she refers to herself with a very highly convincing level of dignity. Unlike many other well-known billionaires who push the celebrity status with the 'catch-me if you can' persona, Ms. Tilton does not do showboating and is a convincing communicator. Ms. Tilton speaks in very clear language, with open facial composure and non-verbal eminence. She occasionally references highly sophisticated investment terminologies which, if you are not fully in connection with as an investigator, you will be left very far behind. Yet, she is far removed from the school of business cliché impressiveness.
- Lynn Tilton has been established as not being a fraudster. She was accused of being one by the SEC, who arguably tried all kinds of tactics and tricks to stifle her defending herself, as it was clear that they could not match her at these business levels and exact contexts.
- Perhaps the biggest mistake that the SEC made and you will make if you take the same approach, is seeing this matter as a personal must-win battle, instead of a reasoned, measured and proportionate fraud investigation. It seems to be an unfortunate case of authorities forcing the facts to fit. Otherwise they would not be in the process of being sued, and Lynn Tilton has never lost a case.

The below is a means of helping you to gauge your way of thinking in terms of ascertaining where your strengths and vocational relevancies in fraud investigation are to take you. We made mention in Chapter 1, for example, of the Herculean demands made on the professional involved with insurance fraud cases. The table opens out the business contexts.

Activity

As a means of taking a brief acid test on this, give a brief verbal response to what is meant by the business-colloquial terms in the box below. These are not in a particular context. They are chosen randomly for you to check for yourself how engaged with business-speak you are. If you are going to apply fraud investigation skills to fraud definitions, a grasp of these kind of business environmental 'triggers' will help.

Just respond to each of these terms as quickly, accurately and as simply as you can. Please be honest with yourself if you don't know. Don't guess for answers.

(Explanations to these are in the appendix of this chapter)

the 'Bottom line'	'Seed Funding'	'Diversification'
'Insider Trading'	'Equity'	'Incremental Revenue'
'Intellectual Property'	'Hedge Fund'	'Procurement'
'Supply Chain Analytics'	'General Reserve Fund (GRF)'	'Crowdfunding'
'Capital'	'Bonus Scheme'	'Balance sheet'
'Venture Capital'	'Accure'	'Bitcoin'
'Kpi'	'Underwritten'	'Whistleblower'

- Review your responses to the above and reflect not so much on what you do or don't know in business, but what notions appear in your mind about what situational and business areas of fraud you could operate in. For example, (with due respect to the industry concerned) you may totally reject any notion of being involved in 'high-end' sophisticated finance and investment areas. This is not being disrespectful to anyone, but you probably don't even talk in the same language as they do. It is a sophisticated area and you need to train for it as well as 'knowing your fraud'. But this could be for you, or you may choose to work in an entirely different area.
- Likewise, would you be able to approach a 'crowdfunding' issue and investigate fraud activity within it? Would you feel comfortable? (Crowdfunding carries fraud risk similar to 'Ponzi schemes' of misrepresentation of an investment and the use of 'middle-men' whereby the unscrupulous will latch onto a perfectly *bona fide* business entity.)

If you extract 2 or 3 of the above terminologies from the list provided, you could now apply points of vulnerabilities to fraud. For quick examples for now, I have chosen these two:

- **'The bottom line'** – A fundamental and coverall risk of fraud is misrepresentation of the bottom line, which really amounts to a snapshot of an entire company's financial standing. If this is wrong, you can wager that fraud is present somewhere, especially in the accounts. Certain ingredients of the fraud behaviour informing the bottom line statement are fictitious sales, overstated revenues, and understated expenditure, predicted sales recorded as actual sales, accounting period abuse and manipulation.

- **'Bonus Scheme'** – Probably quite straightforward in spotting points of fraud vulnerability in an occupational fraud scenario. The manager for example, who falsifies KPIs to misrepresent (exaggerate) performance, or forges sales results to get a bonus she/he would not otherwise receive (a case also shored up by a breach of fiduciary trust besides the misrepresentation).

These two are simple examples, and at this juncture, I will inform you that the engagement with fraud scenarios will step up a gear when we engage with extended scenarios (such as procurement and others), but that is after we involve our thinking with certain fraud psychologies coming up next.

Now if we compare some lesser known 'fraud speak' such as, 'Supplier fraud', 'Upcoding', 'Unbundling', 'Overservicing', and 'Non declaration', imagine the scene if a 'fraud' investigator meets an industry professional from one of the settings above. It takes little imagination to see the solid barrier to communication appearing like a wall directly between them. The conversation will be a very testing one, and few if any issues will be reconciled because of it. I have encountered more than one meeting of this nature, whereby an in-house meeting in an organisation becomes a contest in who can cram in the most clichés. Most of the discussion will be about each asking the other to clarify what they say, or, after little time, simply giving up. People, especially corporate people, rarely listen to anyone or about anything outside of their situation or anything that is not in alignment wih their personal self-promotion agenda. They simply programme themselves about what they are going to say next. The same applies to some enforcement officers who either cut themselves off from business nuances or try to impose an alien authoritarian presence on a business setting. That does not work either.

Therefore the onus is on the fraud investigator to engage with business perspectives. You are there to bring in a presence of investigation that the ones you are meeting cannot do themselves, and give confidence to your contacts and clients (who are invariably your fraud victims). But that is not to mean you must take an MBA or something. Nor does it mean you kowtow to corporate protagonists who like to show off. Cutting through this maze as well is a part of what you need to do. You have the job of reconciling the issues in order to carve out a way forward into a serious criminal issue.

As an example, as a police officer, I had a case to investigate of a fraud offender who was committing numerous fraud activities simultaneously. Of course, Chapter 4 in this book is about investigations and *practicalities*, drills into skills, planning and overcoming barriers and 'where to start' in an investigations context, but at this stage and to inform the meaning, the case involved false accounting, credit card fraud, insolvency fraud, perjury, misrepresentation (of the bottom line), misrepresentation and 'scamming' of suppliers to his business and his own customers.

CASE **STUDY**

'SG'

The offender, SG ran a business in selling furniture and leather settees, 3-piece suites and the like.

SG rented a sales warehouse in the North of England to display the various settees open to the public. Customers would place an order and pay a deposit for the suites, and then be told they will receive delivery of the furniture in the next 7 days. But they did not.

SG was taking orders from customers and suppliers of the furniture (located all over the UK) at the same time, but not paying the suppliers. He would order settees up the value of 100,000 pounds over a certain period, sell them, keep the money but not pay the suppliers.

At the same time, he would sell the suites on display 'privately' and keep the money.

That group were never accounted for by SG. Therefore very irate customers called the factory store to ask when they will get their suites they had paid a deposit for (usually a minimum of 200 pounds a time) only for the phones not to be answered.

Some customers converged on the store personally, but the place was now deserted.

At the same time, the supplier companies were sending piles of demand letters, invoices and reminders, the value of which by then was accruing up to nearly a quarter of a million pounds for orders made over a 4 to 5-month period.

This however did not prevent a full creditors' meeting whereby SG had to present a proposal to the supplier creditors of a pay-back plan.

Reluctantly and regrettably, the creditors (representatives from the supplier companies) voted not to bankrupt SG by creditors' judgement provided he agreed to swear an affidavit at the Civil Court to honour a 3-year payback promise to each creditor. It never happened. Furthermore, the affidavit was falsified on several key points.

SG then had the impudence to go to another completely new supplier he had not dealt with before, and took a supply of 20 settees, sold those to 'private' (unaccounted) customers and then he disappeared altogether.

The case overall had 14 victims of the customers who had ordered settees and suites from the warehouse. There were 12 furniture suppliers who SG had fleeced also. Hence, I took 26 witness statements and handled 48 exhibits.

One poor lady had suffered a heart attack from the stress and humiliation of being scammed. Other victims were teachers, managers, and people from all kinds of backgrounds.

Then I made a basic revision of the civil procedure rules and that of insolvency and business conveyance (in furtherance to my claim of the importance of knowing your business as well as your fraud).

I arrested SG and spent more than 7 hours interviewing SG in two 'sittings' with his lawyer present. Eventually SG was sentenced in the Crown Court on several counts of theft and fraud.

Rounding off this issue, recent dialogue which centrally included Rodger Fuller, a Senior Partner of the Financial Crime Advisory Group based in the UK, who succinctly captured the meaning and need to know your businesses as well as your fraud, if you are going to be any good at catching fraud offenders, and overcoming heretical barriers. It was aptly put, that 'sound bite' policing has no credibility especially when a statement from the Head of a National Crime Agency in the UK in regard to countering fraud and money laundering is so poor that it means nothing. In the context of corrupt London bankers or corrupt bank employees, most counter-fraud professionals know that fraud is an ever-present – but worse, an ever-enlarging – risk of fraud and money laundering.

In this context, Rodger Fuller 'deliberately' (in his own words) spent several months working for one of the largest financial institutions, because as a member of law enforcement his previous experience of commercial banking was limited to prosecution investigation, and it was clear (to him, and well put) that he needed to properly understand those risks. He also respectfully suggested in 2015 that the Head of the UK National Crime Agency would benefit from something similar or maybe to take some real professional advice before making pointless political publicity statements. Calling for dynamic action in the financial fraud environment by the NCA, not pointless words, would be far better for the health of our economy and national security. This also highlights the disconnection between the police and business, created by their unwillingness to involve themselves with business above anything higher than low-hanging fruit level.

Police units, such as the Insurance Fraud Enforcement Department (IFED) dealing with scams against insurance companies ('cash for crash' schemes) are praiseworthy in principle, but likewise the more cynical see this as not being about reducing fraud per se, (as the research shows also) it is more about maintaining profits in a commercial deal, with police officers being used as glorified lackeys for insurance companies. This, as opposed to really reducing fraud, because end-user customers see little if any benefit to them by way of their premium payments being reduced when set next to the numbers of arrests of alleged insurance fraud offenders. The classic police obsession with herding numbers of arrests for appearances' sake but with a low number of convictions. Even back in 2011, of the 260 arrests, less than 8% of those arrested actually appeared in court, with only 12 convictions. There were 76 cautions (and how does this reduce fraud?). This is a dangerous approach, as it invites abuse of powers, grounds to appeal, continuing breaches of Article 6 of the European Convention on Human Rights, and clear evidence of police impartiality being effectively bought by insurance companies.

And in furtherance of the need to simply bridge this 'business gap', Rowan Bosworth-Davies, a former Scotland Yard detective with vast experience, makes the case very clear in his series of superb articles which address this issue. Rowan elevates his experience in this very way. He can speak with the most superlative authority on issues like the 'Forex' Market crimes, and articulate finitely on the heuristics and cronyism in business environments at the very pinnacle of British business, in banking and financial institutions in the City of London. Realism and objectivity make up all of his submissions and assertions, and the point is that Rowan chose to 'know his business' whilst enforcement officialdom still choose not to, or better put, pretend not to at certain times and in certain beneficial commercial enterprises.

Failure to see the connection with organised crime and security by these authorities and the predecessor outfits (now disbanded) is not particularly surprising to see. And this banal insistence of over-categorising and pigeon-holing crimes leaves no connectivity to business in so many aspects, as we have touched upon here should happen.

2.3 THE VARYING PSYCHOLOGIES OF FRAUD

Why fraud is unique as a crime

To make a simple distinction it may be useful to see cybercrime as a 'conduct' crime and economic crime a 'result' crime. Qualifying points are:

- It is now (very) rare that the perpetrator of a fraud case has direct interpersonal contact or involvement with the victim. This is especially so in cyber-related fraud.
- There is no 'scene of crime' in fraud. The fraud crime is discovered (much) later.
- Consequently to that, there are mostly no 'clues' or leads as in scenes of crime for other offences. You must follow the skill. For example, telemarketing and Internet fraud, identity theft and credit card account thefts, are among the most prominent of these.
- *Investigation* of fraud demands a level of conceptual thought, creative thinking (away from the policy) and an ability to decipher evidence from a range of information sources.
- Victims of fraud are very often reluctant to report fraud at all. This is equally so at corporate identity level. Even then, fraud victims are not the 'easiest' victims to support. To be a victim of fraud is to be *prima facie* made a fool of. Victims will say 'It's not easy to talk about this'.
- A certain 'sensitivity' comes into fraud and fraud victims that is absent from other crimes. Victims of fraud vary in disposition as the fraudsters do with their schemes.

Victims and 'victimhood' (in fraud)

Fraud is debilitating to human kind. That is the raw truth. So as harsh as this may seem, it is the root of ALL fraud investigation cases (when you clearly establish fraud in a case). You must, with no grey areas, establish that fraud is present in the case. Even if emotional dialogue raging about 'ethics' and right and wrong and insouciantly applied dishonesty is brought in by one the parties to the case, you will have a scenario of dishonesty in its basic sense but you do *not* have fraud. Your work-day knowledge of fraud definitions appropriate to you should be set and automatic by now.

As crucial as the understanding of the definitions of fraud themselves, is the understanding of who is a victim. We can, for example, briefly step outside the constraints of fraud and refer to one case involving causes to promote new measures to combat 'cyber-bullying'. But into the mix came the opposing arguments that the measures were too draconian and were stifling rights, endorsed by the vociferous use of accusatory terminology such as 'trolls' or 'cyber bullies' for disagreeing with a particular consensus. Interestingly, therefore, we can learn that a new set of accusatory cliché-led names which are flung around openly are engineered by self-appointed victims. This in turn ought to make you as an investigator of fraud cautious of hearing and responding to parochial terms and trendy buzzwords which some people use to reinforce an argument, and have no hesitancy in flinging mud to say what the other is saying is 'criminal'. Whistle-blowers are often subjected to this kind of treatment, and often by officialdom.

With this problem, also it is common to hear politicians, even prime ministers and presidents, make meandering speeches, conveniently rolling all manner of fiscal and financial crime issues erroneously into one, with totally confusing pronouncements to go with it. According to some political rhetoric anyone who has an offshore bank account has to be a tax evader, a fraudster and money launderer all in one. Equally also, the failings of certain EU governments, for example Greece, to set effective tax collection procedures suddenly gets to be the fault of the entire community who are all labelled as tax evading criminals, just to plug financial holes caused by incompetent top-tier management and even ministerial incompetence. Fraud victimology can therefore take a peculiar turn.

Also, following numerous banking scandals, with direct complicity in money laundering and tax evasion costing billions, many have a problem seeing a bank as a 'victim' of fraud. But they are, and on a daily basis.

Some excellent studies on victims and 'victimhood' have been produced. The Zur Institute in the United States has presented many underlying issues about victims of crime. Amongst these was a paper titled, 'Rethinking "Don't Blame the Victim": The Psychology of Victimhood'. Albeit the research focuses mainly on violent crime and violent issues, one point of reference is that blame of the victim is as counter-productive as the 'politically correct' attitude of non-blame, because it produces a climate that forbids exploration of the role of victims. This is a point well made, because investigating fraud, with all of its nuances, and in all manner of scenarios, must entail examining the history of the victim, the involvement of the victim and what informed the misrepresentation against them.

With this, victims can tell us much more than we may first think, but we need to obtain such detail from them. A victim, for example, is the one and only person who can direct you to other victims in the same chain of fraud activity, or at least make you aware of them.

Likewise in our fraud context, it can be argued that social media is now a massive creator of fraud criminals, who were once victims. I presented at a conference in Bogota in 2012: 'Social Networking as Facilitator of Fraud'. Ninety-six per cent of people under age 30 have joined a social network. Twitter has 75 million users, and an equally extravagant number of users are on LinkedIn and Facebook. One impulsive but not too unexpected comment was once made to me by a senior director of a large Middle East based steel company where internal fraud was bordering on rampant. Before I delivered a training course in-house he said, 'We have enough problems here, Ian, are you not teaching people how to commit fraud?'

My response was politely and merely to point out that social media can do a far better job at that than I can, and of course is permanently accessible. That was not to be 'smart' or anything like that, it was a true-life reference to the fact that there are thousands of videos online on how to hack for one example. There are even very professional and 'modularised' training programmes with 'learning outcomes'. Following this trend therefore, the amount of identity (ID) theft rockets in number on a daily basis. Online fraud victims grow in number but their numbers are counter-balanced – even exceeded – by this first-hand social media guidance on how to commit fraud which creates offenders at rate arguably faster than any other fraud offender motivational context. The victims see how easy it is so they try it on themselves. Yesterday's fraud victim is today's fraud criminal (more in Chapter 3).

Point: An understanding of some key concepts of 'victimhood' is not a strictly academic exercise. This awareness can help you with time management of your case work if, for example, you are dealing with a case whereby the victims come to you via a third party.

I received a referral for a case in South Africa because the (numerous) victims had been to the police in ones and twos but had got nowhere, largely due to the monetary 'price' the police in some jurisdictions put on being a victim. Namely, if the case is below certain value, then it is 'officially' not fraud. This is of course absurd, but it is policy. Therefore victims were in desperation about what to do after being conned out of thousands in a real estate scam. These victims will not – or ought not – present any challenges to you in preparing a case, as they will have no knowledge of fraud in the formality sense, and you can benchmark the evidence and prioritise it. This is in complete contrast to a fraud case involving a corporate scenario, whereby you may encounter a mix of company cultural attitudes and policy formalities to the organisation being a victim of fraud.

Of course, collecting and classifying evidence of fraud is fundamental to your work (as we will profoundly address in Chapter 4) but establishing who a victim is, and why, is also a clinical and exact way of thought for an investigator, and in fact a critical element of your work, but as simple as this sounds, it is a point often overlooked or taken for granted. In other crimes there is usually a scene of crime, as a break-in, or a clear result of crime, such as a physical assault with resulting injuries to the victim. In fraud, unless you have a cyber-related fraud attack, whereby a system is hacked with a full-on 'smash and grab' style hacking attack, there is mostly no scene of crime. Victims of fraud discover they are a victim when it is way too late, but then you really need to see documentation for example, or 'result crime' evidence of material losses to fraud. Information that can be instantly assessed as providing grounds for an investigation, and not for going into sterile arguments or meaningless banter. Equally, do not be led to think that a genuine fraud victim is not so because they took a risk, or 'it was their own fault'. If, and only if the evidence is there, you have a case. Misguided, inappropriate moral judgments do not come into it.

Hence, it is a major professional failing to be led by protagonists who either subtly or vocally misapply fraud elements to try either maliciously or emotively to persuade you that they or someone else is a fraud victim. Know in your own mind professionally that this the case.

To support you also, an invaluable move for any investigator is to involve your work with and put pertinent questions to our relevant psychologists. Although they both work closely with the legal system, *criminal* and *forensic* psychologists have different focuses. A criminal psychologist evaluates criminals exclusively. A forensic psychologist in contrast works with all types of court cases, including civil matters not involving just the offenders, but the victims also. Much of a criminal psychologist's work is done on a theoretical basis, but a forensic psychologist tends to evaluate persons already identified by the courts. Therefore by the time victim or witness or both is 'identified' by the courts you will have derived for the court, a clear account of the status, disposition of and effects on the victim.

A consultation with a forensic psychologist on a particular case can also expand on the issue of victimisation to add a zeal to your case. The International Institute of Investigative Psychology (IAiP) is a leading organisation in this area and it is well worth researching their resources.

A final important point is made about offender-to-offender fraud. As one former FBI career officer was asked, 'Should we care if one crook bilks another?' 'Absolutely. The cheated one will find an innocent victim to absorb his loss.'

A cluster of informative dogmas to help to advance conceptual thought of fraud and fraud offenders

- ▓ Impulsive fraud.
- ▓ Systemic fraud.
- ▓ 'Organised' fraud?
- ▓ Fraud Offender profiling:
  - ▓ Profiling: where it lies in fraud.
  - ▓ Profile differences between theft and fraud offenders.

Important distinction

Although they both work closely with the legal system, *criminal* and *forensic* psychologists have different focuses. A criminal psychologist evaluates criminals exclusively. A forensic psychologist by contrast, works with all types of court cases, including civil matters not involving criminals. Much of a criminal psychologist's work is done on a theoretical basis, before a perpetrator has even been identified, while a forensic psychologist tends to evaluate persons already identified by the courts.

Two distinctly different approaches to fraud offending

It would be useful at this point to tie in the above, and we can then address them separately. To further this point, I have had opportunity to meet two gentlemen and discuss informally their cases, which are widely known (one of whom even had a movie made about him). The distinctions between the two discussions in relation to the state of mind and informing their motivation to misrepresent, sets out an interesting balance of learning outcomes in this context. Accounts as follows:

Humberto J. Aguilar: a former US Attorney, practised law, until he was indicted for money laundering in a Federal District Court and fled to Spain where he was arrested and extradited. He laundered over $100 million by way of extensive global travel and opening up bank accounts for Colombian Mafia members. He was later sentenced and served 7 years in prison. A debrief of Mr. Aguilar's account was that his behaviour was to always plan ahead; suitably achieved by putting into action the creation of a false corporate image of numerous corporations around the world and with that, hundreds of bank accounts under those corporations and with hundreds of letters of recommendation from bank to bank. Aguilar paid prostitutes to use their names on forged bank reference letters. What he created was a simple highway of well-constructed lies before him; a red carpet of crime with well-coordinated movement to convince the bankers and insurance companies that he was not only legitimate, but that he was the kind of individual worth doing business with. He would never travel anywhere to open bank accounts and to effect movements without having letters of introduction from one banker to the next. On the odd occasion he was mildly challenged in a bank about the legitimacy of the money being deposited, Mr. Aguilar would merely pronounce and emphasise his lawyer status, and lie accordingly to have the bank account processed.

Nick Leeson: known as the 'Rogue Trader'. A former derivatives broker whose fraudulent, unauthorised notional trading directly caused the collapse of Barings Bank, the United Kingdom's oldest investment bank. He was sentenced to 7 years in prison in Singapore. He later became an active keynote and after-dinner speaker and advises companies about risk and corporate responsibility. I asked Mr. Leeson two rather blunt questions: one of them was, 'Why did you not get caught?' (as it was not because he was investigated and caught, but rather a case of his bank empire in Singapore collapsing around him leaving the whole thing visible as a bomb crater of his own making, which caused him to flee the country). His reply was simple, that outsiders 'did not know the business' (his exact words) and leading up to that he was also able to fend off audits and inquiries to enable his seamless fraudulent trading. The other question I asked him related to his state of mind, in that what elements of fraud were practised first in his scheme of fraud activity, and how these developed in his mind to drive his actions? Mr. Leeson said (as he often does publicly) that it was never his intention to bring the bank down. This is a valid and certainly honest reply, given that his next comments were to affirm that it had got to a stage whereby the urge to do what he was doing, totally unchallenged, had completely overtaken his whole way of thinking, on a par with a gambling addict. He had lost the sense of right and wrong, which foreshadowed his fraud and continuing 'fraud thinking' as a normative way of things for him.

Composite Summary

A simple analysis of the accounts of Humberto Aguilar and Nick Leeson presents a stark if not completely opposite approach to fraud in their way of thinking – as fraudsters.

Mr. Aguilar said it was fun to try to beat the system by creating the sort of schemes meant to circumvent the guidelines against money laundering that were created by the financial and governmental institutions. Nick Leeson was totally the opposite. He did not use his position in the same way as Aguilar (who arguably was part of organised crime with his Mafia associates) who planned his fraud and money laundering meticulously and with an ability to exploit an accomplished professional skill to achieve it. He also evidently has what psychologists refer to as a semantic memory, being of declarative or explicit memory. A man with a massive intellect, and being a senior lawyer, he had a strong general knowledge (facts, ideas, meaning and concepts aiding his planning in crime) of protocols, the law, interweaved with his experience.

In contrast, Nick Leeson, was a brilliant and talented banking professional who was one of the youngest ever senior heads of Banking Operations and put in charge of the entire Singapore operation for Barings Bank. His 'thinking' then departed from coldly utilising his skills as Aguilar did. His thinking drove him relentlessly, so much so that he became a nervous wreck (and later kindly wrote a book about dealing with stress) and unlike Mr. Aguilar, had no thought of wanting to beat the system. Leeson had carte-blanche authority himself.

Narcissist leadership and inevitable fraud

Narcissist leaders and managers can be quiet, they can be loud, but they are all scheming, manipulative and cowardly. It is only the outward persona that differs and to what level of conspicuous presence they work, operate and live in. The narcissist is centrally about 'Me, myself and I' and no one else matters. Many 'make things happen' positively, but the trouble is, they drag fraud in behind them. Objections then get suitably stamped on.

But this is another stark but suppressed area of fraud offending 'creativity' because it is conceptually hidden and hardly ever discussed in management and leadership contexts. (Your first port of call will be to investigate the accounts, and see whether what you expose align with the company 'tone' set.) Likewise, on the 'fraud side' we as profilers and investigators pay little heed to this area of what makes a person commit fraud. Investigative psychology therefore surely should accommodate this problem.

Hence, the inevitable connections that form fraud offending tendencies with certain leadership notions and traits certainly exist. It is possible to give predictable and proven connections with salient points of fraud offending, and especially pinpoint where and how the narcissist leader will commit corporate fraud, aided by unethical, reckless materialistic, cognitive leadership thinking and then breeding it in others.

Impulsive fraud

Following on, it may be inferred that impulsive fraud is a part of rational choice, if rational choice theory forms patterns of behaviour in societies that reflect the choices made by individuals as they try to either maximise their benefits, or just get by. This may go part way to explaining the creation of certain identities of some geographical regions which are labelled as being more corrupt than others.

Of course, people make decisions about how they should act by comparing the risks and benefits of different courses of fraud action. Consequently, patterns of behaviour develop within the country or wider society that result from such rational choices. However, there is a danger that corporate stereotyping then takes over. Research projects and 'findings' are based on questionable research parameters. For example, if in Nigeria corruption is a way of life then it may also be suggested that London is the money laundering capital of the world. But it is not said. Yet, evidence exists and is even provided by the police force that banks cover up the extent of cybercrime losses. London also has been at the centre of some of the most serious fraud and money laundering cases there have been in recent years. The geographical and social environment, therefore, is not a true and single indicator of financial wrongdoing and rational and implicit impulsive choice to commit it. Being more attracted to the immediate value of the target.

Studies on continuing impulsive fraud are rare. To mirror other areas of human impulse takes us to a close analogy that some fraud offenders are like impulsive or 'consumerist' buyers. They make quick decisions about what they choose to do then and there. Personal characteristics of their mood, emotions, and personal culture can all play a part in these instantaneous decisions. Thus, profiles of fraud offenders can and do include some of the same characteristics as impulsive consumers.

Broadening the subject to the academic field in this area, one excellent analogy is made by Dr. Liane Leedom, who in her study of the 'sociopath' presented a three-tier model: *The Inner Triangle*, with a supporting definition.

Dr. Leedom analysed the criteria for antisocial personality disorder (stated in the American Psychiatric Association's Diagnostic and Statistical Manual of Mental Disorders, Fourth Edition (DSM-IV)). Two of the three findings of by Dr. Leedom are (1) lacking the ability to control impulse and (2) lack of moral reasoning.

My own insights and experiences show that fraud offenders who offend by impulse (the dictionary definition of 'impulsive' being 'a sudden strong and unreflective urge or desire to act') offend according to their day-to-day surroundings and personal habits and routine. It is merely one glimmer of motivation or nuance that completes the impulse to do the deed.

With relevance to fraud offending I would suggest that such an analogy with Dr. Leedom's work is a sound one, and thus fraud-sociopaths (my term) with such a mental state are interlinked. This is a dangerous combination in my view. These are my reasons:

- That impulsive fraudsters are not so much more difficult to catch (fraud is fraud), but much more difficult to present for what they really are. It takes little imagination to relate to both the persona and personal agenda of Bernie Madoff. And even then, how long did it take to catch him? Madoff I would say is (or was) not a compulsive fraudster. It just became a state of normality for him after four decades of practice and criminal conditioning. Madoff was certainly not a 'chancer'. His empire, his sycophants, his colluders, the inept auditors and inept and corrupt investigators, the self-serving corporate culture he set for himself and worked for so long makes Bernie Madoff not just an infamous fraudster, but a distinct example of a systemic fraud offender who had also built a corporate empire around him to shroud it.
- Following on, regarding the highly important task of reporting fraud cases, many police reports especially often fail to present any aggravating features. This makes it much easier for defence lawyers to pile up extraneous mitigation around a client for whom this case is 'out of character' or commiting fraud was a 'momentary lapse of judgment.'
- But it is no good just castigating defence lawyers. Lawyers have a duty to their clients, and lawyers cannot be criticised when it is we who write outcomes reports of fraud cases which are so bland and uninterestingly written with a misguided understanding of objectivity that they fail to provide even a hint of the severity of the offender's actions. (This is not to be taken to mean that we can or should lie in, or embellish, reports.)

Likewise, the incessant and irritating call for reforms to the law and to give more powers to enforcement authorities to make it easier to catch criminals is an equally sterile argument. Massive criticism of 'snooper powers' is well founded.

- Equally the numbering format of some HR-style reports also can water down the seriousness of a case. These are endorsed with so much really short-sighted professional guidance at times, with the stock 'keep it simple' advice (which brings an added danger of missing other offenders in the same case, because this indulges a way of thinking that is more robotic than productive).

▪ If you have the skill, a balanced and proportionate account of the offender's conduct can be presented and understood by any reader. (More of how to sharpen that skill in Chapter 4.)

This overriding point of impulsive fraud offending is supported by studies carried out by the Association of Certified Fraud Examiners (ACFE), which shows that most occupational fraud offenders are first-time offenders. Even as far back as 2002, the *ACFE Report to the Nations* (and subsequent reports) presented that 68% of offenders convicted had not been charged before, let alone convicted. This is a huge number. It also says much about the complacency when we deal with a 'first-time' offender, in that many investigating a fraud case are taken in by an offender's appearance and sometimes innocent persona, and especially applicable is the medium of the language used. Creating empathy is often viewed to be the role of the investigator (which it is) but often it is created by the offender. Hence, as the interview or investigation progresses the substance of the evidence and seriousness of the case gets lost along the way.

If we visualise an 'organised' mafia-type offender before us it is easy and often the case that we go into the breach of this following this quirky hypothesis. Some one-hit frauds secure enough criminal proceeds to retire on.

Impulsive decision making and working memory

First, certain fraud victims are highly susceptible to being fraud victims due to their impulsive tendencies.

Decision-making processes that dominate short-term over long-term consequences of fraud actions, are classified as impulsive or temporally narrow-minded.

There have been interesting experiments in this regard. One of particular relevance to us is when monetary rewards were real rather than hypothetical. Therefore the 'chancer' such as the hacker or 'phishing' email offender (who certainly follows a pattern of behaviour) to those offenders who can actually see the benefits before them, such as a manager who can falsify expenses, knowing that no one checks them.

The ACFE of course provides other important findings in key areas, such as covering gender issues among fraud offenders, departmental breakdown, and tier levels of high-level perpetrators who actually cause the greatest damage to their organisations, more so than 'the workers'. Frauds committed by owners and executives are more than three times as costly as frauds committed by managers, and more than nine times as costly as 'employee frauds'. Executive-level frauds often also take much longer to detect (the Bernie Madoff syndrome and that alluding to cases such as Nick Leeson). Also, approximately 77% of the frauds exposed in the ACFE studies were committed by individuals working in one of seven departments: accounting, operations, sales, executive, the upper management, customer service and purchasing and finance.

▪ Therefore working conditions in-house form part of the working memory, as much as the outside societal environment.

Systemic fraud

A term often heard is the 'systemic failing' or 'systemic problem' in an organisation.

- An important distinction is made between systemic fraud and institutionalised fraud (or other institutional problems).

Some globally set examples may help with understanding and distinguishing systemic fraud from other categories:

- In 2014, Kabul, Afghanistan, an EU report confirmed rampant fraud in the Afghan Presidential Election in December of that year.

A campaign team led by Manawar Shah came under intense threat on the day of the Afghan election, ironically from those who were supposed to be keeping order, namely government officials, security forces and supporters of one of the candidates, Ashraf Ghani.

Mr. Shah's team members were reportedly beaten and prevented from using their video equipment and cellphones, in incidents taking place in Khost Province. They were supposedly watching for fraud but unable to document it. Just in one polling centre, Mr. Shah said, they observed just 500 voters and election officials casting multiple ballots, for a total of 10,531 votes.

Equally, an inherent issue was President Hamid Karzai, who 'referred' an operations officer to the Independent Election Commission, relating to him as his 'nephew' (an expression of his favour rather than of actual kinship). The official was Zia ul-Haq Amarkhail, a young officer who had worked in the field operations of the commission and knew his way around the system. Mr. Amarkhail met frequently with senior aides to the president at the palace, though election officials were supposed to guard their independence.

Early in the election run-up, Abdullah campaign officials produced a set of audio recordings in which Mr. Amarkhail, other election officials and Ghani campaign workers could be heard directing various officials in the practice of 'ballot-box stuffing'.

That episode and others like it led to accusations of a conspiracy with systemic fraud by Mr. Ghani, along with election officials and President Hamid Karzai trying to rig the vote, plunging the country into crisis and creating a new threat of factional violence. This is after years and millions of Western aid spent building it.

- In Kenya in 2015, dozens of prominent Kenyans are among the 175 people named in an investigation being undertaken by Kenya's Ethics and Anti-Corruption Commission.

The above-mentioned people were under investigation for issues ranging from planting potatoes on government land, to approving 'sweetheart' deals for favoured firms, land-grabbing and using millions of Kenyan shillings in public funds to bribe Members of Parliament, with former government officials as suspects. There were 124 cases at various stages of investigation.

Some instances of this investigation are:

- One official who used his office in 2006 to deny former Kenya Railway Corporation employees a chance to purchase houses set aside for them to buy.
- The former Secretary to the Cabinet is also being investigated over irregularities in a Sh1 billion interior ministry tender.
- Two ministers concerning the irregular disposal of a parcel of land in Westlands Nairobi, for Kenya Sh320 million, with the then minister allegedly pocketing a Sh5 million bribe.
- The same two are named among half a dozen others over the irregular procurement of a ranch.
- One other being probed over the purchase of a parcel of land on Loita Street, Nairobi, from Kenya Commercial Bank for Sh220 million before 'flipping' it to a buyer waiting in the wings for Sh650 million.
- Electoral: two politicians being investigated over the procurement of electronic voter identification devices.
- One government minister accused of abuse of office for allegedly making trips abroad and failing to account for the funds.

Systemic fraud reaches into many areas, stemming from a range of situations, but a common thread among them is the drivers of the behaviour are at senior levels – many of them in government. Also, senior business hierarchy, such as in the following cases:

- Cases involving SERCO and G4S, the world's largest security company (who at the time of writing are still under investigation by the UK Serious Fraud Office).
- An official investigation into 5.9 billion pounds of outsourcing contracts held by these firms found evidence of 'inconsistent management' in 22 out of the 28 contracts across eight government departments and agencies.

The review found that there were 'key deficiencies' in invoice and payment processes that led to overcharging. That review was ordered in the wake of the scandal involving SERCO and G4S's 'tagging contracts' in relation to the electronic tagging of offenders. Both SERCO and G4S agreed to repay the Government £68.5m. The scandal concerned the Ministry of Justice being charged for the tagging of prisoners who were either found to be dead, back in prison or overseas.

- Another case of this is A4e, who like SERCO is a contractor for the government's welfare-to-work schemes, a similar business operation. A4e, which stands for Action for Employment, was established in Sheffield, England in 1991.

Leaked documents in March 2012 concerned 'systemic fraud at A4e', the Welfare-to-Work firm, which knew of widespread potential fraud and systemic failures by management. Auditors found staff claiming tax-payer funding for putting people into jobs which did not exist or which did not qualify for payment, and generally fabricating claims and falsifying paperwork. Auditors said that they could only be sure that A4e was entitled to the money the company claimed in 70% of the cases.

Margaret Hodge MP, chair of the government Public Accounts Committee, said of the document: 'This appears to be devastating evidence of systemic fraud within A4e. Either A4e failed to act or to inform the Department of Work and Pensions (DWP) or they did inform DWP and the department failed to investigate properly.'

Ms. Hodge urged the department to suspend all its contracts with A4e immediately.

Police were already investigating claims of serious 'financial irregularities' at a company which was being paid £200m a year by the government for training the unemployed and getting them into long-term jobs.

Specific incidents: A4e

In Edinburgh one client walked out of a job after two hours complaining of sore feet and never appeared on the potential employer's books, but A4e still claimed for a job outcome.

In Liverpool, the auditors could find no trace of a man who was supposed to have found work at Royal Mail and no trace of the man who was supposed to have employed him.

In Bridlington, a cafe owner told an auditor that he had never even met a man A4e had claimed for and he wanted to know why A4e kept asking him to sign blank forms.

In 2013, in Sydney, Australia, the consumer rights campaigner Denise Brailey exposed what she described as 'Australia's subprime crisis'. In doing so Ms. Brailey made public 2500 private emails and bank documents.

Ms. Brailey claimed that lenders and mortgage brokers fabricated documents to provide more credit for certain borrowers. She urged an investigation by corporate regulators to investigate the banks and other lenders over alleged 'systemic fraud' in the 'low-doc' market. Low-documentation loans are made to borrowers such as business owners who can't prove a regular income, but the borrower signs a declaration as to estimated income. The loans usually carry a higher interest rate than other loans, as they are seen as more of a pay-back risk.

The Australian Securities and Investments Commission, which oversees lending in Australia, said there was 'no evidence' of fraud. However, Ms. Brailey replied that the ASIC is being 'tricky'. More than 100 of her members sent their evidence to the ASIC and they all received automated rejection letters telling them to 'get a lawyer'. Ms. Brailey also stated that the release of her data proved the banks were pulling the strings, using mortgage brokers as 'agents' to push credit on those who could not afford it. Most of the loans are secured over property. Ms. Brailey said many of the loans became due for refinancing and consequently the Financial Ombudsman Service (FOS) has reported a 'spike' in the number of complaints.

Included in the emails made public are the passwords for a programme called the Service Calculator. The mortgage brokers would enter these passwords to access the banks' portals to determine whether a loan would be approved.

This was described as the 'smoking gun' that everybody refuses to talk about and which the regulators and the FOS refuse to investigate.

▨　A final point to round off this context is to highlight the increasing reliance of company staff engaging in systemic fraud to plead that what they were doing was a 'mistake', or 'I was just doing my job'.

A fair measure of this test is provided by statutory stipulation in the United States:

The difference between fraud and mistake, under the False Claims Act

The False Claims Act envisions a broad definition under 31 U.S.C. § 3729(b) for when a defendant 'knowingly' makes a false or fraudulent claim to the federal government:

> Knowing and Knowingly Defined— For purposes of this section, the terms 'knowing' and 'knowingly' mean that a person, with respect to information—
>
> 1.　has actual knowledge of the information;
> 2.　acts in deliberate ignorance of the truth or falsity of the information; or
> 3.　acts in reckless disregard of the truth or falsity of the information, and
> 4.　no proof of specific intent to defraud is required.

Interestingly, the burden of proof is lowered in this statute, presumably to bring some balance of fairness. It was tested in the case of *Grogan v Garner*, 498 U.S. 279, 288-289 (1991).

Realtor, John Owens, brought a claim under the False Claims Act ('FCA'), 31 U.S.C. §§ 3729, et seq., against First Kuwaiti construction firm, his former employer. He alleged that the firm billed falsely for deficient work in connection with construction of the US embassy in Baghdad and that it retaliated against him for actions taken in furtherance of his FCA contentions. The district court granted summary judgment to the defendant.

The essence of the realtor's claim is that the defendant failed to live up to its contractual obligations. He produced no evidence either of knowing misrepresentations on the defendant's part or of having been mistreated for any actions taken on behalf of his FCA claims.

> The district court's judgment held that the congress crafted the FCA to deal with fraud, not ordinary contractual disputes. The FCA plays an important role in safeguarding the integrity of federal contracting, administering "strong medicine" in situations where strong remedies are needed. Allowing it to be used in run-of-the-mill contract disagreements and employee grievances would burden, not help, the contracting process, thereby driving up costs for the government and, by extension, the American public.

The case itself is an example of when faulty government contracting work is not quite bad enough to warrant liability in fraud against the contracts in place. The defendant there apparently messed up some of the building work, but no worse than that relating to other contracts with similar claims, and more importantly, no worse than envisioned by the contract itself. The 'whistleblower' (as he was casually referred to) thus couldn't muster, at least in the Circuit Court's eyes, enough evidence to show the defendant even 'recklessly disregarded' the falsity of the claims it submitted.

'Organised' fraud?

The term 'organised crime' has become as well-known as it is misunderstood. Naturally, criminal gangs responsible for people trafficking, drug smuggling and the like exist prominently and are easy reference points. In money laundering, these include for example:

- Colombian cartels (drugs).
- Mexican cartels.
- Russian Mafia.
- Japanese Yazuka (finance – banking).
- Italian Mafia.
- Chinese Triads.
- Turkish & Kurdish Gangs.
- Nigerian (phishing scams).
- Balkan Gangs.
- Hells Angels – motorbike gangs (Scandinavia).

The above list is shown because many of the situational money laundering schemes by those groups especially include fraud. The banks can now be safely added to the list.

Definitions of organised fraud exist, and are even legislated for, as in the state of Florida, USA: 'the intentional misrepresentation or concealment of information in order to deceive or mislead.'

In the UK, the Insurance Fraud Enforcement Department also known as 'IFED' is a specialist police unit dedicated to tackling insurance fraud. They have addressed the problem of 'crash for cash' fraud schemes, where offenders deliberately cause car crashes, and stage them in such a way that blame and therefore liability for causing the crash is on the other party. The objective of course being to be awarded compensation (by fraud). Certainly this is one clear example of organised fraud, given its widespread national and repeated patterns of occurrence.

However, when it comes to wider aspects of fraud, the narrow way of thinking of organised fraud is swayed, both politically and practically. There is a banal insistence, including among academics, that organised fraud and 'white-collar crime' are separate entities. Moreover, the official diktat from national crime-fighting agencies is that professional criminals are not from mainstream professions or legitimate organisations, when the reverse is true. As noted earlier in this chapter, a valid argument is put forward that the banking community is a part of organised crime, as much as any so-called organised crime or mafia-style organisation. The 2015 conviction of Tom Hayes of Barclays for 'LIBOR' fixing adds to this.

Settings for fraud activities in the context of crime networks, fraud opportunities and of a victim-centric typology of fraud clearly attach to the mechanics of so-called organised fraud as above. Picking and choosing who is a group or gang, who is criminal, and who is not, when both behave in exactly the same way is often a mere public relations exercise. Hence it is only the political representation of them that confuses and misleads.

Added to this is the ever-present collaboration between offenders in frauds in different fraud settings. Often, both co-offenders and victims in face-to-face (which is rare) and remote targeting yield and overcome barriers to growth of 'fraud as business'.

Further, the globalisation of crime is centrally part of the dependent relationships between patterns of business, consumer and investment activities.

Enforcement authorities and the organised crime dialogue and its constructs should be less obsessed with the structure of groups and more with the people involved, and objectively so. The illicit and largely licit world of fraud is made of many players. It is inescapable that there are small mobile groups or individuals who are capable and can transplant techniques of fraud activity wherever they go.

Another distinction to be made is that between 'organised' and 'organising' fraud. There is no point in pondering or attempting to classify these issues:

1. The ease with which offenders find the accomplices necessary to help to commit fraud on any scale; and
2. The breaking down of the elements of 'criminal organisation' (not 'a' criminal organisation) into its constituent parts (i.e. termed as 'script analysis' by Cornish, 1994; and Cornish and Clarke, 2002).

It really is best and helpful to think of the tasks that need to be performed to commit fraud and the range of places where they need to be and are performed (because all of the incessant talk about 'the' globalisation of 'crime' is in the main achieved only locally).

This small table helps put into perspective some components that make up organised fraud attacks, which infuse with fraud generally:

Financial Services	Cheque fraud
	Counterfeit intellectual property and products sold as genuine
	Counterfeit money
	Data-compromise fraud
	Embezzlement
	Insider dealing/market abuse
	Insurance fraud
	Lending fraud
	Payment card fraud
	Procurement fraud
Non-financial services	Cheque fraud
	Counterfeit intellectual property and products sold as genuine
	Counterfeit money
	Data-compromise fraud
	Embezzlement
	Gaming fraud

Fraud offender profiling

Profiling: where it lies in fraud

The Radex model, using Multi-Dimensional Scaling (MDS) procedures, allows specific hypotheses to be developed about important constituents of criminal differentiation:

Salience; MDS analyses reveal the importance of the frequency of criminal actions as the basis on which the significance of those actions can be established.

Models of Differentiation; research reviewed mainly supports distinctions between criminals in terms of the forms of their transactions with their explicit or implicit victims.

Consistency; offenders have been shown to exhibit similar patterns of action on different occasions. The most reliable examples of this currently are in studies of the spatial behaviour of criminals.

Inference; under limited conditions it is possible to show associations between the characteristics of offenders and the thematic focus of their crimes.

(Cited from, Offender Profiling and Criminal Differentiation, Professor David Canter.)

There is strong debate in psychology circles as to whether psychological profiling should be seen as a scientific endeavour or merely as subjective deduction.

UK psychologist David Canter has been critical of the FBI's approach to profiling, stating it to be 'unscientific'. He has a point, when it is compared with Garberth (1983) who saw offender profiling as a combination of brainstorming, intuition and educated guesswork, largely an inferential process similar to any other psychological evaluation.

Canter is right in my view. Other experts also suggest that police officers might be more seduced by the academic standing and status of the profiler than by the actual usefulness of their material. Gudjonsson and Copson (1997) suggested that it is easy to understand why there is confusion about what profiling involves as it is 'neither a readily identifiable nor a homogeneous entity'. Indeed the same authors noted that little has been published in the academic literature on what profilers actually do and how they do it. Hence the mixed understanding of profiling.

Yet, profiling fraud offenders forms a central variant and attracts all manner of both personal and societal ills. For example, pathological gambling or an insatiable addiction to gambling. This is the case of the Cambridge University finance officer jailed for stealing £300,000 to fund a bingo addiction (2015).

With the below case also, it demonstrates that any fraud prevention controls were applied very late, if at all. Staff familiarity and heuristics played a strong part in the length of time it took to apprehend this offender.

In regard to the 'gender-bias' of reporting fraud, it is not for this book to attempt to compete with well-known annual reports of fraud, such as from KPMG etc., which are well structured and informative. However, both the research methodology and the assumptions made – that the majority of fraudsters are male, aged from their mid-30s

CASE **STUDY**

Jacqueline Balaam, 41, was a trusted finance officer at Pembroke College but also was a secret gambling addict. Balaam opened an account with 'Jackpotjoy' (the UK's biggest online bingo site) in 2006 and over the following eight years paid in £324,425 of her own money.

She won up to 15,000 pounds each time but continually reinvested her winnings instead of cashing them in and put on more bets totalling £6,383,126, but withdrawing only £87,600.

To feed her habit Balaam abused her position as a purchase ledger clerk at Pembroke College for 18 months. She duplicated invoices and paid the money from those into her own account. Balaam was also in charge of paying suppliers who provided goods and services to the college, and paid them using the BACS system on a weekly basis.

Over 18 months Balaam duplicated 77 invoices and targeted the suppliers who paid the college the most frequently. By the end of the fraud she was making payments into her account four times a week. She would then go back into the accounting system and change the details back to those of the supplier to cover her tracks and made sure they were still paid.

The college uncovered this crime during an internal audit in January 2014.

Police also found that Balaam had also stolen more than 3,000 pounds over four years from a social club where she volunteered as treasurer.

to 40s, employed by a company or organisation for more than ten years, and holding a senior managerial position, and so on, – are based solely on occupational fraud scenarios. Therefore the scope of research falls short of the seeing the clear shift from male to female fraud offenders.

Moreover, the divide of opinion between the corporate and the academic worlds is as wide as ever on this topic. They are no closer to agreement on a definition for this type of crime than they were before, with most disagreement being around whether the emphasis should be on the offender or the type of offence. Originally, white-collar crime and criminals were evidently viewed as offender-based definitions of fraud, which focused on the status of the offender in society, rather than on the criminal act itself.

The changes in the role of women in society and the workplace have developed more opportunities for them to commit fraud. Moving away now from the cases such as that of the Cambridge University finance officer above, research has shown a positive correlation between the growing numbers of women in work and workplace crime, especially fraud Therefore, there is no reason why we should not view women as potential fraud offenders to the same degree that we do men. But women still appear to be less in the spotlight when we discuss fraud and the 'average fraudster' who according to the certain reports is still profiled as male.

Undoubtedly, where women are concerned, research has tended to focus on lower tariff fraud, such as benefit frauds: in other words, on crimes of need rather than greed. Moreover, research has also focused upon the basic nature of female fraud offending; that being the perception of having broken both the criminal law and additionally a social code of what is perceived to be 'feminine'.

So-called pink-collar or female fraud was first highlighted in the 1980s but, since then, there has been little recognition of women committing such crimes, with the media focusing mainly on celebrity offenders like Martha Stewart. Given that women now make up nearly 50% of the British workforce, what kinds of frauds are they involved in, and do their methods and experiences differ from those of men?

One study by Dr. Janice Goldstraw-White raised the question, why is it so difficult for us to see women as potential fraudsters? There is no female 'frilly cuff' to match the male 'white collar'. And very well put, given there is no notable difference in the crimes for which they had been convicted, nor their *modus operandi*.

What was found also was that women fraud offenders were mostly more remorseful than men, and pleaded guilty more often.

Profile differences between theft and fraud offenders

One key difference between fraud and theft and offenders is the mental ability to reason in fraud to deceive as opposed to the opposite inclination to take something without permission. Of course, in the latter case, the emergence of identity theft and fraud make some thefts more sophisticated than others; however, this should be viewed in the wider context of problem solving, in which the solution to this particular problem may take into account the targets of theft (for example, vehicles and their contents, the locations in which vehicles are parked, and the potential victims of theft), as well as the offender.

Naturally, issues of theft are as diverse and scattered as fraud, if not more. There are, for example, research papers into specific areas such as art theft. It is not the purpose of this book to fill in a void of research between theft and fraud. One reason is that most scholarly articles roll them up into one.

Likewise, crime classifications in different countries are at odds with each other. The FBI makes a distinction between the levels of crimes against property and defines property crime as burglary, larceny-theft, motor vehicle theft, and arson. In another category offences include bribery, counterfeiting, forgery, vandalism, embezzlement, extortion, and fraud. A peculiar mix really. The UK Home Office does not classify fraud as crime at all. In a quite chaotic situation, Action Fraud, the reporting facility, can only record NFIB classified fraud and cybercrimes. Where other notifiable offences are apparent the victim will be referred to the police (who invariably do nothing). Likewise, non-NFIB recorded frauds and cyber-enabled offences remain the responsibility of the police to record (i.e. other fraud and forgery or blackmail offences committed through social media and chatrooms).

But a very interesting distinction made by an Australian researcher (Clive Williams, 2005) was the presence of gender identity, masculinity, and that stealing cards was more of a showing off crime than an acquisitive one.

This is balanced with a project to research the profiles of robbery offenders in Canada (1995), which engaged with the explanations for robbery being linked to issues such as mental health or social problems. Offenders themselves point to the obvious – money for money's sake is usually low on the priority list (as opposed to fraudsters) and thus thrills, drugs and peer influences are the main reasons for taking or attempting to take something of value from a victim. Thus it is a distinction that certain theft-related crimes, such as robbery, develop from a subculture of violence and should be classified as a violent crime instead.

But similarities are few. In the overwhelming majority of fraud cases, financial gain is the intended result, without the need for acts of bravado. Likewise, it is not so much educational standards, but fraud offenders learn processes and cultures before exploiting them. Opportunist frauds such as phishing and other direct scam-orientated frauds show more planning than spontaneity. In any case, it is rare that a fraud offender goes in for public posturing. Likewise, fraud offenders tend not to belong to groups described as being asocial, as having to steal to seek attention from others; or those brought up in a familial environment whereby just taking something is normal behaviour.

This brief account of the profile differences between theft and fraud offenders is to inject some differences of the linking and end-result motives of offenders engaged in criminal activity with dishonesty as the central characteristic. One common denominator is theft and fraud feeding certain addictions or habits, like the cases referred to in this chapter.

Why do 'good people' do bad things?

But are we not already bad? Is it that fraud is a ready outlet for human behaviour in greed and opportunism? The propensity to commit fraud arises far quicker than it would to commit other serious crime. Yet fraud is a crime that wrecks lives also.

In the general study of so-called 'psychological traps' that lead 'good' people to commit fraud, some are plausible in that regard:

Social bond theory   In large organisations, employees can begin to feel more like numbers or cogs in a machine than individuals. When people feel detached from the goals and leadership of their workplace, they are more likely to commit fraud, steal, or hurt the company via neglect.

The 'Galatea effect'   Self-image determines behaviour. People who have a strong sense of themselves as individuals are less likely to do unethical things. Alternatively, employees who see themselves as determined by their environment or having their choices made for them are more likely to bend the rules, as they feel less individually responsible.

Time pressure   In a study, a group of theology students were told to preach the story of the good Samaritan, then walk to another building where they would be filmed. Along the way, they encountered a man in visible distress.

When given ample time, almost all helped. When they were deliberately let out late, only 63 percent helped. When encouraged to go as fast as possible, 90 percent ignored the man.

Acceptance of small theft   There are many small temptations in any workplace. Stationery, for example, is frequently taken by employees.

Those small thefts are ignored. So are slightly larger ones, like over-claiming expenses or accepting unauthorised business gifts. It doesn't take long for people to begin pushing the limits.

Conspicuous consumption   Extreme wealth, or environments that reflect it, can lead to unethical behaviour. For employees, seeing excessive bonuses or perks that they don't share leads to feelings of injustice and jealousy which may lead them to unethical behaviour.

The Pygmalion effect   The way that people are seen and treated influences the way they act. When employees are viewed suspiciously and constantly treated like potential thieves, they are more likely to be thieves. This effect occurs even in employees who aren't initially inclined towards unethical behaviour.

Reactance theory   Rules are designed to prevent unethical behaviour, but when they're seen as unjust or excessive they can provoke the opposite reaction.

This is known as 'reactance theory'. People resent threats to their freedom, and they often manifest that resistance by flouting certain rules.

The blinding effect of power   Powerful people appear more corrupt because they're caught more publicly. A study found that when given power, people set ethical rules much higher for others than they do themselves.

The foot in the door   When a figure in authority asks someone to skirt the rules, they want to seem like a team player. Giving in modifies self-perception. A person may begin to think of themselves as extremely loyal, someone who gets things done. In that frame of mind, they may be willing to do increasingly unethical things.

Cognitive dissonance and rationalisation   When people's actions differ from their morals, they begin to rationalise both to protect themselves from a painful contradiction and to build up protection against accusations. The bigger the dissonance, the larger the rationalisation, and the longer it lasts, the less immoral it seems.

Problematic punishments   Rather than being about whether something is right or wrong, it becomes an economic calculation about the likelihood of getting caught versus the potential fine.

Lack of sleep and hypoglycemia   Research has found that tired participants asked to complete math tasks significantly over-report correct answers. While being tired or hungry won't make someone commit fraud, it leaves them more open to moments of weakness.

Escalating commitment   Fraud offenders often start out in minor frauds and build both misplaced trust and familiarity which favours the offender and paves the way to more serious fraud activity.

The 'compensation' effect of 'ethical credit'   Sometimes people, having been moral and forthright in their dealings for a long time, feel as if they have banked up some kind of 'ethical credit', which they may use to justify immoral behaviour in the future.

Negative consequences of transparency   Transparency usually serves to reduce unethical behaviour, as it increases the likelihood of getting caught. Experiments examining the publication of conflicts of interest have found the opposite effect. The effect comes from something called 'moral licensing'.

Bad communication – a classic   Issues of corruption and morality are often treated as black and white, wrongdoers are badly punished, and grey areas are not discussed.

That can lead to an environment where, rather than sounding out ideas that border on unethical, people push and test their limits.

The pressure to conform to crime   As an analogy with prison rioting, whereby those inmates who refuse to take part in it are subject to violence, fraud occurs in similar way. That being, in order to fit in with a group, people do things they might not otherwise do, or have not done before. That can lead them to ignore all manner of protocols and even compliance requirements. There are also the added issues of ludicrous company target-setting for sales and the like, merging in some ways with the Pygmalion effect.

Predictive modelling?

Predictive modelling is a mechanised form of profiling, now most commonly done by IT and specialised software. Or could it be argued that this is not profiling at all? Either way, the means of automated fraud prevention by profile or prediction needs to be viewed with caution. Predictive modelling is used by financial experts to study trends and analytics, but can be argued to be out of place in fraud. A model stretched from one sphere of work to an entirely different aspect in crime.

For a long time, inputs like this have been marginalised by the 'solutions' business contingent, who are seemingly more focused on profiteering from the existence of a problem than informing the actual addressing of it. Many have put profit before safety, and followed a line of 'innovation' with a dangerous obsession. I could apply one parallel here of my own, whereby so-called anti-fraud and money laundering 'solutions' have become a sales plaything, but a huge legal pitfall is created in many cases. Of course businesses are here to make profit, but many simply cross the line when it comes to this perverse exclusivity of any fallout from ill-conceived business innovations and models which are damaging to safety in all aspects. We will see the dangers brought by 'Bitcoin', and why the banks are in opposition to it.

The 'predictive model' sellers who claim to 'innovate' fraud prevention shamelessly go into the market with an approach of structuring misleading marketing, and in fact pitching products that do not achieve anything in terms of helping businesses or victims of fraud. Incidentally, of course, the banks have no problem with splashing out millions in customers' money and are easily talked into buying worthless IT 'solutions' in money laundering 'prevention and detection' – often authorised by risk managers who want to hold on to their jobs. Spending customers' money like water just to make themselves look good. We had a similar trend when CCTV became the rage as a cure all 'innovation' in crime prevention. But what we have is millions of CCTV cameras with no discernible drop in crimes.

Hence many argue that sellers of predictive modelling have a sales plan which hijacks the terms of crime prevention to make it plausible. In one meeting I had in The Netherlands with a predictive modelling IT company, the Head of Sales made this viewpoint clear enough. His exact words were, with hands waved in the air, 'We don't care about money laundering, Ian, we just sell software'. Yet their sales pitches claim the opposite.

Certainly, scoring and modelling systems are competent to make business decisions (whether to pay or not to pay an insurance claim) but claims of 'innovations' are not about preventing fraud they are about maintaining profits.

There were also serious problems in the UK in 2012 whereby predictive modelling systems in banks went haywire, and at best caused an automated risk process by staff blindly following a system. The result was innocent customers being 'blacklisted' and being classified as money launderers. Many customers sued, and rightly so.

2.4 CONTEXTS, AND LEADING TO CROSS-ACTIVITIES OF FRAUD

Golden rule: follow the behaviour, not just the 'type' of fraud

Of course, the structure and method of understanding fraud and its varying methods of offending are crucial to its study. Some cases, of course, fit easily into a 'type' or category, such as card fraud, insurance fraud, or securities fraud; but fraud, it has to be said, is one of those crimes in the eyes of both enforcement and prosecution authorities that is subject to 'death by policy'. Over-categorising fraud creates problems. The incessant straitjacketing and typecasting of fraud is now a nigh on permanent way of presenting fraud crimes as 'types' and they are often discussed and reported as such. Very convenient in some aspects, but the problem is that a huge amount of fraud goes undetected, such is the strangulation and single-focus on a fraud activity.

Hence, the less discerning cling to their 'types' of fraud, which in my view has a severely limiting effect on enforcement. Here's a 'type' of fraud, and here is another 'type' of fraud, so if it doesn't tick the box it isn't fraud?

The case of SG described earlier is a classic example of the above situation. Suffice to say, had it been left to the police and resource deployment (or lack thereof) then SG would have probably got away with several counts of fraud also.

When in this kind of territory, unfortunately, our enforcement authorities with a wider remit (e.g. the benefit fraud investigators who struggle to deal with more than one 'type' of fraud) such as the police are entrenched in the way of thinking of such a case being a 'civil matter', when a closer engagement with the actual law at their disposal would allow an ability to problem solve and apply the relevant reference points of fraud evidence just as easily as they can dismiss it as a 'civil case'.

Hence, the disconnection between the law and enforcement manifests itself here.

Financial fraud – corporate contexts and entities

Business assets

Something valuable that a business entity owns, benefits from, or has the use of, in generating income.

An asset can be:

1. Something physical, such as cash, machinery, inventory, land or buildings;
2. An enforceable claim against others, such as accounts receivable;
3. Rights, such as copyright, patent, trademark; or
4. An assumption, such as goodwill.

Assets shown on the company balance sheet are usually classified according to the ease with which they can be converted into cash.

Intangible assets and intellectual property theft

Company reputation, name recognition, and intellectual property such as knowledge and know-how, intangible assets are the long-term resources of an entity, but normally do not have a physical existence. They develop their value from intellectual or legal rights, and from the value they add to the other assets.

Intangible assets are generally classified into two broad categories:

1. Limited-life intangible assets, such as patents, copyrights, and goodwill; and
2. Unlimited-life intangible assets, such as trademarks.

Unlike tangible assets, intangible assets cannot be destroyed by fires, or other accidents or physical disasters, and can help build back destroyed tangible assets.

However, they cannot normally be used as collateral to raise loans, and some intangible assets (goodwill, for example) can be destroyed by carelessness, or as a side effect of the failure of a business. Conversely tangible assets add to the company current market value, intangible assets add to its future worth.

- ▧ Intangible Assets are a major risk area of fraud, if management of the company financial operations is poor, or there is excessive bureaucracy and an indulgence of 'cultural norms', writing off some fraud to business loss, or cases of blind familiarity (such as in the case of Jacqueline Balaam earlier in this chapter, who got away with fraud for far too long, by operating in an area very much in keeping with this section).

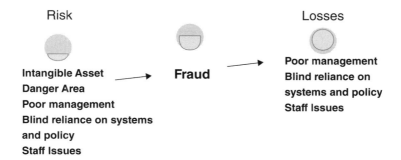

Risk

Intangible Asset
Danger Area
Poor management
Blind reliance on systems
and policy
Staff Issues

Fraud

Losses

Poor management
Blind reliance on
systems and policy
Staff Issues

You may deduce from the above illustration that the company concerned learned nothing in terms of assessing risk of fraud in this context. The risks identified on the left of the illustration actually occurred and losses materialised when the company was hit when we see the end-result on the right. But the losses were avoidable.

Physical financial processes take a different risk approach than those business functions which are all about the human element, whereby counter-fraud efficiency often stops dead and falls flat. So long as unmanaged operatives are allowed to work with no professional reference points against asset security, then fraud will follow.

Getting staff buy-in is not such a massive or even impossible task as many would have us believe. Failure to manage (not dictate) can and does eventually lead to disaster.

Intellectual property theft

'If there is no enemy within, the enemy outside can do us no harm.'

African Proverb

For example, one director of a consultancy company (company A) hijacks the training programmes of that company, which specialises in training, and uses these to advertise the entirely separate business interests of her own consultancy. The separate consultancy is about education management. The offender director concerned, (besides not knowing what fraud or money laundering actually is) does not name the product but makes a clear and detailed reference to it in her own separate business marketing, in such a way that there is no other possible basis on which the property concerned could have come into her knowledge and then possession, other than by stealing it. The subtle disguising of the programme makes no difference to this. Hence, using products (fraud training programmes) from company A, of which she is a director, and for whom she operates in a formal capacity, in order to promote her own separate small company, constitutes fraud against company A.

Outcomes of the above case are:

- A clear conflict of interest concerning a director, which has been duly exploited.
- If business is secured on the basis of the misleading marketing of the separate consultancy, then this will amount to fraudulent trading, given that the smaller company cannot deliver on the promise it makes in the marketing of it.

- The only remaining possibility is to steal the entire training programme and use it by way of delivery by a professionally appropriate trainer. The originating entity could not possibly have been produced by the offender, even if the offender carried out some admin work on it, dressed up to be 'developmental'. But in any case, this does not placate the misappropriation of a physical product and the inherent intangible asset. Hence, if training marketed under the director's separate company is taken up by clients and fees are paid, then that would be fraud against company A. Blatant misrepresentation and an equally blatant breach of fiduciary trust to company A. The case facts complete the offence.

If intellectual property theft is committed on a large enough scale, it can demolish entire businesses.

In a comprehensive 2013 report, the Commission on the Theft of American Intellectual Property (in the US alone) reached agreement on its investigations and set out recommendations after a thorough investigation of 'one of the most pressing issues of economic and national security facing our country'.

Key Findings   The impact of international IP theft on the economy:

- Hundreds of billions of dollars per year. The annual losses are likely to be comparable to the current annual level of U.S. exports to Asia – over $300 billion.
- The Cyber Command and Director of the National Security Agency (NSA) commented that the ongoing theft of IP is 'the greatest transfer of wealth in history'.
- Loss of jobs.
- A drag on GDP growth.
- Investment and economic growth.
- Innovation. The incentive to innovate drives productivity growth. The threat of IP theft diminishes that incentive.
- Long supply chains pose a major challenge.
- Stolen IP represents a subsidy to foreign suppliers that do not have to bear the costs of developing or licensing it. In China, for example, where many overseas supply chains extend, even ethical multinational companies frequently procure counterfeit items, or items whose manufacture benefits from stolen IP, including proprietary business processes, counterfeited machine tools, pirated software, etc.

Hence, this is not to be underestimated as a fraud threat, at any level.

Trade secret theft and corporate espionage

Theft of corporate trade secrets is raised by cases such as those of companies like U.S. Steel and Westinghouse Electric, in 2014.

The (US) Defend Trade Secrets Act, introduced in April 2014 to give trade secrets the same legal protections as other forms of intellectual property, estimates the financial loss due to these types of thefts and frauds at between $160 billion and $480 billion each year.

The following are suggestions to better protect your company from being robbed of its most prized property.

Laptops Taking a company computer on a business trip is a normal way of life, but needs some precautions. Loose security could be disastrous to your business. Make sure the laptops only contain documents essential for the trip. You may also want to think twice in some places about using a hotel Wi-Fi. Offenders can set up fake Wi-Fi services to download all your banking and company information.

Policies Documents that are true trade secrets should have protocols in place that ensure they do not get into the hands of people who really do not need them. If you put policies and protocols in place first, then if they are stolen you have a reasonable argument that they are trade secrets because you took responsible steps to protect them.

Departing employees When an employee gives notice, depending on your business, it may be prudent to ask for an IT audit of the employee's business emails. A key vulnerable time.

Bring-Your-Own-Device (BYOD) Bring-Your-Own-Device policies can be high risk. It is suggested instead that buying your employees smartphones is better as you can control the information flow, and yes it is expensive, but a great investment. Employees often have two or three devices, which means company information could be on their phone, laptop and the like. The single, company-issued device is easily wiped when an employee leaves. If you cannot afford devices for everyone, an alternative is having employees sign consent forms that explain the company will need to wipe parts of their devices before they depart.

Corporate Espionage Organisations can research and collect public sources of information in the public domain, but sometimes offenders will obtain material in unlawful ways.

Motivations Rational Choice Theory does not apply to a corporate espionage, whereby there exists a 'predator employee' or inside person whose purpose is to steal from the organisation, be it assets or trade secrets or intellectual property. One theory is summed up by the acronym **MICE**: *Money, Ideology, Coercion* and *Ego*:

- **Money:** The prospect of financial gain can be a strong motivating factor for many, either to supplement their income or to alleviate financial difficulties.
- **Ideology:** In some cases, people will simply spy because of their sense of patriotism, or cultural or religious beliefs. With the rise in globalisation and the shift from military powers to economic powers, corporate espionage has become an important arm of warfare among superpowers.
- **Coercion:** The threat of scandals aired in public can be a strong motivating factor for executives who are blackmailed into providing sensitive information.
- **Ego:** The sense of importance linked to accessing and possessing sensitive files or documents can be enough for some to enter the world of corporate espionage.

Also, individuals can hold grudges that can motivate offenders to sell trade secrets externally. 'Secrets' can include customer data held by those organisations – even public sector ones – that hold a massive amount of personal data, which naturally is confidential, such as the insider selling of customer data to external marketing companies.

Therefore it is clear that although stealing combined with competitive intelligence is not new, it certainly has become easier with the introduction of universal high resolution cameras (smartphones), miniature storage devices that hold massive amounts of data (USB drives) and advanced tools of human manipulation (social networking).

Does corporate espionage happen frequently? Yes. When we combine competitive pressures to outshine the competition with easy-to-use espionage tools (smartphones, Wi-Fi hacking apps, Facebook).

From an external attack perceptive, 'E-espionage' is the unauthorised and criminal access to confidential systems and information for the purposes of gaining a commercial or other advantage. Corporate espionage has followed technological change. It is no longer necessary to photocopy or photograph sensitive documents because they now, of course, exist in digital form.

The UK Centre for the Protection of National Infrastructure (CPNI), summarises the risk, in that espionage against business interests comes from many quarters.

In the past, espionage activity was typically directed towards obtaining political and military intelligence. This remains the case, but in today's high-tech world, the intelligence requirements of a number of countries also include new communications technologies, IT, genetics, aviation, lasers, optics, electronics and many other fields.

The threat against national interests is not confined to that country. A foreign business intelligence entity operates most effectively in its own country and some countries therefore find it easier to target certain national interests at home where they can control the environment and where a business traveller may let their guard drop.

Financial statements

A financial statement (or financial report) is a formal record of the financial activities of a business, person, or other entity. The four main types of financial statements are:

1. **Statement of Financial Position** (also referred to as the Balance Sheet) presents the financial position of a business entity on a given date. It is comprised of the following three elements:
   - **Assets:** Something a business owns or controls (e.g., cash, inventory, plant and machinery, etc.).
   - **Liabilities:** Something a business owes to someone (e.g., creditors, bank loans, etc.).
   - **Equity:** What the business owes to its owners. This represents the amount of capital that remains in the business after its assets are used to pay off its outstanding liabilities. Equity therefore represents the difference between the assets and liabilities.
2. **Income Statement,** (also referred to as the Profit and Loss Statement or 'P and L' statement) reports the company's financial performance in terms of net profit or loss over a specified period. The Income Statement is composed of the following two elements:

- **Income:** What the business has earned over a period (e.g., sales revenue, dividend income, etc.).
- **Expense:** The cost incurred by the business over a period (e.g., salaries and wages, depreciation, rental charges, etc.). Net profit or loss is arrived at by deducting expenses from income.

3. **Cash Flow Statement**, which presents the movement in cash and bank balances over a period. The movement in cash flows is classified into the following segments:
   - **Operating Activities:** Represents the cash flow from primary activities of a business.
   - **Investing Activities:** Represents cash flow from the purchase and sale of assets other than inventories (e.g., purchase of a factory plant).
   - **Financing Activities:** Represents cash flow generated or spent on raising and repaying share capital and debt together with the payments of interest and dividends.

4. **Statement of Changes in Equity**, (also referred to as the Statement of Retained Earnings) details the movement of the owners' equity over a certain period. The movement in owners' equity is derived from the following components:
   - Net Profit or loss during the period as reported in the income statement.
   - Share capital issued or repaid during the period.
   - Dividend payments.
   - Gains or losses recognised directly in equity (e.g. revaluation surpluses).
   - Effects of a change in accounting policy or correction of an accounting error.

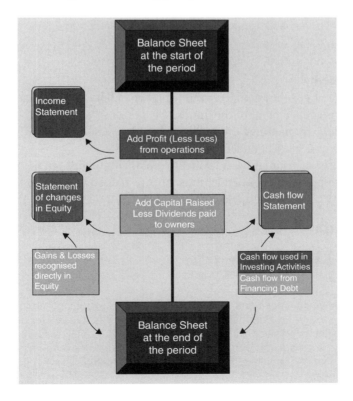

Specific Financial Statement Fraud Scenarios

CASE **STUDY**

Case 1.

The accused, N, was employed as a Senior Bookkeeper from March 2008 to May 2011. The company provided accounting, bookkeeping, payroll and tax services to its clients, being small and medium-sized businesses.

According to her employment contract the accused's duties, functions and responsibilities were to:

- Oversee the entire bookkeeping function of clients that had been allocated to her;
- Undertake any payments of suppliers as requested;
- Receive their payments for compliance in respect of VAT, and other statutory requirements;
- File money received and receipted and ensure correct deposit of funds into account concerned;
- Capture and reconcile credit card, cash book and other cashbooks of the clients.

Between September 2009 and May 2011 the offender transferred money from her clients' accounts into her personal cheque account. The investigation revealed that the supplier's invoices used by the accused in support of payments reflected the bank account details of the accused.

- Supplier invoices used in support of payments/transfers of money were forged.

Lessons Learned:
- This is a classic case of an underrunning breach of fiduciary trust as well as misrepresentations at each point of the frauds.
- The offender demonstrated an intelligence and a persona to play the role she was performing as a fraud offender.
- The response when caught was to offer to repay. This turned out not to be a genuine offer. The response of the offender must be investigated as much as the crime itself.
- This activity could have crippled the business.

CASE **STUDY**

Case 2.

Miss X held various positions at the apparel company including Administrative Assistant to the President and Director of Human Resources. Her duties and responsibilities included sales and marketing, accounting, human resources, merchandising; and she had authority to approve and sign purchase orders, invoices, and cheques in amounts of less than $75,000, if these matters were in the normal course of business.

For approximately nine years, between 1999 and June 2008, Miss X generated fictitious invoices and submitted those invoices to her employer for payment. Since her duties gave Miss X authority to approve and sign purchase orders and cheques for amounts up to $75,000, she would approve those fake services invoices and ultimately transfer those funds into her personal bank accounts. According to court records, in August 1999, Miss X created a fictitious business entity to facilitate the fraudulent scheme.

The money was used to pay for her son's college tuition and to finance trips to Disney World, the Bahamas, Europe, and Australia. She also installed a $20,000 home theatre system with these proceeds.

Lessons Learned:

- This conviction was the defendant's third guilty verdict for embezzlement from an employer. Case after case continues to show that past behaviour is a predictor of future behaviour, but must be used as informing an investigation as opposed to jumping to an evidential conclusion.
- No proper screening and background check was done on Miss X before she was hired. Had a criminal records check taken place, Miss X's two prior convictions for embezzlement from former employers would have come to light.
- The offender's duties gave her the authority to approve and sign purchase orders and cheques for amounts up to $75,000. No single employee should have the ability to perform any high-risk financial task without supervisory oversight and verification.
- Miss X had authority to approve and add vendors to Accounts Payable authorised vendor payment lists without impartial verification that those vendors were legitimate businesses.

Further Examples of Financial Statement Fraud

Improper Revenue Recognition – 1   Premature revenue recognition; recording financing arrangements as sales; manipulating long-term contracts; channel stuffing; and improperly recognising sales with conditions and consignment sales are several of the many ways discussed during this session that revenue can be improperly recognised.

Improper Revenue Recognition – 2   Improperly classifying certain sales transactions can take a wide variety of forms, including recording outright fictitious sales, improper recording of gain contingencies, manipulating sales to related parties, and undertaking bill-and-hold schemes. This addresses several improper sales treatments, as well as indirect methods of revenue manipulation, and how to identify and investigate these schemes.

Improper Deferral of Costs and Expenses   The improper deferral of costs and expenses often does not leave an audit trail. A simple change in accounting methods can shift current expenses to an earlier period.

Improper Asset Valuation   Improper valuation of accounts receivable, inventory, business combinations and fixed assets, just to name a few, are some of the methods used to produce fraudulent financial statements.

Improper Recording of Liabilities   Failure to record liabilities, changes in accounting assumptions, off balance sheet entities, and manipulation of reserves are some of the popular methods in the hands of the fraudster.

Inadequate Disclosures   Management has an obligation to disclose all significant information in the financial statements. Inadequate disclosures of related-party transactions are among the most difficult financial statement frauds to detect.

Emerging Issues in Financial Statement Fraud   As accounting standards change and the financial reporting landscape evolves, increased opportunities for financial statement fraud emerge.

Finding Evidence in Financial Statement Fraud

Financial Statements   Financial statement fraud is one of the most common frauds there is. It often involves so-called 'topside' journal entries that produce a desired effect. A particular kind of 'truth'. That truth not necessarily being accurate or legitimate with numbers.

Accounts receivable activity takes place in a subsidiary ledger. All totals feed into the general ledger, which in turn informs the financial statements. However, as their name implies, topside journal entries are not made in subsidiary ledgers because fraud in the transactions in subsidiary ledgers is easily visible to employees.

In this context, offenders also try to hide their activity from internal and external auditors. Companies routinely post voluminous numbers of transactions, and auditors can examine only limited samples at any one audit, whose monetary value equals a set and in fact undisclosed minimum amount. Hence, if fraud offenders learn the auditors' criteria, it's a simple task for them to keep fraudulent transactions below that threshold amount and greatly reduce the chance the auditors will ever notice their illegitimate entries (similar to money laundering and suspicious transactions).

Know your business – much can be learned from studying the audit process and its objectives. The better understood, the more capability of obtaining and analysing information, such as comparing their company's financial ratios to industry standards and prior periods and related business cycles. For example, if a ratio value doesn't make sense to you, the task then is to identify the people responsible for it, in all positions in the company (avoiding simply assuming that if someone tells you they plug in a number to make the financial statements look better, you have fraud). Simple.

Even if you are not trained as an auditor, you can gain insight into that profession by exploring the auditing standards issued and enforced by the US Public Company Accounting Oversight Board (PCAOB), a private-sector, non-profit entity set up in statute by the US Sarbanes-Oxley Act, with quasi-governmental regulatory powers and responsibilities.

To support this, these are the common red flags of financial statement fraud summarised:

- **Fictitious revenue.** One of the oldest financial statement schemes around. Involves posting sales that simply never occurred.
- **Unusually rapid revenue and/or profit growth.**
- **Readily noticeable internal control weaknesses.**
- **Noticeably 'aggressive' financial actions by senior management.**
- **Personality or character flaws of the CEO and or other executives.**
- **Unusual increase in assets – the other side of the entry to mask fictitious revenues.**
- **Customer records have key data missing such as addresses and telephone numbers.**
- **Unusual changes in ratio patterns – such as a spike in revenues with no commensurate increase in accounts receivable.**
- **Shifting expenses from one entity to another or reclassifying liabilities as assets** (such as WorldCom when they improperly reported $3.8 billion in expenses as capital expenditures).
- **Use of different audit firms for different subsidiaries or business entities.**
- **Recurring negative cash flows from operations or an inability to generate cash flows from operations while reporting earnings growth.**
- **Invoices and other liabilities go unrecorded in the company's financial records.**
- **Writing off loans to executives or other parties.**
- **Failure to record warranty-related liabilities.**
- **Disclosure notes or reports so complex and difficult to understand that it is almost impossible to determine the actual nature of the event or transaction.**
- **Discovery of undisclosed legal contingencies.**
- **Unusual or unexplained increases in the book value of assets such as inventory, receivables, long-term assets, etc.**
- **Odd patterns in relationships of assets to other components of the financial report, such as sudden changes in the ratio of receivables to revenues.**
- **GAAP violations in recording expenses as assets.**

'Beneish Model'

A mathematical model and IT tool that uses financial ratios and eight variables to identify whether a company has manipulated its earnings. The variables are constructed from the data in the company's financial statements. Once calculated, they create an M-Score to describe the degree to which the earnings have been manipulated. The eight variables are:

1. DSRI – Days' sales in receivable index.
2. GMI – Gross margin index.
3. AQI – Asset quality index.

4. SGI – Sales growth index.
5. DEPI – Depreciation index.
6. SGAI – Sales and general and administrative expenses index.
7. LVGI – Leverage index.
8. TATA – Total accruals to total assets.

When calculated, the variables are combined together to achieve an M-Score for the company. An M-Score of less than -2.22 suggests that the company will not be a manipulator. An M-Score of greater than -2.22 signals that the company is likely to be a manipulator.

An outcome from the above tends to give evidence of fraud as an organisation.

Accounting

Drawing back in again to situational and underpinning fraud activity, we look at the baseline and core issue of much financial fraud: Accounts.

Definition of Accounting Fraud:

The intentional misrepresentation or alteration of accounting records regarding sales, revenues, expenses and other factors for a profit motive such as inflating company stock values, obtaining more favourable financing or avoiding debt obligations.

The above definition draws together a set of fraud offending behaviours, which are set out in this chapter, but it is important that we realise such areas that attract different fraud actions.

As a headline, some of the most infamous so-called accounting scandals are:

Enron   Few corporate scandals in history are as well-known as the Enron case. In 2000, Enron was one of the most prolific corporations worldwide. However, due to significant misrepresentations in its financial statements, the US company made the headlines with one of the most spectacular bankruptcy stories ever.

Swissair   Switzerland's former national airline company was completely dismantled due to a miscalculated expansion move. In less than a year, the Swissair fleet was grounded and the corporation liquidated.

Jérôme Kerviel – Euro-market Downfall   This trader caused mayhem in European trading markets when he used the computers of Société Générale to engage in unauthorised trades. Kerviel caused the bank to lose nearly €5 billion Euros.

Tyco International Ltd   In 2002, two Tyco Executives were charged with a $600 million fraud. Both were indicted on charges that they obtained $600 million through a racketeering scheme involving stock fraud, unauthorised bonuses and falsified expense accounts.

- **Accounting with financial statement fraud can be more prevalent in company mergers and acquisitions.**

Fraud offenders in this context do not worry about losing money if they acquire a company that might have fraudulently overstated its assets and hidden liabilities to run-up its market value. Honest acquirers would run in the opposite direction. But fraudsters see this as an opportunity to commit a larger fraud afterwards, in which they write off much more than they overpaid.

The concept of fraud by both participants in a merger and acquisition, whereby both have misstated their financial status, is a matter of finer investigation. A current high-profile dispute exemplifies this, with each party to a massive acquisition accusing the other of false statements. In 2011, Hewlett Packard bought UK software maker, Autonomy, for $10 billion. But the following year, wrote off most of the deal's value, alleging that $5 billion of its charge was due to 'a wilful effort' on behalf of certain former Autonomy employees to inflate the underlying financial metrics of the company in order to mislead investors and potential buyers.

Typical day-to-day accounting fraud is done by way of:

Accounts Receivable (internal fraud committed by employees)

Cashiering   These types of schemes may or may not involve connivance especially if the organisation's internal control system is too loose.

Lapping   Lapping is the most common type of fraud committed by employees who handle cash and cheques and recording at the same time. Simultaneously it involves employees who enjoy good relationships with customers as they are entrusted with money intended as payment for an instalment that is due.

- Under this fraud activity, an employee intentionally excludes cash payments received from customers who are taking advantage of the discounts given for early settlement of instalment payments due.
- The employee pockets the cash payment and uses another customer's payment to cover for the previously disregarded payment transaction.
- Transactions lap on top of each other, as various cash collections are applied as payment to cover for the previously stolen funds.

For example, payment from customer A is pocketed; later customer B pays but it is applied to customer A's account. Then comes customer C's payment but it is applied to customer B's account. However, successive customers D, E, and F issue cheques as payments; hence their payments are difficult to manipulate. Customer G arrives the next day with a cash payment, but it is used to take care of C's account; and so the chain continues.

- During days that no payment transactions are received, the offender employee ensures that the accounts receivable will not go unpaid beyond its maturity date.

This is to avoid any customer complaints that may stem from receiving a billing statement reflecting late payment charges against his account.

▪ In cases where no other payments are eligible to cover the unrecorded transaction, the employee will be forced to pay the maturing account. This is to prevent the account from going awry which could lead to the discovery of his fraudulent act.

▪ The offending employee's activity is exposed once he is unable to raise enough money to cover the unrecorded cash payments.

▪ In some cases, an internal auditor will note the discrepancy of the dates the discounts were computed as against the actual dates the payments were reflected as reduction of the accounts receivable.

▪ If it can be established that there is a pattern by which the discrepancies of dates occur, this should prompt the internal auditor to send out letters to specific customers whose accounts were affected. The latter will be asked to confirm the records of the company against the receipts they are holding as evidence of payments and to note down any differences.

Skimming   Skimming (fraud) is the misappropriation of cash from a business prior to its entry into the accounting system for that company. Skimming is one of the smallest frauds that can occur, but it is also amongst the most difficult to detect, if you allow it to be that is.

The meaning of Skimming: Skimming is also known as an 'off book' fraud because the cash is stolen before it is entered into the bookkeeping system. Skimming in business is the most difficult to detect because there is no direct audit trail that can be followed to the source. Often skimming is discovered by accident, or if a company suspects that it is happening (which is rare, or better put, preferably ignored).

CASE **STUDY**

Skimming: Case Study affecting a small business.

N owns a café and delicatessen.

N has noticed that the cash account has been decreasing, hence engages a mystery buyer, M. After observing the employee cashiers the buyer/investigator notices that one of the employees is pocketing the cash when the exact cash amount for an item is paid.

M explains this to N. When the exact amount is paid the employee can simply pocket the cash because there is no need to open the cash register for change, hence no sale is recorded. This equals skimming.

Skimming: Other Examples

1. **Gasoline Pumps** – The skimming device is installed inside a gas pump in minutes and is not visible to users. A gas pump key can fit pump housings in multiple stations, allowing for quick and easy access. I think this could have been where my card was skimmed. I get gas in a lot of tourist areas around Orlando where criminals are more likely to go after the pumps.
2. **Handheld Devices** – Fraud offenders can take your credit card and quickly record the information with a swipe on these small devices. Beware of the only times your card is out of your sight and not in your possession. In fact, don't allow it at all.
3. **Keystroke Loggers** – This device can be attached to public-use computers, like those found at the library, or credit card point-of-sale devices to record passwords and other personal data. (They can also be downloaded onto your computer as malicious spyware.)

CASE **STUDY**

Skimming: Case Study in a larger business scenario.

A ferry system operator employed 200 ticket sellers at numerous terminals. The owners noticed a problem when conducting testing at one ferry terminal. A ticket taker collected a fare but failed to enter the cash receipt transaction on the cash register and didn't give the customer a receipt.

CCTV was used to film the employee on numerous occasions and determined that the individual was regularly skimming revenue. For example, the employee failed to record over 100 transactions during just one working shift. The employee also kept track of the irregular transactions on a piece of paper in the ticket booth and removed currency from the cash register throughout the day.

The employee admitted misappropriating funds for 13 years, which was substantiated by the deposit activity in the employee's personal bank account and a change in lifestyle after beginning employment at the terminal. The employee said that other ticket takers were skimming, which was later confirmed by CCTV recordings of another employee. A second employee admitted misappropriating funds over three years.

Cards   Credit card fraud falls into two categories: behavioural fraud, and application fraud.

Application fraud is when offenders obtain new credit cards from card issuing companies by providing false personal information and then spend as much as possible in a short time. Some credit card fraud is still whereby situational *behavioural* misrepresentation occurs, with either stolen or cloned credit cards. But most credit card fraud occurs when details of legitimate cards have been obtained fraudulently and sales are made mostly on a 'Cardholder Not Present' basis, where this is allowed. Sales include online and telephone sales and e-commerce transactions where only the card details are required.

The issues around 'faster payments' are currently in various stages around the world. In many regions, they are only recently catching on the problems it brings.

2008 was a major developmental time for the card industry. At that time, the core attention for most banks' strategies was on moving into Faster Payments, to enable the customer to enter the online banking portal easily and safely, not through the use of intrusive authentication methods. Another element that framed the faster payments strategy was the emerging of the digital world, and therefore, fraud and cyber data to be incorporated into a single platform, so as to make decisions and risk reviews more potent against the fraudsters and provide a better experience both for the bank and the consumer. There was a vision that eventually came into reality, and with that leap in fraud management and customer protection, many elements of a bank's cross-channel fraud strategy changed on a notable 'go live' day in 2008. Hence as the general counter card fraud strategy developed from then, it was noticed that it required careful thinking about what channels and events could be made faster and better. Even then, those channels and events included online banking, and telephone banking including Interactive Voice Response (IVR).

Therefore, financial institutions have had an opportunity to, as the old adage says, benefit from 'lessons learned' in what went well with faster payments launches from global markets. In the UK, for example, a customer can send payments up to 100,000 British pounds in seconds, heralded as innovation that benefits both consumers and businesses. Of course, much has changed since Faster Payments was first launched, however mobile banking is now in the hands of nearly every customer. Data breaches have exploded, and cards are often embedded in your mobile device as a portable wallet.

The 'Fraud Hub' – the real-time ability to interconnect data from cyber-digital end points, log in, service use, enrolment, and money movement across all of your customers' interactions, channels, products and services – has been argued to be the way forward to support faster payments in 2015 and beyond.

One learning point is that credit card fraud security has been improved but human fallibility has not. Among the same pitfalls are:

▨ Using free Wi-Fi access at your favorite coffee shop, fine but fraught with danger if checking your bank balance. If you are using an open wireless network, it is easy for hackers to intercept online transactions, passwords and other private business.
▨ A text message on your cellphone from your bank which asks you to log into your card account immediately, but you did not contact the bank? This should set alarm bells ringing.

Banks can only give out advice and terms and conditions of card use so many times.

ATM and Credit Card Skimming   Credit card fraud is a wide-ranging term for theft and fraud committed using or involving a payment card, such as a credit card or debit card.

The intention mostly is to obtain goods without paying, or to obtain unauthorised funds from an account. Credit card fraud is also a helper to identity theft.

Although the occurrence of credit card fraud is limited to about 0.1% of all card transactions, this has still resulted in huge financial losses as the fraudulent transactions have been large value transactions.

London (2012). ATM thefts, skimming and cloning 5000 credit cards and stealing approximately £1000 from each ATM. Traced to Romanian gangs operating in the UK.

Adu Bunu, convicted for credit card fraud, took a picture of his baby rolling in cash stolen from British ATMs (rare behaviour for a fraud offender, as they do not usually boast publically).

New York. Cyber-criminals stole $45 million in a few hours by hacking into a database holding data of prepaid debit cards and then alerting accomplices around the globe to empty cash machines. The case involved thefts from ATMs using bogus (cloned) magnetic swipe cards.

CCTV footage showed one of the offenders, his backpack packed with cash. Other rather boastful criminals (unusual for fraudsters) took photographs of themselves with wads of cash, posing in Manhattan.

Prosecutors called this activity a 'virtual criminal flash mob'. The offenders could use any plastic card to withdraw the cash – an old hotel key card or an expired credit card – as long as they had the account data and correct access codes.

Part of the problem lies with universal magnetic stripes on the back of the cards. Many countries have largely abandoned cards with magnetic strips in favour of ones with built-in chips that are nearly impossible to copy. But because US banks and merchants have kept to using cards with magnetic strips, and they are still accepted in many places in the world, it remains a major fraud risk.

Other fraud attacks against banks

The financial institutions remain the principal target for fraudsters. Of course cybercrime has propelled fraud against banks. The 2014 report of PricewaterhouseCoopers' Global Economic Crime Survey concluded that 39% of financial sector respondents said they had been victims of cybercrime, compared with only 17% in other industries. Fraudsters are increasingly using technology as their main crime tool.

Implicit new and historical threats lie in:

▪ Money service businesses.
▪ Currency exchangers.
▪ Credit/debit cards.
▪ Phone hacking and threats to banking.
▪ Shared value cards – prepaid and gift cards have become commonplace in the retail environment, but these cards have no direct ties to individual bank accounts.
▪ Privately-owned ATMs.

- Micro-structuring.
- Trade-based money laundering – trade price manipulation.
- Internet/mobile payment systems.

CASE **STUDY**

Bank Muscat – Sultanate of Oman, 2013.

Twelve travel cards were compromised in a single day on February 20, 2013 with a total transaction value of 15 million Oman Rials.

Experts in bank card operations in Oman said the fraudsters must have bought the travel cards and duplicated them several times to use them from multiple locations outside the country. Investigations in that regard led to India. They managed to penetrate the database of the bank to use the cards from at least 10 to 15 locations on a single day. They were aided by internal collusion in the bank.

Hackers used compromised access to RBS Worldpay systems to increase the withdrawal limits on the counterfeit debit cards under their control, as well as other deception involving siphoning stolen funds into accounts linked to the cards.

These events were caused by intrusions into the processing systems used to process the prepaid cards, and the transaction limits are overridden on a group of cards, the hackers clone these cards and engage 'runners' to make repeated ATM withdrawals on these card accounts on a Friday night, right after the ATMs have been loaded with cash for the weekend.

In best practices, many look for indicators of fraud, i.e. the financial institutions who deal in 'red flags' in suspicious transactions, in insurance fraud, looking at claims whereby dodgy facts inform the crooked claim or at the point of application which bases the case of fraud to follow. Then the analytics of fraud patterns, or even when data analysis reveals fraud (if the data is subjective enough and can then be objectively assessed as evidence of such, including fraud which is implicit within cybercrime).

Shell companies

Those within an organisation with authority over disbursements may also create shell companies that they control. Such is the ease with which one can set up a company, certainly in name. Fraudulent shell companies often will use a P.O. Box or residential address as a business address. Sometimes the owner of the shell company could be the spouse or other close relative of the perpetrator, and their names or addresses could be used to set up a shell company. These shell companies then bill the organisation for fictitious goods and services. The offender is usually in a position to approve charges, or has authority over staff who approve payments on behalf of that organisation. As the payment is made to the shell company, the offender has stolen funds from the organisation.

But often the billing documents from shell companies do not have the authenticity of legitimate companies. For example, the use of a shell company was discovered when a secretary noticed that the street address of a vendor was the home address of her supervisor. In another instance, fraud was revealed when it was observed that invoices from a vendor that were months apart were sequentially numbered. The implication therefore was that the victim organisation was the only customer for this vendor. On further investigation, the fictitious vendor was exposed.

Likewise, shell companies can, at times, sell legitimate goods to the company but at an inflated price. The shell company purchases the goods needed by the organisation from legitimate vendors and then resells to the organisation at an inflated price. The individual(s) who own the shell company pocket the difference. Such schemes are known as pass-through schemes.

Verifying the list of vendors and ascertaining their legitimacy is an effective way of uncovering the use of a shell company. Data analytic techniques could be effectively employed to analyse large amounts of vendor data to identify anomalies and suspicious activities.

The Enron case increased wider awareness of the use of shell companies to commit fraud. Even though shell companies were used by Enron for fraudulent purposes, they were not used to embezzle from the company, but rather to falsify their financial statements. Enron's use of shell companies is an example of management fraud where the victim was not the organisation but the investors and other third parties.

Ghost employees

A fraud scheme involving payroll is where corrupt human resource managers or payroll managers create *ghost employees*. The ghost employee is what it suggests, and this could be a fictitious person or a family member of the perpetrator. By means of falsifying personnel and payroll records, a ghost employee is added to the payroll and hence the offender collects monthly wages. The potential loss to the victim organisation of a ghost employee scheme could be enormous due to the recurring nature of the theft. After the offender has successfully created a ghost employee in the payroll system, the regular process of issuing salary ensures a steady stream of funds to the perpetrator. When successfully done, unlike the schemes of a shell company or skimming, the offender in regard to a ghost employee scheme does not have to engage in any further maintenance of the fraudulent scheme. As there are no recurring actions on the part of the perpetrator, the data shows no unusual patterns.

The existence of ghost employees can be difficult to detect by performing trend analysis or investigating unusual patterns; instead, they can be identified by comparing different databases. The perpetrator could have access to a couple of databases and thus might be able to alter them. However, she will not be able to include the ghost employee in other essential databases to which she has no access. Because the ghost employee does not work at the company, there is no documentation of work performed by this employee, no vacation days taken, no performance evaluation report, and the like. Reconciling employee data across various functions of the organisation can help to detect ghost employees. Data mining and statistical techniques are helpful in identifying the fraud, as this is not usually picked up by basic auditing, as fake records can easily be compiled to suit.

Inventory shrinkage

When inventory is sold and the corresponding sale is not recorded (as in skimming, discussed earlier) or when inventory is stolen, the offender has to amend the unaccounted decrease in inventory balance. Inventory shrinkage is the reduction in the inventory balance due to theft or waste. Investigating the causes of inventory shrinkage can in turn help expose fraud schemes. Although some amount of inventory shrinkage is routine and expected in the normal course of business, abnormal shrinkage or a pattern of shrinkage are red flags. Such patterns and trends, if identified through statistical procedures, require further investigation.

Documenting inventory shrinkage can be difficult for many organisations to detect due to their accounting systems for inventory. There are two common methods to account for inventory: the *perpetual* system and the *periodic* system.

In the perpetual method, every transfer in and sale of inventory is recorded. But with the periodic method, the inventory balance is estimated or computed at periodic intervals. Usually only one of the two inventory systems is used in an organisation. To effectively detect inventory shrinkage, a perpetual system has to be implemented to maintain running totals of the inventory that can be verified periodically through physical observation. Discrepancies between the two balances indicate the amount of inventory shrinkage.

Offenders have been known to conceal inventory shrinkage by altering either the perpetual inventory records or managing the physical count.

A critical internal control procedure, segregation of duties, prevents the perpetrator from altering records to conceal the theft of inventory. For example, an item could be reported as broken or perished prior to its theft by the perpetrator, thus the records are adjusted prior to the actual theft of the inventory item. In the most egregious cases, the inventory items are replaced by empty boxes, giving the illusion of inventory.

Fraudulent conveyancing

A fraudulent conveyance is often a means to fool auditors about the financial standing of a company just prior to sale or merger. It is also used as an attempt to avoid debt by transferring money to another person or company. Usually in a civil cause of action, the fraud arises in debtor and creditor situations, particularly with reference to insolvent debtors. The cause of action is typically brought by creditors or by bankruptcy trustees.

A transfer will be fraudulent if made with actual intent to hinder, delay or defraud any creditor. Thus, if a transfer is made with the specific intent to avoid satisfying a specific liability, then actual intent is present. However, when a debtor prefers to pay one creditor instead of another that is not a fraudulent transfer.

There are two types of fraudulent transfer: Actual and Constructive.

- Actual fraud involves a debtor who, as part of an asset protection scheme, donates his assets, usually to an 'insider', and leaves himself nothing to pay his creditors.
- Constructive fraud conveyance does not relate to fraudulent intent, but rather to the underlying economics of the transaction, if it took place for less than reasonably equivalent value at a time when the debtor was in a distressed financial condition.

Importantly the distinction between the two different types centres on what the *intentions* of the debtor are. For example, where the debtor has simply been more generous than they should have or, in business transactions, the business should have ceased trading earlier to maintain capital.

Procurement – a main scenario reconciling fraud and corruption

Procurement is the acquisition of goods, services or works, or the providing of goods or services externally. It is an objective that the goods, services or works are appropriate and that they are procured at the best possible cost to meet the needs of the purchaser in terms of quality and quantity, time, and location.

Procurement fraud brings together a crossroads of economic crime. In fact, economic crime in bidding and tendering from contracts scenarios is more aligned with corruption than fraud.

The mechanics of procurement involves 'the movement of raw materials, components, finished goods, supplies, services, documents, money, between a supplier and a customer from start to finish'. The threat of internal and external fraud attack lurks within these operations. Abusing the authority of senior responsibility provides a separate fraud and corruption threat which will affect the company and its employees.

One daunting fact is that the scale, organisation and complexity of procurement fraud is now at unprecedented levels.

This section is designed to provide a firm base of understanding of fraud in a procurement context, to show a degree of competence and proficiency in both protecting yourself and your clients.

Procurement is divided into 2 main elements:

- Bids and Tenders.
- Supply Chains.

This section will also construct the applicable fraud and corruption behaviour characteristics, and distinguish these in the different parts of procurement business operations and what attracts fraud criminals and how they operate in procurement scenarios.

It is important to stress that bids and tenders tend to entail more activity on the corruption side of economic crime, whilst supply chains are more about fraud itself. However, there are elements of both crimes (fraud and corruption) in both procurement elements which we will identify and apply.

Procurement – fraud definitions: recap

- ※ False representation.
- ※ Failing to disclose information.
- ※ Breach of Trust.

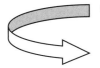

  - ※ Possessing, making and supplying articles for use in frauds.

Fraud in the pre-contract award phase   Much of the fraud occurs in an organisation's external environment, either with or without the knowledge of those involved in the procurement process.

Fraud in the post-contract award phase   The nature of fraud in the post-contract award phase focuses firmly on contract management, specifically on payments made on contracts. Most public bodies use an electronic accounts payable system, with key controls around separation of duties between requisition, ordering, checking receipt of goods and services and authorising payment.

Fraud itself might occur during the bid preparation process if costs are inflated or when a request for bids gives advantage to a certain firm. Public agencies typically place advertisements to solicit bids from competing companies. When planning or budgeting errors undermine competition, it might be considered *procurement fraud*. Fraud can also occur when a government employee gives confidential information to a particular supplier (as in our section about corporate espionage).

Procurement fraud transforms to corruption which can occur during the selection process, typically when bribes or kickbacks are offered in exchange for awarding the contract to a certain company. Government employees commonly rank submitted bids to evaluate which firm can provide the service at the best price. The policy at some public agencies requires two or more people during the bid consideration process to ensure fairness.

Public employees might commit procurement fraud by deception. They might split goods or services into two separate contracts to avoid going through a formal approval process. Public bodies that oversee spending typically set a threshold for contract approval linked to a certain monetary amount. If an employee deliberately splits the order to avoid scrutiny, he or she might be accused of this type of fraud.

Suppliers might also cheat the public during the bidding process or after a contract is awarded. Bid-rigging occurs when companies conspire to submit high bids that give one firm an advantage. A contractor that wins the bid might agree to send subcontracting work to a competitor who submits a high or unacceptable bid. These conspiracies give the appearance of competitive bidding when none exists.

- ※ Another form of procurement fraud happens when a contractor inflates costs of materials or falsifies documents submitted to support these costs.

- When a firm charges for work that wasn't performed or materials not provided, it represents fraud.
- In some cases, a contractor might substitute defective or inferior products to increase profits. Some public agencies ask for documentation to confirm certain materials were used and their cost.
- Controlling procurement fraud in an emergency situation is typically more difficult.

If a natural disaster occurs, public agencies generally lack time to solicit competitive bids and follow the normal procedure when awarding contracts.

In some cases, there may be a sole source of the services the agency needs in an emergency, which eliminates opportunities for competition.

Bids and Tenders

- *Know your business.* Procurement is a huge area of both business and unfortunately, fraud. Hence it is crucial that, if you are involved in investigating or risk-assessing in a procurement context, the backdrop of the business function is clear to you. It will also serve to avoid assuming certain bid criteria are fraud, when they are not.

In business, *bidding* is a recognised way of competing with other businesses for a contract to do a project. The hiring client examines and compares bid proposals from the different businesses to choose the firm with the best overall proposal. Bidding is used for many types of business work and supplies that range from construction projects to medical equipment. Companies inviting bids from contractors or suppliers usually specify how the winning bid will be chosen.

Sometimes, the bid-requesting firm doesn't decide the winning proposal from the bids alone. Instead, it creates a short list of possible contractors or vendors.

A conflict of interest (COI) occurs when an individual or organisation is involved in multiple interests, one of which could possibly corrupt the motivation for an act in another.

The presence of a conflict of interest is independent from the execution of impropriety. Therefore, a conflict of interest can be discovered and voluntarily defused before any corruption occurs. A widely used definition is: 'A conflict of interest is a set of circumstances that creates a risk that professional judgment or actions regarding a primary interest will be unduly influenced by a secondary interest.' Primary interest refers to the principal goals of the profession or activity, such as the protection of clients, the health of patients, the integrity of research, and the duties of public office. Secondary interest includes not only financial gain but also such motives such as the desire for professional advancement and the wish to do favours for family and friends, but conflict of interest rules usually focus on financial relationships because they are relatively more objective, fungible, and quantifiable.

Bidding on Government Contracts   Private businesses that want to bid on contracts or do business with government agencies refer to laws on government contracts to ensure that they are compliant with the rules that are required by local, regional, or national laws.

Government Bidding   One of the purposes of government contract law is to ensure equality in the bidding process for government contracts.

Contractor Bidding   To become a general contractor, known as a main contractor in Europe and a prime contractor elsewhere, the bidding party must show a willingness to undergo background criminal and financial investigations. This is also generally required for someone who wants to become a security contractor. If bidding for a contract with the military, for example, examination of financial and criminal records will be part of the process.

Competitive Bidding   Competitive bidding often begins with a request for proposal (RFP), which is issued by the entity seeking services or by an outside consultant who is managing the search process. A document is released either to the public or on an invitation-only basis. Qualifications for the contract are outlined in the RFP and, as a result, mostly qualified firms reply to the invitation in the competitive bidding process. In order for service providers to respond efficiently, a question-and-answer (Q&A) period will be established between the bidders and the issuer or consultant. Following that Q&A period, a deadline for submissions is enforced.

A bid template is an outline document format used by organisations bidding either to receive funding for a project or to win a commercial project. In some cases, there is a standard bid template issued by the organisation that is considering the rival bids.

Another option is for an organisation that carries out multiple bids with multiple organisations to have its own bid template. This will be a standard document outline accessible to, and used by, all staff. The major advantage of this is that it makes it easier for managers and finance departments to review bids before approving them for submission. It also makes sure that less experienced staff make sure to include all the details that the company believes are important to mention in bids.

In some cases, the organisation that will consider the bids will issue its own standard bid template (not doing so will raise a red flag in itself).

Closely studying and completing the bid template may also give some insight into what the organisation assessing the bids is looking for, thus giving indicators of fraud in that scenario if that is the intention.

Procurement: Supply Chains   Definition of 'Supply Chains':

> 'The movement of raw materials, components, finished goods, supplies, services, documents, money…between a supplier and a customer….. From start to finish'.

Example of an industry procurement project:

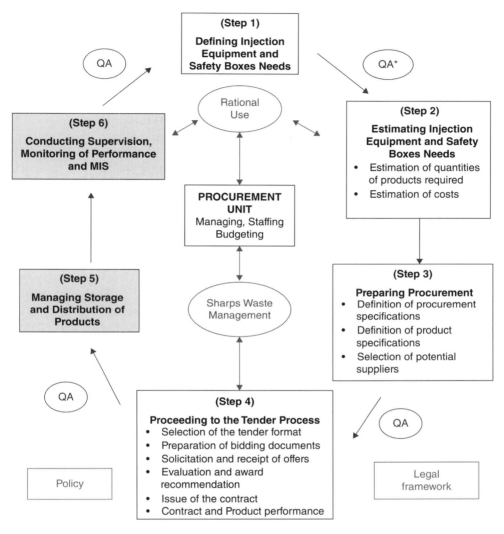

(Step 1)

Defining Injection Equipment and Safety Boxes Needs

QA

QA*

Rational Use

(Step 6)

Conducting Supervision, Monitoring of Performance and MIS

(Step 2)

Estimating Injection Equipment and Safety Boxes Needs
- Estimation of quantities of products required
- Estimation of costs

PROCUREMENT UNIT
Managing, Staffing Budgeting

(Step 5)

Managing Storage and Distribution of Products

Sharps Waste Management

(Step 3)

Preparing Procurement
- Definition of procurement specifications
- Definition of product specifications
- Selection of potential suppliers

QA

(Step 4)

Proceeding to the Tender Process
- Selection of the tender format
- Preparation of bidding documents
- Solicitation and receipt of offers
- Evaluation and award recommendation
- Issue of the contract
- Contract and Product performance

QA

Policy

Legal framework

*QA: Quality Assurance

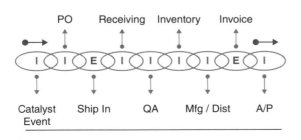

Inbound Supply Chain

PO   Receiving   Inventory   Invoice

I   I   E   I   I   I   I   E   I

Catalyst Event   Ship In   QA   Mfg / Dist   A/P

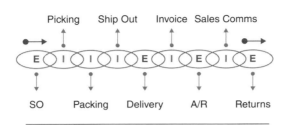

Outbound Supply Chain

Picking Ship Out Invoice Sales Comms

SO Packing Delivery A/R Returns

KEY VULNERABLE POINTS FOR FRAUD IN THE SUPPLY CHAIN

- ▪ **Occupational** – Using one's role to benefit personally.
- ▪ **Organisational** – The organisation is corrupt, mostly due to upper management failure.
- ▪ **Operational** – When gaps in systems and processes enable illicit behaviour to occur.

POINT TO NOTE: ISO Quality standards do not cover fraud risk.

Procurement and Import and Export

CASE **STUDY: INDIA**

NEW DELHI / MUMBAI, February 2014

India's central bank ordered banks to tighten monitoring of export finance deals after investigators uncovered an invoicing scam they suspect is part of a multi-billion-dollar scheme to exploit Western financial sanctions against Iran.

Although the Reserve Bank of India's ruling made no mention of the scheme that targeted UCO Bank, an RBI source familiar with the matter said it was related to a probe into the suspected misuse of up to $3.2 billion in export advances paid out by the bank.

'Banks should exercise proper due diligence and ensure compliance with KYC (know your customer) and AML (anti-money laundering) guidelines so that only bonafide export advances flow into India', the RBI said in a circular to banks posted on its website.

Under a provision in US sanctions law, Iran can accumulate oil export revenues with its Asian buyers and use the funds to buy essential imports.

Allegedly, a group of nine Iranians who entered India on student visas set up shell companies in a provincial city to tap into these funds held at the state-owned UCO Bank.

Under Indian rules advances for exports, or for the re-export of goods imported into India, should be covered within 12 months by proof that an actual delivery is made. The shipments, which included purchases of diamonds for re-export to Iran, were never made.

Investigators also confirmed 9.25 billion rupees ($150 million) in suspect transactions involving eight firms. The real figure could be as high as 200 billion rupees ($3.2 billion).

SUMMARY **POINT:**

■ *'Procurement'* has an innocuous title, but pools a massive area of fraud activity.
■ Supply chain and trade based money laundering fly into the frame already. Likewise corruption exists in this area more than fraud does, so the skill is to set out a case which clearly presents which financial crime falls where and how that fraud scheme operates.

A case study which presents a classic case of procurement fraud and thereby contains both fraud and corruption (and money laundering) is the case affecting the supermarket giant Sainsbury's and its customers.

CASE **STUDY**

John Maylam, a director of Sainsbury's (Sainsbury's 'buyer') accepted £5 million in corrupt payments from a key supplier, was lavished with 'excessive gifts and hospitality' by David Baxter, a director of Greenvale, which supplies half of the supermarket giant's potatoes.

Between January 1, 2006 and January 1, 2008, Maylam received cash payments of hundreds of thousands of pounds from Baxter, ran up a £200,000 bill at Claridge's Hotel in London and had a £350,000 holiday at the Monaco Grand Prix. Maylam received payments via an account in Luxembourg set up by Greenvale (Baxter). Additionally, Maylam claimed expenses of £20,000 (€23,800) a month.

Baxter (Greenvale) funded the extravagant gifts by overcharging Sainsbury's for its potatoes in a £40 million contract sanctioned by Maylam – collectively inflating the price Sainsbury's paid for potatoes from the firm and overcharging the supermarket by £8.7 million. Greenvale would then obtain ongoing 'profits' based on the overcharging. Greenvale disposed of some of this revenue via legitimate vegetable sales outlets. Andrew Behagg Greenvale's chief finance officer. He made no personal gain, but signed-off Maylam's ludicrous expenses claims, 'knowing his company would not be paying, but Sainsbury's would'.

Outcomes:
■ **Baxter:** Fraud – false representation – Corruption: giving bribes (and Money Laundering).
■ **Maylam:** fraud –-false representation – Corruption: receiving bribes.

Case Components:
■ Manipulated contracts (fraud).
■ Financial statement fraud (falsified expenses claims, internal audit documents falsified).

▨ Documentation forgery (fraud).
▨ Understating revenue (fraud).
▨ Fraudulent conveyancing (fraud to pass an audit).
▨ VAT Fraud: 'carousel fraud' (fabricated tax returns).
▨ Conflicts of interest (corruption).
▨ Paying or accepting bribes (corruption).

Evidence – Fraudulent contract drawn up by Maylam, which misrepresented to his own company (Sainsbury's) the actual status of pricing with Greenvale (following inducement from Baxter to do this). Continuing overcharging following the first-point deception, the illegal profit margin would kick-back automatically to Baxter (Greenvale) who would from time to time heap more cash payments and lavish gifts on Maylam.

Applying the Three Cs model:

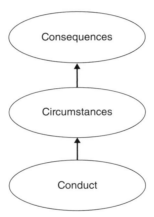

Conduct – Maylam was able to collude with Baxter, his key contact at Greenvale, to artificially inflate the price of potatoes from the firm to a higher rate than the one previously agreed with Sainsbury's. The normal variation in the price of potatoes, depending on the volume and quality of crops, allowed this to go unnoticed, with the surplus money put into what the defendants called 'the fund'. The money laundering evidence was of the disguising of the proceeds of fraud by selling some of the proceeds by smaller vegetable sales outlets.

Circumstances – It was this 'pot' that paid for Maylam's bribes, with no-one else from Sainsbury's knowing of its existence.

Consequences – in essence, Sainsbury's were being bribed with their own money!

Healthcare

Fraud in healthcare is an enormous area, which unfortunately is marginalised in public thinking, yet it is major area of fraud.

Mostly, cases like the following make the headlines.

CASE **STUDY**

Doctor Farid Fata, a prominent cancer doctor in Michigan, USA admitted to intentionally and wrongfully diagnosing healthy people with cancer.

Fata also admitted to giving them chemotherapy drugs for the purpose of making a profit. The cancer doctor's guilty plea shocked many in the courtroom.

Fata owned 'Michigan Haematology Oncology' which had multiple offices throughout Detroit. In court, the doctor named numerous, dangerous drugs that he prescribed to his patients.

As each count was read out, he admitted, 'I knew that it was medically unnecessary.' 'It is my choice.'

At the time of this publication, the prosecution are seeking a sentence of life in prison for 'the most egregious' healthcare fraud case ever seen.

The prosecution stated that in addition to insurance fraud, which involved a $35-million Medicare fraud scheme from 2009 until the present, Fata also harmed, and in some cased subsequently killed, his patients with dangerous chemotherapy drugs they did not need. According to government records, Fata's medical practice included 1,200 patients. Fata was administering chemotherapy to people who didn't need it, essentially putting poison into their bodies and telling them that they had cancer when they didn't have cancer.

Outcomes:

In 2010, Angela Swantek, a chemotherapy nurse and a 'whistleblower' of the cancer-treatment doctor informed the state medical authorities. She wrote a letter suggesting an investigation that day. But the reply received was to say they found no proof of wrongdoing at Fata's office, following which she noticed patients receiving chemotherapy incorrectly.

Fata admitted he put greed before the health of his patients, putting them through unnecessary chemotherapy and other treatments just so he could collect additional millions from Medicare.

Lessons Learned:
- Kneejerk covering up by the authorities. Atrocious apathy in such a case.
- An abject failure to investigate at the outset. Even a professionally qualified and experienced expert witness rejected as a nuisance whistle-blower.
- Lives lost.

Other instances of healthcare fraud

External:

Claiming a free prescription when one is not entitled to (takes money away from other frontline patient services and, in sufficient fraud volume, reduces the amount of money available to spend on patient care).

And, as referenced in Chapter 1 those cases which are internal fraud activities:

- **Upcoding** – refers to a provider's use of CPT codes to bill a health insurance payer for providing a higher-paying service than was performed.
- Asserted to be fraudulent practice used by providers who are trying to cheat the system so they will be paid more money than they have negotiated with those payers.
- **Upcoding** is recognised as being costly for individual patients and for taxpayers.

In opposition, in a 2012 US report one school of thought asserted that up-coding is not fraud. Hence we see more political forces at play in the healthcare industry in a fraud context:

Medicare and other payers require that doctors use a convoluted coding system for billing medical visits based on their documented complexity. The system is overly-complex and, for years, doctors have even been tasked with remembering the numerous elements required to justify the level of the visit (1 through 5), and then documenting the details required to support the billing level.

The end result: most physicians, with limited time and partial recall of the complicated rules, pick the code that they feel best encompasses the visit level based on perceived complexity.

It was further argued, that in the past when doctors dictated or handwrote patient notes it was more difficult to include all of the historical factors required to support a higher level billing code. The use of electronic health records, however, has made the process easier by automating the incorporation of past medical history, medications, allergies, social history and family history into clinic notes, thereby allowing physicians to justify a higher level code.

SUMMARY **POINT:**

I totally disagree with this whole approach, simply because replacing efficiency with artificial speed is a fatal error in fraud prevention thinking and practice. The incessant clamor for IT 'solutions' (my word in this context) again overtakes all manner of fraud detection benchmarking and drags the whole procedure along IT channels, and when fraud does occur it has become lost along the way and is exposed far too late, and has by then cost far too much. This approach also simply distances and disconnects fraud as a danger from medical care and related industry issues and entities.

Fraud *is* a fact of life in healthcare and whilst everyone knows that the primary duty and approach of doctors is to treat and care, the definite and real and objectively measureable presence of fraud, including so-called 'up-coding', is as present as the mountain next to Mount Everest. This kind of professional sullenness against fraud is like an office manager working in a hospital who says cleanliness is not their responsibility. It is like seeing the building on fire but arguing it is not their role to switch on the fire alarm.

Granted that professionals need to be allowed to focus on what they do; however, to take the problem out of the professional remit or situational and wider medical environments, and even worse, to try to automate the process in order to over-simplify the problem for themselves, so as a natural consequence that it (fraud) goes away anyway, is a mistake. This is not to suggest that doctors condone, indulge, encourage or do not care about fraud. It simply represents a lack of willingness to address or even engage with fraud by way of this complete rejection and playing down of fraud from its true scale and magnitude and the clear cut and proven particular way in which it happens, and see fraud in healthcare as completely someone else's problem.

Other examples of fraud in the healthcare industry are:

- **Unbundling** – refers to dishonest medical professionals who bill separately for individual medical procedures that would otherwise be grouped together into a single bill. Health authorities often pay less for certain medical procedures when grouped together. Hence some healthcare providers commit fraud by engaging in such a practice.
- Adding fictitious episodes.
- Substituting uncovered services with covered services.
- Peddling fake medication and pharmaceuticals.
- Overcharging for prosthetic devices.
- Doctors taking bribes to refer patients to certain private healthcare schemes.
- Doctors taking bribes from patients to put them higher in a treatment waiting list.
- Billing medical authorities for non-existent diseases.

Insurance

This includes any act committed with the intent to obtain a fraudulent outcome from an insurance process. This may occur when a claimant attempts to obtain some benefit or advantage to which they are not otherwise entitled, or when an insurer knowingly denies some benefit that is due.

We have made some references to insurance fraud in Chapter 1. However, a narrow canvassing and inquiry into how the insurance industry manages fraudulent claims amounts to a focus of frauds in the travel, motor, and home and business contents sectors, with fire an increased hazard, especially in the latter case, where large sums are at risk. There are also shipping freight fraud cases (procurement orientated) which attract vested interests of millions in claims, underwriting and litigation. Very often the facts leading up to and including a particular incident which is the subject of a claim are the object of the investigative scrutiny.

The structure of insurance in respect of fraud control is best described, including the important role of loss adjusters, as a number of initiatives at industry level. These appear to indicate increasing recognition of the damage being done by insurance fraud but, for a variety of reasons, many companies are reluctant to take bold and public steps to combat fraud. As with other industries, insurance has of course seen a surge in IT systems (including predictive modelling) but even these lack a fuller capability of preventing fraud because companies rely too much on (fraudulent) customers simply complying with an online or other process and giving 'honest' answers. Some insurance application processes even allow the customer the choice not to follow a bespoke application process and opt out of it, but the insurance company still allows the same customer to open a policy. This is simply like placing a diversion sign around the problem to benefit the fraud criminals.

Generally, the most prevalent forms of insurance fraud are:

Stolen Car: A car owner sells his car to a body shop to be cut up for parts and then reports the car stolen. Or the car is taken to a remote location and is set fire to. The body shop is in on the fraud, so the authorities are never told about the sale for parts. Or criminals sell the car to an overseas buyer, make the transaction without any paperwork, and ship the car overseas and then report it stolen (as per our car smuggling case study earlier).

Car Accident: such as 'cash for crash' incidents as referenced in Chapter 1.

Car Damage: Any form of insurance fraud is illegal and damaging to the insurance company. Some people will report a small car accident, get an estimate for damages, collect the insurance cheque and then not get the car fixed. This is the single most common form of auto insurance fraud going on, and it happens constantly. The people doing it see no harm in it, but the money the insurance company pays out comes from premiums paid by other customers, which will go up the more often this fraud is committed.

Health Insurance Billing: as per the last section. Unfortunately, healthcare professionals will sometimes get in on the insurance fraud act.

Unnecessary Medical Procedures: whereby your doctor is ordering you to go for unnecessary testing, then you may be the victim of insurance fraud, or certainly as per the despicable Dr. Farid Fata and his case, the patient being used as a pawn in the scheme.

Staged Home Fires: Homeowner's insurance fraud costs insurance companies and their customers each year. In almost every case of a staged home fire, the homeowner is not home and can account for his whereabouts when the event took place. Criminals are hired to set fire to the home, or break in and vandalise the home to make it look like the homeowner was victimised.

Storm Fraud: A common form of fraud that happens in the wake of major storms is homeowners will either enhance the storm damage to their home to get more of a settlement, or the homeowner will take advantage of how busy the insurance company is and call in a claim even if there was no storm damage.

Faked Death: This is more common than you may think, even though it has been the plot of many movies, television shows and books. A criminal will take out a life insurance policy on himself and make his spouse the beneficiary. After the policy has been in effect for several months, the insured criminal fakes his death and his spouse is paid the death benefit.

One UK case was the John Darwin disappearance case, the investigation into the faked death of the British former teacher and prison officer John Darwin, who turned up alive in December 2007 in Panama, five years after he was believed to have died in a canoeing accident.

Darwin was charged with fraud, obtaining a passport, and claiming money by deception. His wife was also charged, having claimed the money on his life insurance. Both were convicted and sentenced to more than six years in prison.

Renting and Insurance: Fraudsters who rent homes take out inexpensive insurance policies to cover the cost of their possessions. Prior to moving out of the home or apartment, or when financial times get bad, the insured will sell their possessions and then report them stolen to collect the insurance money.

A final and developing concept in insurance and fraud is about '*cyber insurance*' and the debate going along with it. There are many discussions in the finance and insurance world about who pays out and when and why, if the victim is at fault. For example, if you leave your door open and you get burgled, or you leave the keys in the car with the engine running. Insurance companies are increasingly looking to apply the same principle if you leave yourself vulnerable to cybercrime after being warned to take precautions. Should liability be on the victim if they turn off their anti-virus programs or deselect the malware filters? Or when they fail to change default passwords on their devices when warned to change them?

Telecom fraud

Core issues in telecoms, leading to definitive fraud behaviours and patterns are:

- How mobile networks work.
- Concepts 3G networks subscribers.
- Data International Mobile Equipment Identifier.
- IMEI Subscriber Identity Module – SIM.
- International Mobile Subscriber Identity - IMSI.
- The Luhn Algorithm for fraud identification.
- Subscription Fraud.
- PRS Fraud.
- Interconnect Fraud (GSM GATEWAYS).
- Fraud SMS spamming.
- Dealer commission and corruption.
- Roaming fraud.
- WANGARI.
- International Revenue Share Fraud.
- Prepaid Fraud.

The Luhn Algorithm or formula, sometimes called the Luhn Mod 10 Algorithm or 'Mod 10' for short, is a simple public domain formula used to validate a variety of identification numbers, such as credit card numbers. The algorithm can catch most, but not all, errors in card data entry.

Payment card issuers use the Luhn Algorithm to create valid numbers, and so Authorize.Net (a subsidiary payment gateway service that enables merchants to accept credit and electronic cheque payments through their website) can use the same algorithm to validate the numbers when submitted to their systems. However, the algorithm only checks to see if the card numbers are valid. It does not confirm that the card numbers were issued by a valid card issuer, nor does it confirm that the card numbers are currently associated with active accounts. It is therefore possible for a card number to be accepted by an authoriser but rejected by a payment processor when it tries to process a transaction against that card.

Likewise, because the Luhn Algorithm is available in the public domain, it is possible to generate numbers that resemble card numbers and which pass Luhn Algorithm checks, in an attempt to find valid and active card numbers for fraudulent or malicious purposes. The payment card industry has taken steps to mitigate the risk, but it is important to make clear that the Luhn Algorithm should be used by merchants only in conjunction with other means to help reduce credit card fraud, including but not limited to using the Address Verification Service (AVS) and the Advanced Fraud Detection Suite (AFDS).

Revenue Share Fraud

According to the Communications Fraud Control Association (CFCA), the telecoms industry lost $4 billion to revenue share fraud in 2014 alone.

International Revenue Share Fraud (IRSF) is one of the major fraud threats hounding the telecom industry. IRSF is caused by the artificial inflation of traffic or traffic pumping to the premium rate numbers in the world.

What is needed is an International Revenue Share Fraud tool, a big data analytical tool that detects International Revenue Share Fraud and remediates it in near real time which will avert huge financial losses for enterprise customers, mobile operators, service providers and wholesale carriers.

Typically IRSF involves a nexus between the following:

- ▪ PRN (Premium Rate Number) Aggregators: who obtain a range of fraudulent premium rate numbers (PRN) in countries such as Lithuania, and enter into an agreement with service providers falsely claiming entertainment services.
- ▪ Hackers or the fraudsters who generate traffic. They either hack a PBX of a company, or clone SIM cards and generate millions of artificial calls to premium numbers.
- ▪ Hackers and the revenue share providers share the revenue generated by the fraudulent calls which will be billed either to the end customer or some carrier in the routing flow.

Subscription fraud

In April 2015 a US magazine and newspaper subscription service was accused of charging highly inflated prices for publications they were not authorised to sell.

The nationwide scam targeted mostly elderly readers, allegedly charging them as much as double the actual price for new subscriptions and renewal offers to publications the attorneys general of New York, Oregon, Minnesota, Missouri and Texas charged in simultaneous lawsuits.

The operators of the subscription service and eight other interrelated third-party subscription companies are alleged to have mailed out millions of solicitations to consumers around the country without publishers' permission. The notices date back to 2010, purporting to be magazine and newspaper renewal and new subscription invoices.

Premium Rate Service Fraud

Along with IRSF, PRS Fraud accounts for $6.5 billion in fraud losses, according to a CFCA fraud loss survey in 2014. PRS Fraud and IRSF are similar in nature.

In both cases fraudsters inflate traffic to certain numbers or number ranges which attract higher settlement payments from the operators. However, there is a subtle difference in the way each fraud is carried out.

Premium Rate Service Fraud has been operating much longer than IRSF. Historically the vast majority, if not all, of the PRS Fraud has been domestic (i.e. calls originating and terminating with the same country). The method is that fraud offenders acquire PRS numbers (i.e. chat lines, horoscope, news, gambling, etc.) and inflate traffic to them with the knowledge that the telecom provider will pay them their 'revenue share' at the end of the month.

Because it takes a while for the operator to collect the money from the customer (usually at least 60 days), the elapsed time allows the PRS fraudster to 'disappear' before being detected for fraud.

IRSF in comparison as we have seen, uses assigned country numbers and relies on revenue generated from the terminating fee in that country.

Interconnect fraud

Fraud by way of mobile phone use was a fraud crime that was only committed directly against mobile phone customers, just as other scam activity; however, this has widened and there is now a range of mobile fraud schemes being practised against end-user victims.

What is also unique in this area of fraud is the very open conceptual nature of Interconnect fraud. Therefore very similar to money laundering, those (customers) are actually being used to commit fraud to amass and leverage large volumes of fraudulent revenues. Such customers have no idea they are involved in a fraud (but as mentioned in Chapter 1, liability occurs when the offender knowingly engages in a misrepresentation) so in effect the customers would be witnesses as opposed to being charged as defendants.

Interconnect bypass – also known as GSM Gateway or 'SIM Box' fraud

If customer A makes an international call, the call will pass through a diverse number of telecoms operators who will facilitate the call from one country to the other. Again, like money laundering or, better put, 'e-laundering', this takes place in a nanosecond especially with the high computer speed and memory chips in the increasingly efficient telecoms companies system.

When the call takes place, the mobile companies receive a small payment for electronically facilitating the call across their own network. Finally, the call is received by a local phone operator who will receive a 'termination fee' when the call is finally transferred to the recipient.

Fraud occurs whereby the cost of the termination fee is higher than the cost of a local mobile call. If for example the termination fee is 20 euro cents, yet the local company operator suddenly offers calls at 10 euro cents a minute, the fraud can take place by way of diverting calls from the usual incoming routes or telecoms channels.

In regard to the above mentioned SIM box fraud, SIM Boxes are machines that store massive numbers of SIM cards. Hence, if the possibility of the above cost override of 20 cents is there, the offender can make money from each call if the number is in the SIM card box.

Call termination finds its way into the telecoms system by a naturally occurring business entity whereby mobile phone operators form unofficial partnerships (in a more refined criminal context, these would be called 'cartels', and in my view this no different) and the operators buy and sell 'call termination.' The market conditions for such reciprocal trading boil down the traditional 'supply and demand' phenomena to sell terminations in another country where they are needed. This is open ground for fraudsters, as SIM box fraud offenders will harvest or collect massive numbers of terminations, running into millions, and sell these privately. In usage terms the routes used by phone operators in order to do call termination can result in the calls being diverted by a fraud offender using a SIM box.

Practicality: a phone user would have no way of knowing that the call is being routed by use of a SIM box. The customer may experience some echo or interference. Usual mobile phone services are still available, such as call diversions.

On a higher scale, indeed like money laundering as I referred to and the way fraud funds more money laundering and vice versa, the SIM box fraud is very much a part of organised crime mostly because of the stealth of using it, and it being a fraud crime which is hidden and suppressed within a fast moving consumer industry and consequently the awareness of it is driven down.

So-called SIM Box fraud is one of those 'hidden' frauds, yet as we saw earlier in regard to the costs of fraud, this area is one of the highest yet least known of and even less addressed.

Prepaid fraud

Fraud occurring on prepaid accounts generally capitalises on several points of compromise:

- Prepaid account enrolment.
- Issuance and activation of the cards.
- Loading or funding the cards.
- Purchase transactions or cash access.

But this problem also extends to other risk factors and financial activities, including changes of address, changes to source account information, change in email address and other personal information. Analysing the velocity with which this is done by card-holders and card purchasers, this information can be used effectively to create a more complete risk profile for prepaid card products.

Of course prepaid risk and fraud managers have seen the value of involving the cardholder in fraud mitigation. Examples of this are text alerts that can be sent to the cardholder during a suspicious transaction.

But this can also take the form of simple transaction or balance alerts that keep the cardholder better aware of card usage and may alert them to an account compromise. It is the cardholder who can best recognise legitimate account activity and stop fraudulent transactions then and there.

Although the prepaid card industry has not been hit so hard by fraud as other indus-tries, some points are notable to avoid such situations.

Processors can assist and engage in the fraud mitigation process. As the prepaid transaction volume grows it will be more valuable to issuers and programme managers. As more money is placed on prepaid cards, the prepaid world becomes a more attrac-tive target. Equally, the types of prepaid cards in the marketplace are designed for more transaction velocity and greater length of use. A payroll or general purpose reloadable card, for example, is used for more transactions and has more funds loaded onto it on average over its lifetime than a gift card.

Hence the opportunity is created not only to steal the card information, but the opportunity to benefit directly from the theft (i.e. more funds available once the card is stolen) is also that much greater for the offender.

The ability to both scale transaction volume and also to diminish fraud is of vital importance for the selection of a prepaid processor. Equally, as we know, fraud reduces profits. With large players among retail giants cutting fees for prepaid cards, downward pressure on profit margins seems inevitable and makes effective fraud management for a business critical.

Fraud directly funding terrorism

> A society that applauds innovation in the world of business can hardly expect to
> escape innovation in the world of crime.
>
> —*Leon Radzinowicz, Criminologist*

A common and wholly misleading concept of fraud is that fraud is not linked to terrorism, and that the funding of terrorism is strictly in the domain of money laundering. But nothing could be more wrong.

In this chapter we have covered a range of concepts and dynamics of fraud, but this section represents a drawing together of some concepts and areas of fraud, because to assume that white-collar crime issues are more the province of categorised organised crime, is a perception that is misguided.

- ▨ **Another main point often misunderstood is that terrorists need huge amounts of money to operate. They don't.**

As a police officer in the 1990s I went to the scene of two IRA bombings in England. A main funder of the Provisional IRA (aside from Colonel Gaddafi and Libya) was 'Noraid' – an acronym for the Irish Northern Aid Committee, which was an Irish American fundraising organisation best known for raising funds for the Provisional Irish Republican Army (which its leadership denied, naturally). Hence, I saw the end results of mindless slaughter, whereby an IRA sympathisers' organisation, which pumped millions of dollars into the IRA, directly funded terrorist atrocities in mainland Britain: Hyde Park, Canary Wharf, Warrington, Manchester, to name but some of the bombings which killed a huge number of innocent victims. Aside from Noraid and direct fundraising activities, funding by fraud was not as prevalent then as it is now, but racketeering, extortion, bank robbery, were among the other ways the IRA was funded.

In modern times, terrorist factions such as ISIS enjoy media publicity with their barbarous behaviours and want to be seen to be making territorial gains and at the same time, of course, like to posture about how much money they gain from sympathiser donations and the like, but to say such organisations only get money from this means is a mistake.

Hence, you (really) need to know the links between fraud and terror, because in our last section about telecoms fraud, you could be unknowingly but directly funding terrorism. That is either as a company or as an individual.

Among the fraud activities commonly used to fund terrorist cells are:

- ▨ Credit card fraud.
- ▨ Wire fraud, mortgage fraud.
- ▨ Charitable donation fraud.
- ▨ Insurance fraud.
- ▨ Identity theft.
- ▨ Immigration fraud.
- ▨ Tax evasion.

I once met Gary LaFree, the Director of the University of Maryland's National Consortium for the Study of Terrorism and Responses to Terrorism, and both to me and in his excellent research findings, he made the point clearly enough:

Part of the problem is that it takes so little to finance an operation. For example, the 2005 London bombings cost about $15,600. The 2000 bombing of the USS

Cole is estimated to have cost between $5,000 and $10,000. Al-Qaida's entire 9/11 operation cost between $400,000 and $500,000, according to the final report of the National Commission on Terrorist Attacks Upon the United States.

As alluded to above, the crux of the issue is that terrorist groups require significant funds to create and maintain an infrastructure of organisational support, and to sustain an ideology of terrorism through propaganda. But to commit the deeds themselves, the costs outlined above may prove how cheaply they can do so. Small semi-autonomous cells in many countries are just as capable of conducting disruptive activities without extensive outside financial help. They simply conduct smaller-scale frauds.

Hence, even though the nexus between fraud and terrorism is undisputed, there's concern at state and local levels that law enforcement professionals lack specialised knowledge on how to detect the fraud–terror link because they're more apt to investigate and prosecute violent crimes.

A critical lack of awareness about terrorists' links to fraud schemes is undermining the fight against terrorism. Fraud analysis must be central, not peripheral, in understanding the patterns of terrorist behaviour.

Synergy between Fraud and Ideology

Cyber Crime and fraud has shifted from a criminal inspired activity into an ideology driven terror funding mechanism for African based terror organisations and their affiliates in Europe.

Nigerian advanced fee fraud, also called 419, used to be a criminal instrument to enrich a large number of criminal organisations originating from Nigeria and other West African countries like Ghana, with strongholds in the Netherlands, Great Britain and Spain.

Presently, Cybercrime 419 advance fee fraud (romance scams) being a low probability of detection fraud crime, is the primary funding for most of the African-based terror groups in Somalia, Nigeria, central Africa and East African communities.

African nations are facing more and more terror acts by groups who no longer believe in equality and economic prosperity in their countries. Fraud is the driver of an ideal, not to get profit, as is the case for other fraud criminals in other contexts and concepts. The happy few and elites in every country are benefiting from all the wealth while the majority of the population is starving (to death). It is no surprise that the Islamic voice of 'prosperity being spread equally over all the population' is suddenly very popular in Africa, where the population is denouncing all imperialistic and capitalist influences by the Western world.

Al-Shabaab terror groups in Nigeria and Somalia should not be considered a local and isolated problem anymore. Boko Haram is endangering the government of

Goodluck Jonathan (President of Nigeria, 2010–2015), who was forced to declare a state of emergency in a number of states.

Although Boko Haram seems not to be very well organised, it is very effective in spreading terror in Nigeria and across its border. Attacks in Nigeria have proved that Boko Haram is not only capable of organising and carrying out those attacks but also of raising funds and setting up a financial supply chain based on 419 fraud.

Hence a destabilised Nigeria is not only a Nigerian or African problem, but also a significant regional problem because of the oil wealth and the very large population (largest in Africa and number 8 in the world) of 167 million people.

Moreover, intelligence agencies have identified connections between Boko Haram and individuals in Europe, which creates a scary scenario of Boko Haram conducting terror attacks not only in Nigeria but also on mainland Europe. Currently there are several ongoing operations by European intelligence in Europe, trying to eliminate those cells.

For us one thing is simple: our enforcement authorities should take 419 advance fee fraud more seriously instead of saying it's just another scam. If you were to report this, certainly in the UK to the likes of 'Action Fraud' it would be waved away in an instant.

■ **This also represents a key theme of this chapter; the danger of fixating on 'types of fraud'.**

Breaking this concept down further, it has also been exposed that benefit fraud is now implicit in terrorist financing. Taxpayers' own money is being used against them, as the UK government doles it out in benefits to fraudulent claimants who use it to fund terrorism in Syria and Iraq. Additionally to engaging in fraud, terrorist-funding gangs often use women to smuggle large amounts of money abroad in the belief they are less likely to arouse suspicion.

But a surge in fraud online by abuse of the benefits system, abuse of student loans, etc., represents a new turn in funding terrorism. One clear case of fraud in this context – through the taking out of student loans, whereby finance is offered by the government for mass university education – is rampant. One police investigation reported a number of cases whereby each one could have netted terror gangs tens of thousands of pounds of taxpayers' money. That revelation came as part of 'National Counter-Terrorism Awareness Week' but that has been about it, unfortunately.

It is also highlighted that a number of charities are being used as fronts for terrorist fund-raising. Well-meaning members of the public are being tricked into donating to charities with these kind of end motives.

This is not the first time the fidelity of charities collecting money for Syria has been questioned. William Shawcross, the head of the UK Charity Commission stated in November 2014 that he would deal 'robustly' with charities found to be breaking the law. His words came after doubts arose over the work of a charity which took murdered British hostage Alan Henning to Syria. The director of the charity concerned has been photographed posing with an assault rifle with known terrorists.

Moreover, a spokesman for the anti-extremist think-tank the Quilliam Foundation has said that half of all donations to Syria end up in the hands of terrorists, not those most in need. Political support is from one Conservative MP Philip Davies who said: 'I know the Government has been cracking down on benefit fraud. It seems to me that this shows that if anything, they need to go further'.

Likewise, the Al-Manaar Mosque in Kensington, London, has been linked with this fraudulent smuggling of money to the Islamic State. Amal El-Wahabi, a young Muslim bride and employee of the mosque's own nursery was convicted in August 2014 for a plot to smuggle £15,600 pounds in her friend's underwear to her husband in Syria. She met her drug smuggler-turned-terrorist fighter husband, Aine Davis, better known as 'Hamza' while working at the mosque.

Cyberterrorism

Cyberterrorism is the convergence of terrorism and cyberspace. It is generally understood to mean 'unlawful attacks and threats of attack against computers, networks, and the information stored therein when done to intimidate or coerce a government or its people in furtherance of political or social objectives' (Michael Knetzger, 2008).

Hence, the violent pursuit of political goals using exclusively electronic methods forms the new landscape of terrorism. It is not confined to groups such as ISIS. In addition to cyberattacks against digital data and systems, many people are being terrorised on the Internet today with threats of physical violence. Online stalking, death threats, and hate messages are abundant.

To understand the potential threat of cyberterrorism, two factors must be considered: first, whether there are targets that are vulnerable to attack that could lead to violence or severe harm, and second, whether there are actors with the capability and motivation to carry them out. Studies have shown that critical infrastructures are potentially vulnerable to cyberterrorist attack. Eligible Receiver, a 'no notice' exercise conducted by the US Department of Defence in 1997 with support from NSA 'red teams' found the power grid and emergency 911 systems in the US had weaknesses that could be exploited by an adversary using only publicly available tools on the Internet.

The attack on Sony Pictures in 2015 was another example of how the uptake on cyber-weaponry has surged.

Although many of the weaknesses in computerised systems can be corrected, it is effectively impossible to eliminate all of them. Even if the technology itself offers good security, it is frequently configured or used in ways that make it open to attack. In addition, there is always the possibility of insiders, acting alone or in concert with other terrorists, misusing their access capabilities.

- **Point:** the authorities still display a propensity to address and categorise fraud in too narrow a context.
- It is obvious that, even with fraud reporting centres and hotlines etc., in existence, the information and reports of fraud do not get to the right enforcement departments, if at all. The problem of terrorism by fraud is a massive one, but marginalised in both enforcement and public thinking.

- Benefit fraud enforcement authorities for one are singularly absorbed in benefit fraud *per se* and fail (not only the tax payer) to attach any significance to terrorist funding, with narrow policies and narrow enforcement agendas.
- On a larger and even global scale, the activities of the likes of Boko Haram are equally absorbed in social media and a naiveté that romance or phishing fraud is 'just one of those things' when in fact it is a massive contributor to terrorism.

Stand-alone or peculiar fraud cases of note

Unfortunately, many authorities fall into an exclusivity mine, as often many public sector anti-fraud departments and private sector companies (including the banks) are so absorbed in self-interest they try, inadvertently or otherwise, to operate independently of each other. One fraud offender committing a cross-activity of numerous fraud offences unfortunately often gets away scot-free. Fraud victims canvassed, who report frauds which move or fluctuate across different behavioural scenarios to a particular authority get nowhere, as it does not fit into a computer field or 'type'.

Of course some very exclusive fraud cases take longer, the authorities can, at times, only act when information gets to them, and this can take a long time because of public perceptions and slowness to report it:

- One such case is in 2015 whereby an American woman was charged with fraud after allegedly marrying 10 men over an 11-year period, without getting divorced. Within this case, she was accused of being married to eight of them at once.
- A US man was charged with 23 counts of identity theft in Pierce County, Washington in December 2014 in one of the most unusual cases of food stamp fraud. He is alleged to have stolen money from at least 23 Electronic Benefits Transfer or EBT accounts. This was by generating account numbers of EBT card holders without ever coming into contact with the victims or even getting his hands on the cards and numbers, then charging the cards for purchases from his retail meat business. He would take a known EBT account number then generate more account numbers using a simple mathematical formula that led him to existing subsequent accounts. The formula allowed him to work out what other numbers would be without ever seeing a card or getting the number from a card holder, stealing nearly $10,000.
- In a lesser known or prevalent form of fraud activity, disappearing ink is used on cheques so the hand written content disappears in a short time (sometimes just hours). The offender will write a cheque to him/herself or for an accomplice, mostly whereby the amount is written in disappearing ink but the main content, such as the payee and date etc. are written in standard ink. Alternatively whereby the first digit of the amount is written in disappearing ink and by the time the cheque is deposited and processed, the difference has been paid, secured by fraud.

Other cases demonstrating a cross-over of fraud activities are as follows:

CASE **STUDY: UK (HJ)**

HJ provided fraudulent references to a letting company in order to secure tenancy of a rental house. HJ falsely stated that she was in full-time employment when she was not, but was claiming state benefits. No proper verification took place by the letting company and consequently HJ was allowed residency and moved into the house.

Immediately after gaining tenancy, HJ went to the benefits office and saw her advisors. HJ claimed housing benefits from the benefits authorities, producing the letter confirming tenancy of the house. To claim housing benefit you need to be on a low income or claiming benefits already. Hence the playing off of two authorities against each other.

Outcomes:
- Fraud – false representation – misrepresenting employment status to letting management by claiming to be in full-time employment with salary level above the benefits limit.
- Fraud – false representation – misrepresenting eligibility to obtain housing benefit.

What flowed from this was that HJ went into six months of rent arrears, she did not pay a single bill, squatted in the house for months, and then stole several items of furniture, even light fittings and appliances before leaving. This is a pattern of behaviour HJ had followed at two previous rental properties. Thousands of pounds of tax payers' money stolen. Likewise the gain of an ongoing benefit the offender would not have otherwise had (in UK law only) besides committing fraud and theft set amid those incidental issues.

HJ played the system. She got away with two counts of serious fraud because the local UK police claimed it was a civil matter. On balance, the housing authorities' investigations departments stated that, because it was outside the scope of their policy, 'it would be inappropriate to take action' – even with the confirmed presence of 'benefit fraud' (which went on for 6 months) which was central in the scenario.

SUMMARY **POINT:**

This case is an example of the law being excellent but enforcement being non-existent. Public sector authorities being out of sync with each other. The offender knowing the system better than the authorities. It also showed that the tenancy referencing company did little or no due diligence and any realistic checking of references or background. It shows how fragmented the UK authorities are when it comes to enforcement.

CASE **STUDY**

Johannesburg, South Africa, 2014

In January 2015, RS, a Real Estate Agent operating from Johannesburg, South Africa appeared before the Specialized Commercial Crimes Court in Johannesburg, charged with several counts of fraud.

RS is alleged to have committed systemic fraud, by deceiving customers and drawing them into a fraudulent house purchase 'scheme'. There were 7 victims in this case, to a total of 395 000.00 Rand.

RS focused on properties which were subject to insolvency proceedings (bank repossessions).

Acting as the agent to sell the properties, RS exploited the situation and saw this as an opportunity to market the properties but keep the deposit monies of customers and not repay any of the deposits to anyone. There are even indicators that RS intended to keep the properties and 'sell them' several times over.

RS tried to make this yet more plausible by concocting a 'contract' which had implicit terms, with specific reference to returning of deposits if the offer made by the buyer is not subsequently accepted by the vendor (seller of the house). The evidence is clear however, RS had no intention of following his own contract terms in this regard.

RS then fended off claims to pay back the deposits by using an associate to assist him. This was done by the associate acting as a 'gatekeeper' who would reply by email to victims on behalf of RS, using intimidating language and tactics to block any redress to RS.

RS and 'colleague' even fabricated a fictitious audit to mislead the victims, in that the associate claimed to have 'checked' RS's accounts and work etc. and 'could not find any act of fraud, misconduct and or mismanagement by RS and or the Company'. Clearly designed to make victims give up.

Hence, the use of such an accomplice, to 'play the system', use intimidation tactics.

Likewise, RS could hardly use an excuse of inexperience or 'mistake', given his 17 years in the real estate business.

Eventually, however, the false barriers put up by RS and accomplice were dismantled and RS has been exposed as being a predator of his own customers.

SUMMARY **POINT:**

Another aspect of the case was the questionable processing of the criminal revenues (money that RS stole from his victims) and how these came to be deposited so easily into his bank account. The case implies collusion.

It also shows that fraudsters are not always 'looking over their shoulders'.

2.5 CYBERCRIME AND FRAUD

Cybercrime: a new presence of fraud in the 21st century

Backdrop: The title of 'Cybercrime' first appeared as being a representative name of crime used by 'cybercriminals' via computers across the internet. The cybercrime practices, however, have since expanded the boundaries of so-called 'traditional' areas of crime, bringing in new terminologies for old crimes, such as 'grooming', 'phishing' and 'pharming'. Hence, the term 'cybercrime' has literally exploded, and both repeats and 'innovates' traditional crimes (such as in supply chain and fraud) and relates to hugely topical cases of hacking. For example, in the SONY pictures hacking attack of 2015. Indeed analysts are already stating that wars are being fought by cybercrime means. Day-to-day however, cybercrime is a central mechanism of modern day fraud. Intellectual property theft, trade-secret theft, patents, impersonation and direct theft are among these.

As the world moved into the 21st century and technology's presence in our lives has increased, so has the amount of crime that is committed using the Internet and computers.

Across the cybercrime spectrum, there is a host of serious crimes that have appeared, with child pornography, cyber terrorism (as referenced earlier in this chapter) amongst them. For our purposes we will deal with fraud-related cybercrime.

In one instance, according to the Russian Interior Ministry, the state-run gas monopoly, Gazprom, was hit by hackers who collaborated with a Gazprom insider. The hackers were said to have used a Trojan horse virus to gain control of the central switchboard which controls gas flows in pipelines, although Gazprom, the world's largest natural gas producer and the largest gas supplier to Western Europe, refuted the report.

In our context, cyberspace is constantly under assault. Cyber spies, thieves, saboteurs, and thrill seekers break into computer systems, steal personal data and trade secrets, vandalise websites, disrupt service, sabotage data and systems, launch computer viruses and worms, conduct fraudulent transactions, and harass individuals and companies (Furnell, 2002). These attacks are facilitated with increasingly powerful and easy-to-use software tools, which are readily available for free from thousands of websites on the Internet.

Many of the attacks are serious and costly. The 'ILOVEYOU' virus and variants, for example, was estimated to have hit tens of millions of users and cost billions of dollars in damage. The February 2000 denial-of-service attacks against Yahoo, CNN, eBay, and other e-commerce websites were estimated to have caused over a billion in losses. They also shook the confidence of business and individuals in e-commerce.

Hacking

Most people by now have heard the words 'hacking' and 'hacker' and when canvassed many people think that hacking is all about criminal activity on the Internet. Whilst that of course is true to a large extent, it is not the full explanation. It should be made clear also that hacking as a practice has been happening for over 150 years. Like money laundering, again it is the names and terminology that give different benchmarks and definitions. When we see terms like 'layering' and 'placement' in money laundering (which, as mentioned previously tend to oversimplify the issue) in hacking there are 'classifications' of hacker as defined by Michael Knetzger (2008):

- The 'white hat hacker' could be what is now termed as an 'ethical hacker'. Identifies weaknesses in a computer system or network. Does not exploit the system but provides a report to a customer on its vulnerabilities. In other contexts this would be a 'risk assessment' one supposes, but again, some like to peddle out new jargon and create sub-sets of definitions.
- 'Black hat hackers' have clear criminal intentions. ID theft, DDOS (2014) attacks, and ransoms were among these.
- 'Grey hat hackers' are those who apparently are both of the above, or better put, can choose to be one or the other at a given time. For me, the grey hat hacker does not exist. If one hacks for criminality then one is a criminal, and in this idiosyncratic context of referencing and identifying and defining the criminal hacker does not mitigate that behaviour by doing a white hat hacking the week after. It may hold well in movies where you have a young hacker who is suddenly recruited by the FBI or something, but the development and advancement of training and cybercrime resourcing makes some of these definitions over-engineered and slightly dangerous if we are to allow one hacker to have the best of both worlds.

There are also claims made that hackers are of certain age group, that is 'teenage dominant' (from around 15 to 21?). Of course many 'grow up' with IT and its related outputs and young people are more proficient technically than ever before, but this rather constrained view of hacker profiling has been left behind by the explosion of social media use for one reason: Twitter – the social networking and microblogging service, that has 236 million monthly active users.

In 2015 the Metropolitan Police Commissioner (London) has announced (or at least mentioned in a TV panel discussion) that 300 more officers will be engaged to fight 'cybercrime'. But not a scintilla of mention of FRAUD online. Naturally the front line of crime is in many contexts on the Internet field, but we should not forget that fraud costs the 'occupational' fraud community and victims $3.5 trillion in 2014 (per ACFE figures). Enforcement policy-making lags behind in attacking the causes of fraud in this massive media context. But, as ever, we do insist on pigeon-holing and categorising crimes, and over 'policyfying' crimes, which compounds the fraud problem in social media yet further, and pushes the visibility of fraud even further out of sight. The enforcement wheel against fraud just goes round and round.

Thus, hacking is unfortunately viewed as a social norm, until of course we have cases like the SONY picture hacking or when international political opportunism suddenly arises. But, day-to-day criminal hacking is a massive problem on a massive scale. Not just when a famous movie company is attacked and drags all the media mongering to go with it.

Hacking – how easy is it? **Maybe this case study and the facts to follow will confirm the above and answer this:**

CASE **STUDY**

Hacking Wi-Fi is child's play!

7-year-old shows how easy it is to break into a public network in less than 11 minutes.

Just days after an investigation revealed how much personal information public Wi-Fi networks can 'suck' from phones, a child has shown how easy the hotspots are to hack.

The ethical hacking demo was carried out under the supervision of an online security expert to highlight just how vulnerable the networks are.

On YouTube there are over 20,000 videos about hacking. How to hack this or that, with the most popular of these video tutorials having millions of views!

Naivety also exists whereby many think that simply having (expensive) anti-virus software protects them from being hacked. However, such open availability tutorials can enable the beginner in a short space of time to hack all manner of online accounts, including social media accounts as mentioned, and many online payment systems and even modern smartphones. This was the reserve of only the technically proficient – but not anymore.

The following profile elements can be used to steal or misappropriate your identity:

- Full name (particularly your middle name).
- Date of birth (often required).
- Home town.
- Relationship status.
- School locations and graduation dates.
- Pet names (nicknames, not the name of your dog, etc.)
- Other affiliations, interests and hobbies.

Alerts and triggers and 'Big Data'

Previously, banks could use certain software to look for known signs of fraud-related breaches. For example, company expenses payments made on a Thursday would trigger an alert, as would payments and invoices that do not add up to a contracted amount. Network traffic from malicious IP addresses could be blocked. If, for example, an offender based in Washington made transactions in Tokyo, a red flag would be raised.

Now, offenders know the rules the banks set and how to get around them (often with the help of collusion with corrupt bank employees who help them). Banks have to closely watch the behaviour of people as well as their computer screens and software to observe those anomalies of all kinds, and decode what the peculiarities mean.

Moving away from signature-based systems and rules-based systems, because the bad guys have learned what these signatures and patterns look like and they're creating new ways to hide. 'So what we need is a finer-grained view of the behaviour, then we need the background baseline to decide if this behaviour is outside the norm.'

More proof to the assertion that it is necessary to move to behavioural science and Big Data to detect fraud. Systems use statistics of course, to give indications of how far out of the norm certain points of behaviour are.

Some software programs can consume many kinds of data, including network traffic, mobile app traffic, main banking transactions, and scan for suspicious behaviour that red flags fraud, using pattern definition, pattern matching, and anomaly detection.

This is on a par with putting CCTV in a street. This will record patterns as a baseline of activity. Traffic and people. The difficulty is setting up cameras and software to flag as an anomaly anything outside of that usual pattern.

Systems are tools. Fraud monitoring needs people monitoring.

Phishing and internet fraud

Phishing is an e-mail fraud method in which the perpetrator sends out legitimate-looking email in an attempt to gather personal and financial information from recipients. (Definition provided by Search Security – www.searchsecuritytechtarget.com.)

Fake messages commonly purport to be from well-known sources and endorsed by the words 'trustworthy' or 'reliable' or 'secure' websites. These have included famous household brand names, PayPal, eBay, MSN, Yahoo, and others. Analogous to a fishing expedition, when 'phishing', the offenders bait the hooks on line and wait!

Date:	Tue, 17 Feb 2015 16:37:18 +0400
From:	Amazon.com <"delivers"@amazon.com>>
To:	ianr@............................

Hello,

Thank you for your order. We'll let you know once your item(s) have dispatched.

You can view the status of your order or make changes to it by visiting Your Orders on Amazon.com.

Order Details

Order R:131316 Placed on January 04, 2015

Your requested report is Attached here.

Need to make changes to your order? Visit our Help page for more information and video guides.

We hope to see you again soon. **Amazon.com**

- The above email (not sent by Amazon) is a simple example of a phishing email.

Other examples include, **an increase in the number of victims signing up for free trials for unapproved or misleading pharmaceuticals or supplements.**

This is a full-on scam, usually involving the use of a 'pop up' on your computer screen, or even a text message advertising, for example, a free 14-day trial. In signing up to this trial you are asked for your credit or debit card details and after the 14 days have elapsed, recurring payments are taken. Naturally, the products are either fake or of an inferior quality (including pharmaceuticals or teeth whitening products, food supplements or slimming tablets) and in much the same scheme of things with slick payment processes, recurring payments or continuous payment authorities put in place to make you forget you are paying later along the line. But also remember that this is often more involved and difficult to cancel (purposely so) and make sure you identify who is taking payments from your account.

Here is another example sent to me before the Soccer World Cup in Brazil in 2014:

YEAR 2013 EDITION!! NOTIFICATION LETTER CONGRATULATIONS!!!

This is to notify you that as mandated by the **FIFA Regulatory Act.1982** on Competition, through our affiliated web hosts (**Microsoft Dynamics/Yahoo.Inc**) conducted a comprehensive online Cyber surfing on email addresses of company/ Individuals that are active within the period of the just ended **World Cup in the Republic of South Africa**. The purpose of this programme is for our online Cyber promotion and **Awareness Campaign of 2014 FIFA World Cup** to be hosted in Federative Republic of Brasil (South America).

As a result of this Promotional programme and according to the provisions by **FIFA Regulations on Competition**, a total sum of <u>USD$3,000,000.00</u>(**Three Million United States Dollars Only**) from the FIFA TRUST FUND was allocated to be shared among *Four (4) lucky Winners*. According to the released result by Competition Committee, your email account was among the Four (4) e-mail accounts that were luckily selected to receive a total amount of USD$750,000.00(**Seven Hundred and Fifty Thousand United States Dollars Only**) each and two (2) **VIP TICKETS TO 2014 Soccer World Cup in Brazil.**

With this view, we are highly glad to officially inform you that you have won a total sum of USD$750,000.00(Seven Hundred and Fifty Thousand United States Dollars Only) and two (2) **VIP TICKETS TO 2014 Soccer World Cup in Brazil.** Congratulations!!!   Congratulations!!!   Congratulations!!!

Naturally, the fraudsters who sent this were asking me for all manner of personal data in order to 'claim' this amazing prize.

List of phishing activities

Spear phishing   The criminal's aim is to collate as much 'close' detail as possible in regard to personal data and information of the target to eliminate risk of it being discovered with any immediacy and increase successful and ongoing frauds. This is despite being an open attack (and is in contrast to the extent of trying to create a mirror image of the single-hit fraud victim). This is to make continuing frauds invisible to the authorities. Studies show this to be the dominant fraud activity online which accounted for 91% even back in 2011. Of more interest is the decline of spam emails from 300 BILLION messages per day to around 40 billion coinciding with the surge in spear phishing.

Clone phishing   Cloning, as the name suggests is, about creating identical entities. In this context the fake is created from the genuine. For example, a genuine email sent is then used to facilitate fraud whereby a clone email is produced by criminals and contains a link to induce payments straight to the fraudsters. The second (and third etc.) email is seemingly sent from the original sender when it is not. Of course at the same time, the second email links will very often contain viruses, as Trojan horses and malware to infect machines and open up more fraud or theft activity.

Whaling   This activity tends to be 'commercially targeted' whereby the fraudsters use a kind of senior executive tone. The construct of a whaling email is such that it is often written in legal language, a quality issue (such as ISO, standards and dealing with complaints) even using additional and completely forged court papers, such as subpoenas, and in line with customer service affability, the email will sometimes contain a link to view the documentation purported online. This mirrors court service for the public of course, and is very often fallen for by company officers.

Bitcoin and cloud currency: vulnerabilities

Bitcoin is a form of digital currency, created and held electronically. No one controls it. It is in the main unregulated. Bitcoins are not printed, like usual currencies – Bitcoin accounts are produced by people, and increasingly businesses, running computers all around the world, using software that solves mathematical problems.

Bitcoin attracts a short but serious range of fraud threats. The so-called 'Dark Wallet' application has been the subject of controversy and in turn led to some sudden scrambling to get Bitcoin regulated and subject to formal compliance standards. The risk has been gauged by global financial authority and institutions (argued by Bitcoin exchanges that this is because the authorities want to stamp on business opposition by over-using regulation). To put it bluntly, the banks despise Bitcoin with a passion.

CASE **STUDY**

The case of 24-year-old Charlie Shrem rather crudely labeled as the 'Coin Prince', who was arrested by the IRS. After an involved road of investigation was followed with financial nuances, Shrem was indicted on April 10, 2014 on accusations of 'operating an unlicensed money transmitting business, money laundering conspiracy and willfully failing to file suspicious activity reports with banking authorities'.

On September 4, 2014, Shrem pleaded guilty to a reduced charge of aiding and abetting unlicensed money transmission. On December 19, 2014, Shrem was sentenced to two years in prison for indirectly helping to send $1 million to an entity named 'Silk Road'.

The interesting outcomes and learning from this case are that Bitcoin is not regulated, yet Shrem was convicted of regulation-orientated charges. A case of building up of criminality around the legally-fictitious entity concerned, as supposed to direct non-compliance towards a regulated authority. Moreover, money laundering was the main issue at the beginning, yet was phased out during the process. Reduced to conspiracy, and lying behind the other charges. This shows that the outcome and disposal of a case can take an investigator to a conclusion not foreseen at the start.

Hence the moral of the story is that you are an investigator – not judge and jury.

Digital Currency: Other Dangers

The growing use of digital currency will result in a rise in cyber laundering, as hacking attacks and online scams take centre stage on the Internet. Banks and authorities are affected, as money laundering using online black-marketing routes and other techniques will expand with the use of digital currency.

New techniques of money laundering (using digital currency) include opening accounts with low cost and little known payment gateways, buying digital currencies, purchasing stolen data, setting up online shops with payment gateways, using the bank accounts of money mules to transfer money to different localities.

Digital currency is the alternative to the traditional currency which is used in online transactions. It is very similar to the operations of loyalty points.

A report, 'Laundering in Cyber World – The Digital Currency Way' cited a recent case in the US involving 'Liberty Reserve' whereby a digital currency website was used for laundering at least USD $6 billion by data thieves, drug dealers, child pornographers, identity thieves, hackers and other criminals.

Traditional fraud and money laundering has often been a secondary process, preceded by an illegal activity, such as drug trafficking, but the liberty reserve case shows that data thefts,

(Continued)

hacking attacks and online scams are matching and enhancing the traditional crimes and that digital currency is now at the centre of the money laundering operations. Now the money laundering is expected to grow even faster with the digital currencies.

Currently, digital currencies are neither produced by government-endorsed central banks nor necessarily backed by the national currency. Consequently, digital currency is decentralised, controlled by its users rather than the governments. This means it is anonymous, and that, unlike credit cards and PayPal, which block payments from a number of countries, it enables instant payments to anyone, from anywhere in the world.

That is why criminals, along with some online retailers, are seeing digital currency as a preferred choice, because it is money without any sort of safety net underneath.

Ripple, Microcash, Litecoin, Bitcoin, BBQCoin, Novacoin, RuCoin, Terracoin are some of the popular forms of digital currencies used across the world wide web.

Social networking as a 'facilitator' of fraud

Each month, Facebook's half billion active users disseminate over 30 billion pieces of content.

For many, this realises and involves more frequent, fulfilling, and compelling communication than any other offline or online forum.

Summary Point:

96% of people under age 30 have joined a social network.

Linked-In has 100 million users.

@Twitter - has 75 million users. There are over 200 million individual blogs.

2015. Facebook is about to pass 1.5 billion active users—and 2 billion is within sight.

Privacy first

Although Facebook users have privacy options to control who sees what content, the 133 million active users in the United States lack a reasonable expectation of privacy from government surveillance of virtually all of their online activity.

Based on Facebook's own interpretations of federal privacy laws, a warrant is only necessary to compel disclosure of inbox and outbox messages less than 181 days old.

Everything else can be obtained with subpoenas that do not even require reasonable suspicion. Accordingly, over the last six years, government agents have been digging in the gold mine of personal and confidential information on Facebook.

Key Questions:
- How do online 'social communities' work?
- Social network analysis?
- Fraud, 'shapes and sizes'?
- Hacking – how easy is it?

How do online 'social communities' work?

Social networks are by their very nature all about sharing, sharing experiences, our latest news, likes and dislikes – and perilously, sometimes our personal information.

Whilst we all like to share – and we very much do – there are risks associated with allowing 'everyone' and 'anyone' open access to our personal information, which by its very definition, can be sensitive and, in fact, highly valuable (a friend of mine even puts on there what he had for dinner).

If you post that you are out of town on vacation, if you mention that you are away on business for a weekend, you may leave your home open to assault or robbery. But when it comes to stalking or stealing an identity, use of photo- and video-sharing sites like Flickr and YouTube provide deeper insights into you, your family and friends, your house, favourite hobbies and interests.

Hence people post their most personal and private business and details on there for the world to see. So what is ironic is that if I approached you in the street as a complete stranger and asked you about your private life, or other personal details, you would probably tell me where to go, even if I started by asking you out of the blue, 'Excuse me, how old are you?' or 'Where you are going on your vacation?' Yet many of you are easily inclined to put all of that information on Facebook.

Not forgetting also that personal information is often used to verify our identities with a range of organisations including banks, credit card companies, utility providers and online providers of goods and services.

- **But in 2010, a survey revealed that 6% of social media users claim to have been a victim of identity fraud hacking (Survey by Consumer Affairs (USA)).**

A basic and worrying fact is that fraud by social networking has widened the scope of *victims* immeasurably.

As we have covered earlier, it is rare that fraud criminals have direct interpersonal contact or involvement with the victim. This is what makes fraud cases unique.

It is also a reason that fraudsters attack virtually anyone now.

Victims becoming fraudsters

Such is the speed and growth and ease with which social networking happens, some of the high numbers of victims having their identity stolen suddenly, because of their constant, daily and active use of social networking sites, quickly see how easy it is.

In fact social networking is arguably one of the most prolific areas of creating fraud criminals there is. And to compound the matter further, many of them who turn to crime are in a business environment, given the numbers of businesses which operate and market themselves on social networking sites.

The international dimensions of the web and ease with which users can hide their location all contribute to making Internet fraud the fastest growing area of fraud.

The famous aphorism by Oscar Wilde, 'I can resist anything except temptation', taken in context here, suitably conveys two key messages about fraud being media-facilitated and thereby creating temptation and reducing the ability to resist it: that fraud has exploded in volume and risen in parallel with social media as a medium of communication and networking (the 'process of gaining website traffic or attention through social media sites') and, more scarily, the way fraudsters enter into the world of criminality without even thinking about it.

In a social setting therefore, both the attraction and availability of 'resources' such as those hacking videos (free of course) means that yesterday's fraud victim is today's fraud offender.

Safety culture

Jumping in at this stage is the concept of safety on line. If you are in a business context, you may consider these questions:

- Culture: What is yours? Sales driven? Top-down pressure?
- Training! And more training .. And more...
- Training for ALL – place this in the policy.
- Build anti-fraud training into main training in the business – side-by-side with marketing. Include the dangers of SN.
- Set the boundaries clearly about what is reasonable regarding social networks against the business.
- Enhanced due-diligence.
- DO NOT separate HR policy or procurement policy from fraud policy.
- Frequent data integrity reviews and audits.
- Review reporting social networking use policy. How far does it go?

In a social or personal context, these points are useful to follow:

Preventative measures: practicalities
Never give out your social security number

- Consider unique user names and passwords for each profile.
- Vary your passwords and change them regularly.

- Do not give out your username and password to third parties (even if it helps you connect to others and build your network).
- Avoid listing the following information publicly: date of birth, hometown, home address, year of high school or college graduation, primary e-mail address.
- Only invite people to your network that you know or have met, as opposed to friends of friends and strangers.

Fraud viz-a-viz social networking

Recent research reveals that identity theft affects millions of people a year, costing victims countless hours and money in identity recovery and repair.

It's a combination of factors: a lack of consumer knowledge regarding protecting your identity online; growing comfort with, and trust in, social platform providers; the need for social platforms to generate revenue; and a lack of standards or policing of those standards.

It must also be noted that social media sites generate revenue with targeted advertising, based on personal information. As such, they encourage registered users to provide as much information as possible. With limited government oversight, industry standards or incentives to educate users on security, privacy and identity protection, users are exposed to identity theft and fraud.

Likewise, these platforms have an untold mine of confidential user information, and are likely vulnerable to online fraud attack. On the marketing front, Google patented an algorithm to rate individual influence within social media. Once publicised, it will likely encourage greater participation by active users in order to boost their influence score. It is quite incredible, yet simple.

Business Terminology

Accrue. To increase, accumulate, grow, collect.

Balance sheet. A statement of the financial position of an entity showing assets, liabilities and ownership interest.

Bitcoin. A form of digital currency, created and held electronically. No one controls it. It is in the main unregulated. Bitcoins are not printed, like usual currencies – Bitcoin accounts are produced by people, and increasingly businesses, running computers all around the world, using software that solves mathematical problems.

Bonus Scheme. To reward individual, team, department or company performance or a mixture of one or more of these four types of performance against set targets.

Bottom Line. Refers to a company's net earnings, net income or earnings per share (EPS). Bottom line also refers to any actions that may increase/decrease net earnings or a company's overall profit. A company that is growing its net earnings or reducing its costs is said to be 'improving its bottom line'.

Capital Leverage or Capitalisation. Measures the exposure of a company's surplus to various operating and financial practices. A highly leveraged, or poorly capitalised, company can show a high return on surplus, but might be exposed to a high risk of instability.

Crowdfunding is the practice of funding a project or venture by raising monetary contributions from a large number of people, usually via the Internet. One equity expert defined crowdfunding as 'the practice of raising funds from two or more people over the Internet towards a common Service, Project, Product, Investment, Cause, and Experience', using the acronym 'SPPICE'. A crowdfunding model is set out in 3 stages: a project initiator who proposes the idea and/or project to be funded; the individuals or groups who support the idea; and a 'moderating organisation' (the 'platform') that brings the parties together to launch the project. (Note that, by 2013, the crowdfunding industry had grown to over $5.1 billion globally.)

Diversification. This is a central component to overall investment strategy, whereby an organisation handling investments is seeking to diversify investments across many various geographic locations (USA, Canada, Asia and Europe) and assets, such as equities and fixed income.

Equity. A stock or any other security representing an ownership interest.

General Reserve Fund (GRF). A 'GRF' is the main holding resource for a government and receives all revenues from which all state budgetary expenditures are paid. The transfers from GRF to pay the state budgetary expenditures are endorsed legally. The GRF also holds government assets, including a country's participation in public enterprises, for example the Kuwait Fund for Arab Economic Development and Kuwait Petroleum Corporation, and issues of EU funding as well as a country's participation in multilateral and international organisations such as the World Bank or the IMF.

Hedge Fund. Alternative investments using pooled funds that may use a number of different strategies in order to earn active return for their investors.

Incremental Revenue. This is revenue which increases gradually by regular degrees or additions.

Insider Trading. The (highly illegal) practice of trading on the stock exchange to one's own advantage through having access to confidential information.

Intellectual Property. Refers to creations of the mind, such as inventions; literary and artistic works; designs; and symbols, names and images used in commerce.

KPI. A Key Performance Indicator ('KPI') is a measurable value that demonstrates how effectively a company is achieving key business objectives. Organisations use KPIs at many levels to evaluate their success at reaching targets. High-level KPIs may focus on the overall performance of the company, while low-level KPIs may focus on processes in departments such as sales and marketing.

Procurement. The role of obtaining or buying goods and services. The process includes preparation and processing of a demand as well as the end receipt and approval of payment. It often involves purchase planning, standards determination, specifications development and supplier research and selection.

Seed Funding. A term that can be applied to any finance raised at the outset of a new venture to allow for development. An alternative to 'venture capital' whereby the risks involved in investment may be too high for venture capital investment.

Supply Chain Analytics. Refers to the science of examining raw data to help draw conclusions about information. It is used in many industries to allow companies and organisation to make better business decisions.

Underwritten. To sign up to and accept liability under (an insurance policy), thus guaranteeing payment in case loss or damage occurs.

Venture Capital. Startup companies with a potential to grow need a certain amount of investment. Wealthy investors like to invest their capital in such businesses with a long-term growth perspective. This capital is known as venture capital and the investors are called venture capitalists.

Whistleblower. A person who exposes misconduct, alleged dishonest or illegal activity occurring in an organisation.

CHAPTER THREE

From Fraud Awareness to 'Risk' – A Professional Step

If you are not willing to learn, no one can help you. If you are determined to learn, no one can stop you.

—Anon

 INTRODUCTION

Risk and thinking about risk is about the ability to reason.

In a fraud *risk* context, are these comments familiar?

- 'No-one could have seen that coming...'
- 'We couldn't have legislated for something like this...'
- 'The policy isn't clear.'
- 'Our system obviously needs upgrading.'
- 'A strategic review is needed.'

Given that this book, **Exposing** *Fraud* is predominantly about fraud *investigation*, this chapter does not claim to go into extensive volumes regarding risk, but the proportionate inclusion of risk issues is highly important. In fact you cannot have a book about investigating and detecting fraud without it.

There are a huge number of discussions and a range of statements and works on risk. Likewise with IT solutions, risk management systems abound. This chapter however is a lynchpin only between fraud awareness and investigations; a bridging chapter from definitions and concepts of fraud to risk.

Other salient points in this chapter are:

- Risks are not always visible.
- The misconception and misapplication of 'pseudo stability' in fraud control policy-making (false and naïve governance).
- How over-controlling displaces fraud to the areas where it can manifest and get worse.
- How and why management 'good intentions' actually increase fraud risk, with some harsh realities in addressing fraud 'by volume' and the ability of an organisation to marginalise fraud based upon its ability to identify and detect it in whatever form it attacks or poses the risk of attack.
- Questions the chapter poses also include, does the senior or executive level give proper direction to an organisation, or is the case of anti-fraud thinking something that is stuck on the side of its business objectives?

Wake-up call – impactive case study

CASE **STUDY**

Ambulance service admits contractor not checked properly

A private ambulance operator won a £600,000 NHS contract, despite one of its managers previously running companies owing the same service thousands of pounds. The ambulance service concerned in the UK did not properly check a director of a company providing paramedics before enlisting that company's services.

The same director had previously been involved with three private ambulance firms, all of which went into administration leaving millions of pounds of debts. One of these companies, which provided paramedics, ambulances and donor organ transport, collapsed in 2006. The director concerned resigned just days before it went into administration.

He was also director of one company, which went into administration in 2006. Again, he left less than a month before it collapsed. A third company of which he was initially a director, involving medical services, folded with considerable debts. The director himself was declared bankrupt in 2007.

In a statement the director concerned said there were 'in effect no losses' to creditors in any of the companies he was previously involved with, and blamed another director for the demise of those companies.

After the company collapsed, staff had to take the company to court to recoup £24,000 in unpaid wages.

CASE **STUDY**

And a victim …

One employee, a driver, said she fell behind with her mortgage repayments and was forced to borrow money. The trust approved such a high value contract on a whim.

'I don't understand why companies don't make simple checks before they employ these people to find out what kind of company is it? Who are they employing? What's their history?' The employee knows or cares more about risk than the management!

The answer to those last questions and the cause....
............'What is this "due diligence thing" by the way?'

CASE **STUDY**

The ambulance trust involved said it wished it had made *'much more detailed checks'.*

The Department of Health said a new 'fit and proper person' requirement was being introduced to give the commission powers to remove directors deemed to be unfit.

In 2013 England's ten NHS ambulance services spent £50m on private firms.

One deputy chief executive said: 'In hindsight, clearly I wish we'd done much more detailed checks. I wish the team were aware of the deeper concerns and then I'm sure the contract wouldn't have gone ahead.'

He accepts he may not have done enough to warn other NHS ambulance trusts.

'I took the opportunity on a phone call with other directors of finance to mention what had happened but, because we were consumed with our own problems, I didn't follow that through and I accept that maybe I should have done,' he said.

The concept of tax revenue being someone else's money was obviously lost somewhere en route to this case. It is also the most flippant management attitude to fraud risk one could ever see: the approval of a contract valued at over half a million pounds given over the telephone. Involvement with the director concerned, considering his highly chequered history, demanded even the most basic risk thinking. This health trust was wide open to fraud because the senior officers, such as the one quoted, probably have notions of 'fraud awareness' but leave the risk exposure of their own tax payer-funded organisations as an open door – an embarrassing and total disconnection between the management levels. It isn't even remotely amusing to the employee quoted above who nearly lost her home, through no fault her own.

The last case study is an exact fit into the following problems, all fully realised unfortunately in that particular case:

- Financial loss;
- Reputation;
- Damaged relationships;
- Loss of integrity with taxpayers;
- Negative publicity; and
- Damaged employee morale.

As a basic measure, they should have attempted to:

- Leverage existing fraud risk management processes;
- Evaluate the effectiveness of their risk management;
- Identify ways to improve risk management;
- Integrate enterprise fraud risk management and internal control; and
- Integrate entity performance management and enterprise risk management.

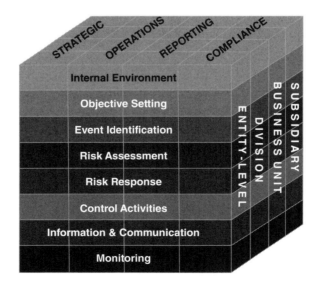

3.1 BEYOND THE DEFINITIONS

Rational Choice Theory

Remaining within the organisation, the Rational Choice Theory (RCT) entails three basic assumptions or propositions of the rational choice perspective. Keel (1997) describes the central points of this theory as follows:

- The human being is a rational actor.
- Rationality involves an end and means calculation.
- People (freely) choose behaviour, both conforming and deviant, based on their rational calculations.

The above theory is modernised from the original theory of David Creasy, a US penologist and sociologist who first developed the theory in the 1960s.

Basically, rationality is a configuration or containing pattern of choices, as opposed to individual choices. Thus, 'rationality' means 'sane' or 'in a thoughtful clear-headed manner'. Rational choice theory uses a more specific approach in that 'rationality' means that an individual acts as if balancing the 'pros' and 'cons' against benefits to follow, an action that maximises gain from (fraud and corruption) crime.

Whilst we have had an engagement with profiling in Chapter 2, at this point, in regard to risk we are able to collate a suitable summary of causes and effects of fraud.

The Fraud Triangle

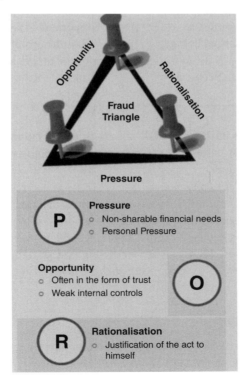

Who commits fraud?

External Offenders?	**Internal Offenders?**
▪ Vendors who intentionally double bill ▪ Vendors who intentionally inflate bills ▪ Fraud rings that target various businesses ▪ Fraud rings that target identity theft	▪ Disgruntled employees ▪ Stressed-out employees ▪ Employees who live above their means ▪ Employees who never take a vacation ▪ Employees experiencing financial difficulties ▪ Employees with drug problems ▪ Employees with gambling problems

Risk assessing as opposed to investigation: the difference

This section is really about pre-empting or seeing signs of fraud as a risk. Auditors play a large part in this area of the operation.

▪ Unexplained variances between budgeted and actual amounts ▪ Large liabilities related to unexpected contracts ▪ Significant internal control issues reported by external auditors ▪ Appearance of personnel living beyond their means ▪ Abnormal changes in account balances	▪ Unusual write-offs or other 'out of the ordinary' transactions ▪ Shortages in cash, investments or other assets ▪ Complaints from taxpayers ▪ Infrequent or late financial reports ▪ Accounting staff is behind 3-4 months on preparation of monthly bank reconciliations

Questions and points why fraud risk assessment is crucial.
- Why harangue those in the company for stealing or bribing when we put them there without checking them!
- Failure to see WHY it happened!
- The attacks may have come from a swamp of hatred, bitterness, enmity, greed.
- What other grievances or motivations feed the phenomenon?
- That swamp is being endlessly refilled and replenished – we fail to TRULY learn from past mistakes, because FRAUD is embarrassing and we don't want others to know. Internally we just want to move on. But there is an *absolute duty* to know why it happened!

Fraud risk assessment

Probably the best fraud risk assessment document template there is from the Association of Certified Fraud Examiners (ACFE) *Managing Business Risk*.

Right to audit clauses

Contractual rights do not go far enough, especially when there is no means of enforcing them. Audit rights can help you to determine whether a party to your contract is complying with their obligations, and determine what your options are if they are not. Marginalising fraud risk is the focal point of this, there is no mystery about the reason why. These points may guide the drafting of a contractual audit clause:

Who? Authorized representatives may conduct the audit, and it may be advisable to allow for an independent third party to conduct the audit. Confidentiality issues and disclosures should be included in the main clauses to cover this.

Where? Meaning which premises you will need access to.

Why? Clearly specify the purpose of the audit. As simple as that may seem, failure to do this will give room to wriggle out of allowing an audit by tying the issue up in petulant bureaucracies. If a clause is not specific enough to avoid the clause being given a very narrow interpretation you will have problems.

Security. Levels of access you will require. Again as ludicrous as this sounds, there have been instances whereby the clause was taken to mean allowing access but did not specify any further access. For example, if the intention is to permit access to a computer to access a database, please specify this.

Right to audit clauses are necessary, albeit there are arguments of pitfalls of having them, but such are the attitudes of some organisations you will encounter this very silly obstinacy, just as I and others have as investigators. I quoted earlier in this book that, as investigators, you will encounter professional pathological game-players besides the fraudsters. This is another area.

Head this issue off, plan out the people problems by ensuring you set out and apply holistic and accurate right to audit clauses, because you will save yourself a whole lot of time, and the courts have clearly stated in many precedent cases that they will not get involved in re-writing the contracts when disputes arise and these *practicalities* occur in regard to parties allowing or not allowing access for the purpose of carrying out audits.

Lastly, is the matter of cost. Factoring a related audit plan into your operational budgeting will be the cost of the audit, and under what circumstances the client will pay for any accrued audit costs.

'Pseudo-stability'

This is a term that is not well known, but the entity and end effects certainly are.

'Pseudo stability' is whereby management simply kid themselves that, if all is quiet across the organisation, then there is no fraud. Equally, the imposing of stifling rules and draconian policy just for the sake of control and stability is, in effect, the same as pushing down on a soft ball full of water. Something has to give, and the problem is displaced elsewhere. The informing effects are unseen until it is too late (hence the opening remarks in this chapter). Stability is achieved, but in theory only, and usually at a creeping price.

Or when fraud occurs time and time again, and the business is on the brink of collapse and then does collapse like a pile of sand, it is no good blaming the last grain of sand for the collapse. The problems that preceded and built up were either not addressed at senior level, addressed badly by those with key and applicable responsibilities, or ignored as an 'it's not my role' mentality among staff working in silos. Problems were allowed to pile up. Even in training programs I have encountered managers from banks saying 'fraud is not my responsibility'. Yes, if you want to quote your job description, but culturally and ethically, this is like saying that you work in a hospital and that cleanliness and hygiene is not your responsibility either. The same one who would watch the building burn down because it is 'not his role' to switch on the fire alarm. All of these attitudes to risk are as unforgivable as they are absurd.

Organisations must work actively on:	And avoid these pitfalls:
▒ *Reducing Risk of Contracts Fraud* ▒ *Creating a Competitive Environment* ▒ *Appropriate Contracts Clauses / Anti-Collusion Clauses and Bid-Rigging Certificates* ▒ *Appropriate Tendering Process and Evaluation* ▒ *Managing the Supply Market* ▒ *Competitive Specifications*	*X Do not expect employees to understand the term 'fraud' without defining it* *X Do not adopt generic control procedures and policies across the business where the risk of fraud varies by business area* *X Do not introduce overly generic training, such as 'e-learning' for 1000 staff across different departments. It may be necessary to tailor training for different roles within your business* *X Do not ignore 'red flags'* *X Do not introduce an anti-fraud policy and fail to follow up on it* *X Do not expect that the existence of an anti-fraud policy alone is enough to prevent and detect fraud*

None of the above happened in the health service case study.

Handling intelligence. Handling information

▒ **Is there a difference between business intelligence and fraud intelligence?**

One part in answering this question is if predictive analytics are involved.

Business intelligence and predictive analytics are a matter of contention in regard to their true efficiency, as opposed to how well they sell software packages.

Automated business intelligence systems focus on the elements and processes within the world of business intelligence and analytics. Fraud is a different matter.

In the modern world of fighting fraud, there has to be a place for technical measures. Gone are the days (in most places I think) whereby there is a team of 20 analysts in a room working into the early hours sifting through piles of documents and information. The benefits of having such an enhanced technical resource should be obvious. But there has been a steering away from the handling of intelligence by this welter of sales of systems which even denounce skills and approaches in the task, by constantly pushing an agenda of reducing the problem and then restating the solution to it as purely a technical one. Phraseology such as conventional analytical intelligence strategy *was* geared towards collecting, managing and reporting on data that can be understood.

Staying with systems, there are some very good systems that can be used in fraud intelligence handling, but must be a support and not a lead.

▪ **Criminal Intelligence is information compiled, analysed, and or disseminated in an effort to anticipate, prevent, or monitor criminal activity.**

The past, the present and the future. One could say that the monitoring and investigation of fraud are one, certainly in some instances.

But as a perceived term, Criminal Intelligence Analysis is a vital factor of effective fraud risk work, at both operational and strategic levels.

Analysts study data related to criminals, crime suspects, incidents, issues and trends. By collecting and assessing this data, they identify relationships or connections between fraud and money laundering in different places.

Objectives
▪ To help to deal more effectively with uncertainty and new fraud challenges.
▪ To provide warning of threats.
▪ To help investigators resource investigations effectively.

Types of Breakdown
▪ Operational (or tactical).
▪ Strategic analysis.

Operational support includes:
▪ Identifying links between suspects, and their involvement in crimes and criminal activity.
▪ Identifying investigative or information gaps.
▪ Profiling of known or suspected criminals. *(The problem with this is dealing only with those you know.)*

Strategic Analysis. Includes the identification of:
▪ The Modus operandi.
▪ Crime trends and patterns.
▪ Emerging threats.
▪ The potential impact of external factors such as technology, demographics or economics on crime.

CHAPTER FOUR

Exposing Fraud: Fraud Investigation at Work

'There is nothing so unnatural as the commonplace.'

—Sherlock Holmes, A Case of Identity

 INTRODUCTION

In previous chapters I displayed underlying causes, motivations and effects, but now we stabilise the work by highlighting the finite behaviour of the 'planner' of fraud and even the serial fraudster. A balance between the spontaneous fraud act and the offender who is constantly predisposed to committing it, and adept at misrepresentation, by act, deed, forgery or silence. As investigators of fraud it is crucial that you appreciate some self-appraisal of your whole approach to investigating fraud, which leads this chapter. Investigation is not massively complicated, but it takes clinical approaches, lateral thinking and character to do it well. This chapter will help you gauge this.

Likewise, we include an element of eye witness testimony, which is all too often now discarded by some as not being 'relevant' (understandable when one becomes conditioned to reading and deciphering masses of data, for example).

Other central themes of this chapter are:

- Collusion and understanding the systemic behavioural fraud patterns that collusion in fraud creates and, for us, the pathway to detecting it.

■ Investigative psychology (as outlined in Chapter 2) has to be included in any credible study of fraud investigation to underpin skills and policy knowledge.
■ Investigative Interviewing has a rightful place here. However, this is kept to a proportionate but lively level of inclusion.

Experience as an investigator of fraud has certainly confirmed my principles that the problems of culture, tone and personalities cannot be left out of a discussion of investigation of any economic crimes. In addition there is strong inclusion (often missed by investigators) of the ability to perceive 'naturally occurring' evidence from one crime to another. Fraud is a 'thinking persons' crime and as such, an intellectual problem to solve.

Therefore, overriding skill, continual unwavering commitment and a willingness to update oneself, to be forward-looking, to take an intellectual approach, makes the skills and embeds the knowledge to help it stay with you throughout your career.

4.1 WHAT IS AN INVESTIGATION?

The word investigation comes from the Latin word meaning 'tracking' or 'tracing'. More practically put, investigation is about closing doors on a confirmed offender.

As with fraud definitions, there are a number of definitions in this context also, which in turn creates a misunderstanding of the role of 'investigation', terms such as due diligence (one term commonly confused with investigations), and auditing. Is this the same as investigation? To some it is, to others it is not. Or enquiry? Essentially, to set out key aptitudes in investigation work, as opposed to having fancy vocational or professional titles, many of which conflict and confuse, it is best to break down the word forming the term *investigation* into more workable subheadings:

■ You *must* be competent in these fundamentals of 'finding out'.
■ You **have** to know the **facts** of the matter.
■ You will obtain these by systematic inquiry, detailed observation, and reflective analysis of information derived from the case and/or those involved with it.
■ Your investigation skills are continuously put to the test in consultations – purposeful conversations or investigative interviews with key witnesses and parties in the case, (who may well become part of the investigation) and third parties.

Fraud investigation is *not* complex. That proposition is just for those who would like us to think that it is, and/or those who *choose* to make it so.

With that last comment in mind, are these comments familiar?

■ 'Did you see anything unusual?'
■ 'There is no evidence.'
■ 'It's only circumstantial evidence.'

- ■ 'It's impossible to obtain.'
- ■ 'That's the guy, I know it.'
- ■ 'There is no other possible explanation.'

The above clichés are common in terms of misguided thinking about investigation. You can see they instantly detract from the ideals detailed above them. Poor company attitudes and cultures also form this corporate and investigative quicksand where the company remains stuck, and any individual flair is stifled.

Additional related 'human issues' of poor investigation important to point out at this stage are:

- ■ Jumping to conclusions.
- ■ Mistaking shrewdness for reasoning. Glorified guesswork is not factual.
- ■ Where the conclusions reached do not represent the investigation that actually happened (an issue which commonly appears at the report writing stage).
- ■ Stepping outside of the professional boundaries or remit (such as in our account regarding expert witnesses, and being unqualified to provide certain evidence).
- ■ Developing 'fraud theories' before getting any evidence.
- ■ At the same time many 'over-think' the tasks before them and by default too readily see a case as 'complicated' or unusual.
- ■ Approaching and treating all witnesses the same.

The above are fundamental in terms of misguided thinking about investigating. The further issues of avoiding conscious-choice investigative malpractice are also covered in this chapter, particularly in the sections on ethical behaviour and investigative interviewing.

With a more clinical approach, more fraud can be detected than by either over-complicating the case, or shying away from investigating part or all of it.

- ■ **Order, method and ability will address all fraud scenarios.**

The first and worst of all frauds, is to cheat oneself.

—*Philip James Bailey*

Investigation work: is it *really* for you?

Some people are simply not cut out for investigation work. So instead of bowling into a shopping list of skills and protocols to ostensibly aspire to (as most training-type texts do) in order to investigate fraud or any economic crime, here at first base, please consider some possible personal (hidden) points to help you ascertain if you genuinely – and with your eyes fully open – are suited to the raw side of criminal investigation. Investigation may seem easy and even glamorous, but it is far from that. Often overlooked also is the truism that even if you work in the corporate (non-enforcement) sector, fraud investigation is still to all intents and purposes a criminal investigation. Also, please understand the following clear points:

- ▥ Investigation can be and is, physically and mentally taxing.
- ▥ Investigation demands determination to ensure a reasoned attempt at resolving a case, as opposed to being seen to follow or merely shadow policy.
- ▥ Being an investigator of fraud (or any crime) is not for you to show how clever you are. You are there to get a job done.

I have met some highly experienced managers in organisations, one of whom, after being in her role for 10 years or more, suddenly found herself with an in-house investigation role, because of rampant internal theft of data and fraud. The training for the new role included the attendance of a fraud and corruption networking conference, which would be 'useful' for her. This manager confided in me that she was 'dying inside' at the thought of suddenly investigating colleagues who she had worked side by side with for years. This kind of case is not uncommon. There are of course some excellent highly skilled in-house investigators around, but many investigators do not receive actual investigations training, as incredible as that may seem, and just 'learn the ropes' or pick things up as they go along.

Even in some police forces, and the criminal investigations departments within those forces, management show an attitude that officers taking an online revision programme will do the trick for them in fraud investigation training. The chief of one police force I worked with in the Middle East openly commented to me that they do not investigate fraud. Any case goes directly to the state prosecutor because his officers either prefer not to or cannot investigate it. The very word *fraud* scares many people but for different reasons.

Behind the training issue, however, we return to the concept above, in that some officers simply steer clear of fraud investigations. The number of times I have heard police officers say 'fraud is not my thing, I was told to deal with it' and also where managers and some auditors put up staunch resistance to the investigation concept and instead prefer to take a 'management' or 'audit' approach. Again, it is not for me in writing this book to try to change human nature and explain the verbal sparring and quirky approaches of other people, namely some professionals, who put up the shutters when it comes to investigating. So no matter how many ways the issue of real time investigating is evaded, it comes back each time to the same question. Is it for you?

Take comfort in the fact that skilled fraud investigators are 'ordinary' individuals after all. The general misperception that investigators are 'clever' or superior is certainly not so. The key difference between the skilled and non-skilled investigator of economic crimes is that the skilled and accomplished investigator *chooses* to think, learn, train, practice and behave as one.

To help you along the way, here are some brief but pertinent questions for you at this point!

Self-Assessment 1

Investigation Notions

1. What is your notion of a 'successful outcome' of a fraud case?
2. If there are three suspects involved in one fraud case, do you regard this as a simple or complicated case? Why do you think this?
3. What is your view of the comment that 'fraud investigation is a war to win'?
4. Do you regard the role of a fraud investigator as being completely practical? That the 'real' learning takes place on the job itself?
5. Is an investigation to you all about demonstrating authority?
6. Are you looking for the offender or looking to blame?

Please write down your answers.

Self-Assessment 2

Do you stereotype?

1. Do you think that people in certain social situations will be more readily disposed to committing fraud? If so, which situations?
2. Do you think that all people who work in banks are involved in money laundering, or have criminal tendencies generally?
3. Does being nationalistic affect your thinking of fraud investigations in any way?
4. Do you use words like 'nerds' and 'geeks' or 'trolls'?

Please write down your answers.

Comments on the questions in Self-Assessment 1: Investigation Notions

1. The 'successful outcome' of a fraud case has been asserted in a wide variety of meanings. The question cannot be answered subjectively. If you are an enforcement officer, prosecution may be your answer, but not all officers think like this. Equally, if your idea of a 'successful outcome' is that anyone convicted of fraud or money laundering should go to prison for 20 years, then this represents restrictive thinking and can lead to fixation on getting a criminal prosecution and doing 'whatever is necessary' to do so.

Conversely, 'getting the money back is all that matters' to some professionals in certain organisations (as often noted in my training courses) denotes a way of thinking of just cutting a deal. It also shows symptoms of the investigative journey you took to get there.

2. The assessment of the so-called complexity of a case is aesthetic. The trained mind in fraud crime detection holds no barriers yielded by volume of facts or number of actors.

3. If you see fraud investigation as a war, then get out of the profession now. The first and main consideration is do not compromise your health. Moreover, do not take this to mean that fraud ought not to be taken seriously. Only the most naïve will discount the influences and clear practicalities of lack of enforcement support, unexpected acquittal, witnesses letting you down, etc.

   ■ There is no point in clinging to the maxim that 'The law is on my side'.

   ■ **Don't try to win a war. Just make sure you don't lose it!**

4. This is best appraised in Chapter 5 (Training). Practical experience is invaluable, but it cannot totally push out or displace academic proficiency.

5. Authorities govern behaviour and apply the law and policy. Rules are there for a reason. But authority should equal integrity. The militaristic authority saturation effect of acting out authority permanently has no place in a professional investigation.

6. Scapegoating leads to massive problems. The end does not justify the means.

Comments on the questions in Self-Assessment 2: Avoiding Stereotyping

1. To demonise sections of society in your *investigative* thinking will, without question, have a conflating effect on your effectiveness as an investigator. For example if people in a certain area in your opinion are 'all the same' – for example benefit fraudsters – you are missing a world of reality, such as the two out of five people in the UK who, without hesitation will commit insurance fraud in some form or other (proved by research).

   So such fraudsters do live in affluent areas and are 'chancers' in the same way as many others in other places. Insurance fraud is not committed by a 'minority' of the population as some would have us believe. Insurance fraud is an unfortunate defining characteristic of the population as a whole.

2. Some banks have a reputation. They have brought the reputation on themselves (with record fines for money laundering, investigations into institutionalised endemic tax evasion, and whistle-blowers exposing corruption supporting that point). In actuality, it is unfortunate for the honest staff who form the majority of banks' human resources that the public image, in keeping with the term 'institutionalised corruption' is subdued by depiction of the organisation having a corrupt or so-called 'toxic' culture. Great offence is taken by the many staff who are not corrupt, and rightly so. As a police officer, I was shocked when my (last) police chief made a press announcement and denounced his police force as being

'institutionally racist', jumping on a political bandwagon and probably working on his knighthood. Racism is not, never was, and never will be among my personal shortcomings, but along with all of my police colleagues, several thousand overall in the force, it was not pleasing one morning to read in the newspapers and on the local television news that we are all suddenly 'officially' institutionalised and labelled as police racists by our own chief officer, via the press. That was a direct public attack on his own officers by a police chief who had never even met me. Later I was refused two teaching jobs with the bold statement, 'You are ex-police, so you could be a racist' without even interviewing me or knowing me. That is what stereotyping causes.

Hence, do not confuse the term 'institutionally corrupt' with condemnation of all who work there. Do not stereotype!

3. Nationalistic pride is one thing, but using it to impose illusions of superiority on another country and its peoples is another. Stereotypical comments or even jokes about other countries should be left in the bar (and to other people). Perceptions must be reasoned.

4. These are common words now which can be taken either as an insult or some kind of parody attachment to competence. A 'geek' can be a highly competent IT person, or used as demeaning term. Hence it can be risky, however you emit these words.

- If you answered **yes** to any of these questions in figure 2 then you stereotype.
- Instinctive denunciation of someone you don't know is an enemy of reasoned thinking. If you stereotype you now need to be honest enough with yourself to admit it, and adult enough to analyse how much and how far you go and in what contexts. Once you do this, you can remove this notable intrusion from your professional work ethic. It can be done, but only if you choose to.
- Please do not see this point as being 'purely academic' or a mere exercise. Too many investigators have crossed the line, which has led to much larger implications, such as court case appeals and law suits. Please think about it.

These basic approaches to test your own approach and notions to investigations are not exhaustive, but they are two key components of it. We need to become aware of how vulnerable we all are to situations and systems that negatively influence our behaviours.

There are some excellent resources available which will help you inform your approach to investigation work. Professor Claude Steele of Stanford University, USA, conducted tests to detect unconscious stereotyping. You may not wish to engage in such extensive studies, but what you do need to do is work out some day-to-day scenarios or social circumstances where you may actually entertain stereotypical notions.

The corporate philosopher, Roger Steare, provides the MoralDNA Profile, which is designed to help you understand *how you prefer* to make good decisions and do the right thing. Be selective in using these resources. So long as you have a healthy approach to the task of investigating and, even better, if you can gain verification from an objective observer or assessor of how you work in all skill areas, it will help.

■ **Do not stereotype!**

Do you think that there is a place for psychometric testing in our profession?

To complete the 'Is it for you' section, as professionals we seek to prevent wrongdoing and engage with and deal with the wrongful behaviour issues when they do happen. So my question is, are selection 'standards' (the word is chosen carefully as opposed to 'procedures') sufficiently accurate and useful enough to appoint people to crucial responsible positions to investigate or control fraud?

It is no secret or mystery that some people are simply not cut out to investigate (as I am not for other roles). Likewise, does the absence of a criminal record and the signing of an ethics policy go far enough to complement 'transferable skills'? Generally speaking, psychometrics involves assessing suitability for a professional role through the measurement of knowledge, abilities, attitudes, personality traits, and education.

Moreover, there are some psychometric tests especially designed to identify people who are most and least likely to engage in unethical and illegal behaviour within organisations. These tests look at attitudes, behaviours and other risk factors associated with wrongdoing.

That is fine, but how about us?

Should there be an added dimension to the means of selecting those of us who deal with the people 'within' (namely, fraudsters) who are likely to engage in unethical and illegal behaviour within your walls? To stereotype for example, as we have put it, is one of the unforgivable sins in investigation work.

For me, the construct of the psychometric test would entail a specific writing of the 'tools' and validation of assessments concerned, such as questionnaires, tests, and personality assessments, to connect with what skills are needed, but also what experiential challenges you may face in your role: non-conformance; breaches, behaviour preceding or leading up to, or forming part of a fraudulent act; culture; internal politics, and more. This is a special edition of such an assessment – for us. I see posts on LinkedIn and I think that many are committed to improvement and progress (hence 'emerging' markets).

I can list a good number of pros and cons, for and against including such a measure or assessment – over and above an application and interview or even a basic competence assessment.

As mere precautionary self-assessment you may want to look into this option to enhance your confidence and that of your team.

Keeping a 'learning log'

In order to face the world on so many fronts in fighting economic crime, we as investigators need to give ourselves a real chance of success. We can read textbooks and articles, go to conferences, and talk all day about 'sharing best practice'. But to self-develop real learning and self-productivity, please equip yourself with the best simple tools and techniques to learn and retain and then apply and re-apply and re-learn as need be.

Keeping a 'learning log' may seem to be applicable only for young students, but it is one of the most latent and productive tools you will ever use – that is, if you are serious in terms of this text about what you do and where you are going and how far. This is NOT the same as keeping a report on a fraud investigation. This is all about you.

What are learning logs? Logs record learning skills and achievements, point out what you need to address, and create a means to reflect on what is learned professionally, or anything that informs professional performance. Students can communicate what they learn through drawing pictures, writing free responses, jotting down notes.

How are learning logs good for investigators? They show perceptions and/or misperceptions of a subject matter. Reactions from those you work with can also tell you whether you are learning and putting your skills into practice in a coherent matter.

A good reflective log will show:

- Some evidence of critical thinking and analysis, describing your own thought processes.
- Some self-awareness, demonstrating openness and honesty about performance along with some consideration of your own feelings.
- Some evidence of learning, appropriately describing what needs to be learned, why and how.

Formats

Your learning log can be a small diary, your personal IT file, Filofax, arch binder, or notebook. The best advice is to find an item and format that suits you and the way you like to receive and then record information and data. Note-taking will certainly be involved. Many people prefer 'visuals', or mind maps. Others take notes by 'key point' or bullet points. Others use linear style note taking.

Specific Open Template	
1. Describe the Experience	2. Review What Happened
3. What Can You Conclude from the Experience?	4. How can you put this Learning into Practice?

Sample of a Narrative Learning Log. (Probably more suitable and closer to the detail)

Date	25/11/2014
What happened?	*Received a series of emails of heated exchanges between an alleged 'rogue' real estate agent and customers claiming he had stolen their deposits in shady house sales deals.*
What if anything happened subsequently?	*Estate agent has 'disappeared' – victims have approached the media and gone onto networking sites to 'name and shame' ....*
	I agreed straightaway to represent the case.
What did you learn?	*To be aware that accurate assessment of a report is vital. This is an emotive issue involving at least ten 'victims'. It felt awkward to refuse at the time. But this could compromise the whole case and HAS alerted the offender (there may be no fraud at all). Am on the back foot. It has taught me to be more assertive and manage the victims next time about 'going public' too early.*

You may devise your own kind of template, but in any case keep a learning log.

' .... I think, therefore I am ... '

—*French philosopher and mathematician René Descartes, also known as the Father of Modern Philosophy.*

About roles (and job titles)

This section is a summarised account of collateral professional roles and titles. Please note also that the use of the term 'investigator' is about the role itself, not job titles.

Auditors

Auditors work in a huge range of industries and sectors, according to the industry standards relevant to them.

- **A generic definition of an audit is:**
  'A systematic and independent examination of data, statements, records, operations and performances (financial or otherwise) of an enterprise for a stated purpose. In any auditing the auditor perceives and recognises the propositions before them for examination, collects evidence, evaluates the same and on this basis formulates the judgment which is communicated through the audit report.'
- **Specific example:**
  Financial Auditor – a person appointed and authorised to examine accounts and accounting records, compare the charges with the vouchers, verify balance sheet and income items, and state the result.

Three broad categories divide auditing:

Internal Audit: An independent, objective assurance and consulting activity designed to add value and improve an organisation's operations. It helps an organisation accomplish its objectives by bringing a systematic, disciplined approach to evaluate and improve the effectiveness of risk management, control, and governance processes. *(Definition provided by the Institute of Internal Auditors, the IIA)*

External Audit: An independent authority outside of the organisation which it is auditing. The focus is usually on the financial accounts or risks associated with finance and auditors are often appointed by the company shareholders.

'Fraud and falsehood only dread examination. Truth invites it.'

—*Samuel Johnson*

Forensic Audit: The uplift to more investigative elements of auditing. Aptly known as an 'investigative audit', in which accountants apply specialist knowledge of both accounting and investigation. As investigators, they seek to expose fraud, mostly missing money and negligence or culpable failings in professional standards.

The illustration below shows some theoretical differences between the Auditor and the Fraud Investigator.

Task	Audit	Investigation
Need	Following an Audit Program	When the need arises
Standard	Quality-led (ISO)	Criminal standard of proof
Criteria	Company rules and principles	Legal liability
Method	Examine financial documentation, or validating professional standards or performance	Handle information, review data and wider occurrences informing a case
Rationale	Professional Skepticism	Finding percipient or other evidence of fraud
Recording	Standard audit documentation. Not fraud evidence orientated.	Holistic evidence gathering, interim reports and benchmarks and managed audit trail
Outcomes	Form an opinion of irregularity, or of possible non-conformance	If applicable, clearly state that fraud is present
Reporting Findings	1. Allude to wrongdoing 2. Confirm wrongdoing	Establish liability against offenders

Reconciliatory Note: Forensic auditing forms the cross-over territory of auditing with investigation.

'Forensic evidence', basically means that the evidence is 'fit for court' and certainly a forensic auditor can be called as an expert witness (see Chapter 1) and this summary provides some input into auditing and investigation occurrences.

Auditors, other than forensic auditors, do not normally look for fraud as their train-ing and accreditation does not usually take them into this kind of professional terri-tory. 'Red flags' is a term that of course has widened and moved into many roles and scenarios but beyond this, auditors do not necessarily seek any advanced or dedicated counter-fraud training.

For example, if a new project is completed within the budget limits it could be easily missed that fraud occurred, because the criteria on paper were met. Equally, the common assumption arises that when an audit is completed and reported, the project financials are correct. A standard audit is balanced between conformance and non-conformance and not really of a construct to expose fraud. The audit remains in a state of equilibrium.

Some further pitfalls of not taking a 'forensic' role or approach are:

1. Predictability: Criminals in other scenarios can weave a story all around the pros-ecution evidence sometimes and in fraud, predictable patterns of audits. As crimi-nals can set their watches by poor security patrolling, fraud offenders can map out fraud activity to align with a predictable pattern of financial audits. Some audit pro-grammes are even circulated months in advance, which makes them 'fraud friendly'.
2. Equally, auditors will incessantly repeat the same format and focus on the same areas and what they are looking for, among the transactions, inventories and records. Fraud offenders can easily read these patterns. Also, if a new auditor suddenly joins the company, the new auditor will invariably be trained and conditioned to be seamless in the auditing operation, to follow the same working pattern which goes on indefinitely.
3. Restrictions brought about by 'Audit Sampling': an auditor can only audit one project at once. Sampling is an audit dominant issue. Hence, if the scope of the business or operation expands, and with that expansion, more information and data grows with it, sampling becomes narrower and efficiency can become lost within the sheer volume of information and data, which increases and never decreases.

Internal control

Distinguishing between Audit and Internal Controls   The internal audit arises from governance, operations, and information systems. The audit also determines the extent of the effectiveness and the extent to which operating and programme goals ob-jectives have been established.

Auditors do not usually get involved in managing control systems as arguably this would create a conflict of interest with their auditing duties and systems they control.

In regard to Internal Controls, they are defined as 'comprising the plans, methods, techniques and procedures used to meet the mission, goals, and objectives of the organ-isation, and to ensure the safety and security of its operations'.

Therefore the process of internal controls is more about 'managing' an organisation and its people, and provides a framework for identifying and addressing major perfor-mance 'red flag' areas and management challenges. Internal control also implies that the whole workforce has a part to play in this, whereas auditing is a strict measure for the auditors.

Risk managers

The role of the risk manager is well known, but few people know what risk managers are. Risk managers are professionals employed as essential officers responsible for keeping a business afloat and maintaining profits.

Risk managers work in a wide variety of businesses and organisations, though as of late, many are found primarily in the banking and financial sector. Specialists working in these organisations are largely concerned with discovering and eliminating fraudulent activities, which could put the business's reputation and success in jeopardy.

Risk management professionals are usually *financial managers* that use specific training, skills and experience to identify possible risks that could result in lower cash flow and higher insurance rates for the business. They assess risks and implement plans and strategies to minimise business losses. Lowering losses also lowers the cost of insurance, resulting in greater revenue flow for the business.

Some risk managers are also highly competent investigators. In Chapter 3 we have a practical application of this area and demonstrate the fusion between investigation and risk (see Impactive Case Study and audit section).

Journalists informing investigation

The definition of *investigative journalism* is different again:

> 'a *type* of journalism that tries to discover information of public interest that someone is trying to hide' (Cambridge Dictionary).

(Conspiracy is also a popular subject for investigative journalism.)

Staying with investigative journalism, I find these essential benchmarks of interest: *(provided by Konrad Adenauer Stiftung's Media Programme for sub-Saharan Africa)*

- An original, proactive process that digs deeply into an issue or topic of public interest.
- Producing new information or putting known information together to produce new insights.
- Multi-sourced, using more resources and demanding team-working and time.
- Revealing secrets or uncovering issues surrounded by silence.
- Looking beyond individuals at fault to the systems and processes that allow abuses to happen.
- Bearing witness, and investigating ideas as well as facts and events.
- Providing nuanced context and explaining not only what, but why.
- Not always about bad news, and not necessarily requiring undercover techniques – though it often is, and sometimes does.

I cannot find a better all-encompassing approach to investigation than this. This is not the usual shopping list of skills needed. The balance across them gives a clear standard of being correct with your facts (and how to be) with a single willingness to step into the middle of an investigation and involve oneself with the more so-called difficult tasks that many instinctively shy away from, in particular, the direct references of 'proactive process' and 'producing new information'.

Journalists investigate to an extent of establishing wrongdoing in a public interest context. But legal implications of getting it wrong are the same for them as for anyone (see 'How far do you go' in this chapter), and whilst some argue that journalists have become 'more powerful than governments', this is not so – a claim verified by the shocking range of examples of ways in which journalists' ability to perform their role is being compromised and undermined.

Hence, journalists are often criticised, yet many enforcement officers who indulge in direct investigative malpractice are rarely taken to account when, for example, they shoe-horn facts to fit particular offences, or they abuse powers and issues of bail, being a daily occurrence. A kind of unofficial accountability appears for journalists, which is running constantly, at the same time as they are being persecuted and monitored illegally. Yet, there is only sporadic accountability for enforcement. And so journalists remain open targets, whilst failings in enforcement and officialdom continue.

The 'psychological contract'

An interesting insertion at this point, and to round the concept of the grey area of commitment (from auditor to investigator for example) or to examine where the lines are drawn between job roles and titles, is to appraise this against the background of the term 'psychological contract'.

First used in the early 1960s it is defined as '...the perceptions of the two parties, employee and employer, of what their mutual obligations are towards each other'. These obligations will often be informal and vague, and so they may be inferred from actions or statements.

The psychological contract is not a legal contract of employment, or of any kind. As a manner of thinking it will, in many cases, offer only a limited representation of the reality of the employment relationship. The employee (auditor or investigator) may have contributed little to its terms beyond accepting them. The employing organisation may impose strong policies, of which some are simply followed blindly, with no room for any flair. You may therefore consider your role to have strict boundaries, and will restrain the effort you put into investigating fraud. Role perception equals role application.

But on the other hand, the *reality* of the situation as perceived by the parties may be more influential than the formal contract in affecting how employees behave from day to day.

Another interesting analogy is that the forensic auditor is usually as qualified professionally as the fraud investigator. Sometimes they are one and the same. Therefore the void in role perception is unmistakable. Are you committed to supporting your fraud victim, by doing that little bit more which is reasonable, legal, ethical and fully professional? Many police and later colleagues shared the same dialogue and experience of doing hours of extra work, staying late, arriving early, even going in on a day off, something which I did many times, but this is not to say those of us who did this are better than others. What the psychological contract does tell us is that we can think about our roles and titles and then each do what we do to inform them, and with that, how we can gauge our commitment to victims of fraud psychologically, and how crossways professionally we interact with each other (*Chartered Institute of Professional Development (CIPD) Journal*, 2014).

4.2 FORMALITIES AND INVESTIGATION GOALS

'A thing is not necessarily true because a man dies for it'

—*Oscar Wilde*

So much is written about the skills of an investigator and *requirements* for a particular role, yet so little is written about what it is we are really aiming for.

Politically, organisations like *Europol* make extensive use of social media to broadcast 'results', which is in fact a similar practice of many enforcement authorities. Whilst successful results carry a modicum of support and reassurance for communities, some of the reporting is over-glamorised and gives a certain indication of politically-motivated or self-serving reports relating to investigation goals, because many results of cases are often prematurely – and hence unwisely – reported. Cross-border operations are one of the main examples of this, whereby the media broadcasting of the seizure of assets in one area merely alerts the criminals in another. Hence the representation of investigation goals and 'results' habitually reflects that investigators often fail to see the larger scenario, or choose to put a stop to a case but on their own politically self-centred terms. Getting the largest slice of the EU budget is also a motivating factor.

London in 2015. Another case in hand as an example of misguided goals and definitional point-stretching is the Conservative politician Jesse Norman who was 'probed' by police over claims he tried to 'bribe' voters with chocolate cake. Not being any kind of political protagonist, it takes just a small element of objectivity to apply this to the points above and see how ludicrous this allegation is. When one attends a business meeting, bowls of sweets on the table are quite a common sight; at events and conferences, large amounts of cakes, sandwiches, pastries, fruit and 'refreshments' are often there. The event is a promotional one of course, added to free gifts of pens, mouse mats, memory sticks, mugs, key rings and others. The attendees are more often than not complete strangers and if the intention is not to develop business and invite new clients then one is not sure what is. But bribery? Therefore to broadcast that a politician is attempting to 'bribe' voters in this context to *that* kind of end result is beyond ludicrous and the most chimerical stereotyping. The knock-on effect is the abject waste of police time, and appalling waste of taxpayers' money. The Bribery Act is not the same as the Representation of the People Act. Practically, if the local community (the voters) do not know the calibre of their local politician or, better put, do not like him or his policies, then they are unlikely to have their political allegiances suddenly transformed and let themselves be politically lobotomised by a piece of chocolate cake. Those who support him will vote for him anyway. But – a bribe?

Hence, to distort and exaggerate the word 'bribe' in a way to suit political or other underhanded motives in a 'mediarised' mud-flinging exercise, is not a proper goal.

The relevance of quoting the above example is to alert you to those who by default distort facts, even words clearly defined in law, such as 'bribe'.

Taking that last example further, when in an enforcement context as opposed to a reporting one, there is the danger of fall-out from it. Certain police investigations are widely condemned as 'witch hunts'. Failure to prosecute one offender often leads to the pursuit of others in a similar group, and they are thereby pre-judged with misplaced assumptions. Pre-judged guilt of offences is fixed at the forefront of investigative thinking before an investigation has even started – by stereotyping. As a result innocent people are spending over a year on police bail before being told there is no further action, which shows a totally crass approach to criminal investigation. It also shows the side motives of some authorities to hide their failure to catch certain criminals by chasing 'others'.

Poor investigation of fraud attracts the same kind of dangers and problems. A former chief executive of a UK hospital, Andrew Breeze was falsely accused of a £2.5 million fraud. The case against him collapsed. 'A case of police of setting out to establish guilt rather than the truth, to construct a case rather than impartially investigate a suspected crime', according to his lawyer. An added complication was using junior detectives more accustomed to murder inquiries to suddenly conduct a so-called complicated fraud investigation (who did not 'know their business') and were led by the 'no smoke without fire' innuendo, but the case ended as it did: as a shambolic embarrassment, and an innocent man severely affected by it.

Finally, let us dispense with the churlish short-cut-to-conviction mentality, whereby one UK local authority benefit fraud team member boasted in the press about IT assisted benefit fraud, 'we don't even have to get from behind our desks'. That kind of very lazy attitude is neither any use to investigations or evidentially to any case thereafter.

The Ethical Rationale of Investigation Goals
- Identifying one or more persons with unique knowledge of the crime.
  - This may not necessarily mean a confession!
- Not being dishonest yourself in trying to prove the dishonesty of someone else (perjury, evidence fabrication).
- Always seek to arrive at the statement of truth in a fraud case which has all other possibilities of doubt removed from it.

'Every truth has two sides. It is well to look at both sides before we commit ourselves to either side'

—*Aesop, Greek author of Aesop's Fables, 620 B.C. – 560 B.C.*

The truth, but which version?

In Chapter 1 we engaged with the 'problem with words' as we all encounter all manner of people who constantly bend 'the truth'. As investigators we have an undertaking to get to the truth.

Versions of the 'Truth'

'We haven't failed, but successfully shown it doesn't work'

—*Boris Veldhuijzen*

Entire newspapers, and publications named 'The Truth' and the 9/11 'Truth Movement', are conspiracy theorists that dispute the media accounts of the September 11 attacks of 2001. Whilst this comment is not in any way disparaging of any of them, we must decide for ourselves, or better put, adapt skill in seeking both actual and natural justice for victims of fraud. Getting to the real truth.

To this end, here we will quickly outline some versions of the truth and what it means in different contexts.

- **Accounting Truth** ('so long as the numbers add up' type truth).
- **Auditing Truth** ('so long as we can tick all the boxes to pass an audit' type truth).
- **Axiomatic Truth** (taken for granted, i.e. 'it seems ok so it must be true' type truth).
- **Mathematical Truth** (highly valuable in fraud investigations, but not on its own. The relationship between mathematical knowledge and knowledge gained from intuition, external fact-finding, and other testimony cannot be addressed by this truth alone).

An interesting modern input about discerning fact from fiction is with the growth of the Internet people are in a unique position to establish things, where previously verifying some claims was difficult for the average person. You need the truth, not a *constructed* truth.

Most fraud cases are decided on a small number of key facts, irrespective of the magnitude of the fraud or the volume of evidence in the case. The main point for me to put here is this:

> The Best Truth is the clinical and unavoidable truth.

How far do you go in an investigation?

This section is to set out a simple ground rule about how far you go into an investigation, and to remove widespread vagueness and uncertainty about the extent of an investigation and, with that point, what kind of *formal* outcome your case will have.

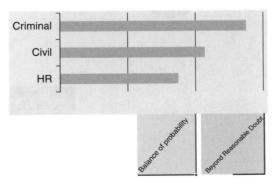

The above will also give indicators of how briskly you need to be able to adapt to a given fraud case. Outcomes of cases will vary and thus your investigation rationale must be adaptable in keeping with both business efficiency and ethical practices.

For example, if you are investigating an internal fraud case where the offender is 'skimming' and you have sufficient evidence in hand to proceed to the outcome stage, is there a need to place a person under surveillance for the next month just to make sure? In a corporate setting, you need to stop the problem and act. The balance of probability standard of proof is met, and thus the offender is dealt with by policy.

Equally on balance, certain enforcement authorities, such as border authorities who deal with tax, VAT and duty issues, being revenue driven, demonstrate a conventional investigational practice of, for example, allowing an offender to continue to smuggle and sell illicit alcohol. The offender is kept under surveillance to allow a case to build, so as to make the offence appear as serious as possible and, at the same time, generate more revenue (and extraneous evidence) by adding this to the court indictment when quantum in lost tax is worked out, despite having ample evidence to arrest and charge the offender already.

All fraud investigations must be proportionate and sensible – and in keeping with human rights laws. Conversely, to say that a fraud case is 'untriable' is to surrender. What is needed is simply to have the right calibre of investigators.

4.3 IDENTIFYING THE ESSENTIAL SKILL SET OF THE FRAUD INVESTIGATOR

'If you can't explain it simply, you don't understand it well enough'

—Albert Einstein

Professional skill set of the Fraud investigator

One point is that investigators need to have a baseline standard in all components of the investigator's skill set. You will excel in some (for example if you work in insurance fraud or trade-based money laundering), but you will never be expert in *all* of them.

The key is identifying with which you are strongest. This may include the fact that you hold qualifications in one or more of the areas, but you may wish to take into account how long it is since you took training or were active in that skill area.

- **You may wish to score from 1 to 5 for how you think you fare in the above skill areas.**
  (5 being the highest)

The industry sector and core competence elements will depend on whether you have an external enforcement investigation role, or an in-house one. If you work for an insurance company for example, you are likely to have a skill correlation between auditing (checking for accuracy of client policies for consistency) with strong policy knowledge and problem solving skills.

Next, is knowing who to involve in an investigation from these areas and at what point in an investigation, if at all.

If you handle a case, and you know your fraud definitions (if you are a 'CFE' for example) you need not go to a lawyer to state that fraud is present, but you may well need a lawyer to examine an involved corporate contract.

Likewise, you are probably more than capable of producing a spreadsheet or a Gannt chart, for example, or a risk assessment report, but intricate IT skills need more specialist application.

Then there are supporting *Application* skills and rationale:
- **Passion** – this is to actually enjoy the challenges!
- **Interest and Inquisitiveness** – questions!
- **Initiative** – take the initiative.
- **Logical thinking, organisation and self-discipline** – be compulsive about checking and re-checking everything you discover, and making sure your case fits together. Remember the legal risks of not doing so.
- **Flexibility** – an investigation can make an unexpected revelation or take new turns.
- **Team working.**
- **Communication skills.**
- **Excellent reporting skills.**
- **Broad general knowledge and good research skills.**
- **Determination and patience** – needs little explanation.
- **Strong ethics** – as alluded to already, rule-bending, perjuring, and recklessly maverick or 'macho' investigation behaviour achieves nothing, other than to get you a reputation you could have avoided by doing the job more simply.
- **Courage** – firmly believe in what you are doing and know why you are doing it at all times.
- Remember: you are only as good as your weakest skill.

Particular talents and skills

'"You will not apply my precept," he said, shaking his head. "How often have I said to you that when you have eliminated the impossible, whatever remains, however improbable, must be the truth?"'

—Sherlock Holmes, The Sign of the Four, Ch. 6 (1890)

'Eliminating the impossible' neatly captures these extended points: that building investigation 'acumen' into the investigation itself will give you a highly valuable additional skill of perceptive thought, whereby you have established the innocent as well as the guilty, and you then can shore up superficial or weak areas in the evidence, ensure that procedure has been followed, and that the chain of custody has no gaps anywhere. Job done.

- **But getting there however needs these elements, with a thorough and discursive treatment of them.**

   Talent. Something you are born with. If you are a musician or an artist, you certainly have a 'gift' which you were blessed with. Therefore 'talent' is your natural ability to do something without really thinking about it. For example, as a soccer fan at Wembley Stadium, I watched in awe as a very young (at the time) Diego Maradona 'dribbled' through an entire team on his own as if they were not there. You cannot coach that kind of talent or you would have a thousand Maradonas. Likewise, Tchaikovsky could not have composed his wonderful music without talent. With that concept, some of the more brilliant fraud investigators are born.

   My friend, Edward Kipngeno Rono was constantly told that his ideas would not work because of corruption. But what he did was build 'IT Skills for Rural Kenya', which became the largest IT community training network in the whole of Africa, creating access to learning and skills for the people in the community who would not have realised this without him. Talent first, skill next, and then unrelenting commitment. Many then commenced anti-corruption projects with their new IT skills. Relevance!

   Skills. 'Skill' is something that you acquire after putting in hard work. This is unlike talent, as it is not inborn, but learned. President John F. Kennedy was a speed reader. He had a talent which he made better by skill. Not everyone is talented, but if you make the effort, you can learn a new skill and yes, there is place for this compartment of working in fraud investigations.

Where skill goes hand in hand with training

Suvorov wrote in Nauka Pobezhdat (The Science of Victory):

'Training is light, and lack of training is darkness. … In the last campaign the enemy lost 75,000 counted, but more like 100,000 in fact. He fought with skill and desperation, but we didn't even lose 500.'

The 200:1 casualty ratio was the direct product of the Russian Army's superior training and organisation.

Formal training and education in relation to exposing fraud is an area we will address closely in Chapter 5. At this juncture we make a natural merging of skills developed by training. Training by thought and by constant application of your skills.

Confidence. Some investigators mistake confidence for showmanship, often by indulging parochial drama in a professional setting. They are too busy showing off. That is why they miss things.

But if you are not confident then you are already at a disadvantage. (Is it for you?) Fear is behind all failure.

Therefore, clearly, training in fraud investigations is not just evidence gathering. One good avenue of training in this context is conflict management training. Imagine the situation when you go to a corporate investigation and you are met on arrival by some *very* hostile individuals who give you all kinds of abuse and accuse you of being some kind of hatchet man (see also Chapter 3 about risk). Assertiveness training between you helps. Also, with reference to training I previously ran, the SAFER model is useful (owned by MAYBO Training):

S	Stand Back	(keep your distance)
A	Assess threat	(because you will get them)
F	Find Help	(if this is necessary then do so)
E	Evaluate	(evaluate what options you have)
R	Respond	(the *right* and professional response then and there)

Training in this regard is so crucial to maintain skills. If you run marathons you need to train, no matter how talented you are. Fraud investigators need to train themselves.

▪ **But for us also, there is a crucial third additive: APPLICATION**

- ▪ This is about *choice* more than anything else.
- ▪ *Choosing* to *apply* the talent, the skill in the right way at all times.
- ▪ This is the point where it goes wrong in investigations for many, both in a personal and organisational context.

In Chapter 2, we appraised the case of Lynn Tilton. Concepts and dynamics of fraud implicitly and unmovably include the fact that successful people and those deemed as criminals, legal and business adversaries (by reason of jealousy or spite) have skills and talents; do not doubt it. The issue lies in the *application*, because some investigative approaches have been disastrous.

Lynn Tilton has not committed any kind of fraud but she was accused of it by investigators who have 'skills' it seems but no talent, or whose application was so unprofessional or wantonly aggressive that the case now stands as it does – in massive litigation. Indeed some of these 'skills' have been highlighted by the exposure of the quirky legal closure tactics employed by the SEC as opposed to getting to any real evidence of fraud. Otherwise they would not be being sued for millions for the incessant repetition of the same approaches and tactics for over 5 years in the same case with the same person.

In the UK, being sued has become the norm for the Serious Fraud Office (SFO) following cases such as the Tchenguiz Brothers, peaking in 2014. The High Court in London concluded that the SFO had fabricated evidence against the two defendants, particularly in the way they obtained search warrants. One of Britain's most senior judges had sat through hours of excuses from SFO lawyers before denouncing the SFO as incompetent (to say the least). Hence the SFO were torn to pieces in court twice, once after the main criminal trial simply collapsed, and then in the High Court when they were sued. The then Chief Executive, Philippa Williamson, resigned in the aftermath of that case (in addition to getting a highly contentious tax-payer funded payoff with other senior SFO colleagues, payments later publicly criticised, and then retracted by the next CEO). The SFO agreed to settle the Tchenguiz Brothers case out of court at over £6 million of legal and other costs to the tax payer. Hence this case, and cases before it have cost the UK taxpayer millions of pounds in a series of botched investigations. Forgive me, but the tired excuse and quasi-political response of 'lack of funding' hardly replaces the need for talent, competent management and having the skills and *choosing* the right *application*, as opposed to false elitism, incessant complaining, investigative malpractice, excuse peddling about how 'difficult' and 'involved' fraud cases are, and 'taking a long time' and a general militant work-to-rule attitude to the good cause of challenging serious fraud. The result being that their successes are a marginalised minority of their case history.

Bernie Madoff had skills and talents, but of course Madoff chose to apply these appallingly for so long to so many victims, but in a similar enforcement twist along the way, there are some profound reasons why it took over 40 years to catch him.

Therefore inflated egos and pretentious or spontaneous responses to the 'can do' cliché will make you uncomfortable from the outset, but to prolong the journey along such a rocky road can lead to disaster. In my situation, I could write out an investigations plan in 5 minutes, but if I were asked to analyse and report on 'meta data' or 'rule embedded analytics' or 'block chain' digital signatures, I will be the first one to say 'I cannot'.

Talent *and the Fraud Investigator* You cannot force a skill into being for yourself if you do not have the talent. Is investigation for you? With our brief but reasonably searching engagement with issues such as stereotyping, this does, as I mentioned, lead to serious problems. Professionals who are in a permanent state of denial about racist attitudes for example, or discrimination or resentment of any kind that affects reasoning, or stretching the laboured point of 'transferable skills' can only hide those for so long before they are exposed.

You must never be critical of anyone in this vocation who admits they are not comfortable with carrying out a fraud investigation, but instead you need to be critical with yourself first of all if you try to kid yourself that you are. Please bear in mind also that the side effect problems (the organisational politics, personal attacks) can be too much. Fundamentally, many people would not be comfortable with the prospect of going into an investigative interview with a bank manager of 20 years' experience who is suddenly suspected of money laundering. So please heed the advice and guidance in Chapter 2 about 'knowing your business' because if you do not you will be eaten alive.

Basic Talent. This is in most of us. For example we know that 3 plus 3 equals 6 and we do not question it, but you would likely find it very difficult to explain why, without *specific talent*. So as a base of inference, in the realm of fraud investigation we need not to go into extraordinary lengths of fact finding, or to mathematician levels of reason and thinking to establish fraud in a case in a balanced legal and business context.

▪ **The moral of that point being, do not over think and do not over explain. Think about what you need to think about and explain when you need to explain in the best and fullest terms required at a given point in a case.**

Specific Talent. This is where we turn in some aspects to the fraud investigator. One could argue of course that learning to drive a car or learning a new language is done from nothing and progresses with training and practice to gain a level of competence. In investigations, this may hold as fair comparison, but only to a point. This is another reason why there is a serious bone of contention about 'types' of fraud, because some types, or better put, cases of fraud demand higher skills than others. Your experience and ability in IT, for example, could entail a role whereby the policy that you follow places a ceiling on the level of certain fraud cases you engage with and to what extent. Or, in a more demanding role situation whereby you perform investigations or provide investigations support across a range of sectors which differ in complexity.

It would therefore be pointless to set out or present a chart of which levels of fraud investigations apply to which kinds of cases. Resources and authorities who deal with benefit fraud for example have a specific remit, but as we have now discovered in Chapter 2, benefit fraud finances terrorism as well. Therefore investigators either need to gain more skills by training, and apply these to the problem, or improve logistical investigation tasks, as it is pointless to identify such a serious problem, which interlinks from a widespread social norm of financial crime to major global terrorist activities, but do nothing to address it other than having a 'fraud awareness week'.

In terms of specific talent, this concept for the professional investigator is essentially made up of two things:

1. **Spontaneity:** Your ability to respond to a situation that sets you apart from standard theorised approaches to investigation. For example, your ability to *delegate* in a fraud case should be instantaneous as you read the scenario before you. Your management talent and skill in this regard should shadow your reading of the case. In a management role, you should not really being going back and starting all over again to

decide who to get involved in the investigation and where in the case and why. You already know.

2. **Creativity:** If you want to be creative and realistic in fraud investigation to benefit co-professionals this is commendable, but please also remember that what you produce has to make sense in business and be achievable and practical.

Creative people bring huge benefits and progress to businesses but managing creativity is something that should not be even tried at all because it cannot be done. Workers congregate around boardroom tables. They think they are having great ideas, but usually they are not. Someone should tell them that you can't schedule inspiration and creativity and that it is wholly unreasonable to expect creativity to flick a switch and the big idea shall spontaneously appear in a 'brainstorm meeting' next Friday afternoon. The irony is that companies actually know they employ people with very active minds, and, many companies talk a great deal about 'fresh thinking' but then try to manage it out, instead of really allowing their staff to tap into intrinsic motivation.

In fraud investigation, there is certainly a place for creativity: in collaboration, meaning working with someone different to you, not what you may first take this to mean. Forming diverse thinking made up of individuals with a wide variety of backgrounds, experiences and opinions that rub against each other is more likely to cause ideas to spark into life.

Creative thinking is also crucial in investigation, because sometimes in fraud there are no mistakes to follow, so you must follow the offender's skill.

Here is an interesting act of creativity:

■ One colleague, Jonathan Le Roux, based in Johannesburg, wrote an article called **'Where fraud is more than just 9 points!'**

In this, Jonathan devised a simple formula to instil fraud awareness for staff, not by renewed policy *ad nauseum*, but based on the famous 'Scrabble' game. His concept is based on the fact that if staff work in a company on their usual jobs, but with lurking fraud vulnerabilities there on a daily basis, they will know but won't readily think of *fraud* cost. So this visual is placed in a way where the points we see on the scrabble rack show business loss and rectification.

Fraud Words		points
l - i- e	=	3
c- h - e -a - t	=	10
b - r - i - b - e - r - y	=	14
c - o - r - r - u - p - t - i - o - n	=	14
s - h - r - i - n - k - a - g - e	=	17
f - a - c - i - l - i - t - a - t - i - o - n	=	17

- If people are unconsciously striving for those maximum points in their 'game' of work. A trigger into the right 'fraudspeak' to get thinking going.
- Following this, the concept that we should be consciously (leading to subconsciously) thinking about the following words when combating fraud:

Correction Words		points
h - o - n - e - s - t	=	9
d - e - t - e - c - t	=	9
e - t - h - i- c - s	=	11
c - o - r - r - e - c - t	=	11
p - r - e- v - e - n - t	=	12

There followed a supporting dual list of scrabble tips applied to business loss to fraud. Example:

> *Scrabble Tip 1:* One triple word score can make or break a game.
>
> *Fraud Tip 1:* One fraud incident in your company can make or break your business image.

We need to reach all involved. So the next time you hear a manager dismissively say, 'just give me the numbers' then here is a workable spontaneous response – brought by Jonathan's talent!

Advancing skill: lateral and cognitive thinking

Cognitive: **of, relating to, or involving conscious mental activities (such as thinking, understanding, learning, and remembering).**

Fraud Investigation: Lateral and Cognitive Thinking

- Starting from the left of the Fraud Investigation figure, a report of **FRAUD** arrives with you. Going horizontally across to the right, this is the *baseline*, which forms and clearly draws your lateral line of thinking.

- Placed on the *baseline* are elements that are *absolutely set* in your thinking. Some 'black and white' elements such as the law form this, and albeit the law is updated and changes, your *thinking approach* to it *never* changes. Moving along the baseline, 'policy' is the same principle.

- When we reach *evidence* and the 'grey area', this is not a confusing area in your thinking. It means that the case evidence can change, for example, by new evidence appearing, such as that data analysis or forensic report you have been waiting for, which puts a whole new slant on the case. Or some other influencing occurrence, such as a witness drastically changing their original account or 'going hostile'. But your knowledge of key evidential rules and principles, the same as the essential elements of your fraud definitions, should be absolutely set and locked into your subconscious. The same with 'facts' and how you think about these. You make a conscious choice to review the law when necessary, and then mentally store it again. Like re-packing your mental suitcase. Then, albeit the 'facts' of a case are reviewed mid-case and change more often than, say, the law and policy, the approach and thinking of them in this context is exactly in the same.

- When we move into a *cognitive* way of thinking, we peel away from the baseline and get to 'information', which is a wider pool of influences in our case and *facts* are taken from it. Then, how you reason this leads to the element of your *enquiries* and how you suspect and apply your scepticism and confront fraud conduct, balanced by how you conduct yourself. This is where you test, probe and thoroughly investigate. Again, your thinking approach is set in line with solid principles of ethics and rule-based protocols (which are often legally-based). The circumstances of the case can change but the black and white position of ethical and professional thought does not.

- The same principles follow all the way to the cut-off point. The *review* along the way does not need to be a complete appraisal of the entire case from scratch. You can save yourself time and maintain your efficiency by applying the Three Cs model again, but this time simply test the evidence against it to first re-affirm that you actually have fraud present as you first thought, or the case is even more serious than when you first took it over, and then you can shore up understanding of the conduct concerned before you present the consequences of it:

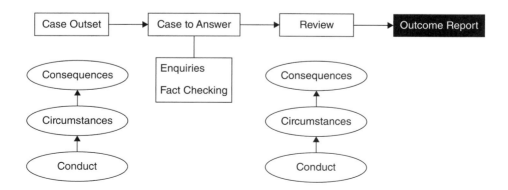

- For the *consequences* part, remember this could equally mean that the person or persons you have investigated are innocent. Part of excellence in investigations is to establish the innocent as well as the guilty. If you 'eliminate the impossible' as was quoted then the innocent parties will be eternally grateful, but at the same time you will avoid some of the highly unprofessional pitfalls in cases that end in embarrassment, before your case turns into a law suit. Some instances and examples of this referenced in this book verify that. Set yourself up in effect to 'work mistakes out' of your investigations as you go. If you make a mistake, which you will at some point, it will be minuscule and openly and ethically correctable.
- The **cut-off point** means exactly that. As an investigator there *is* a point you do not go beyond. You are not judge and jury. You are a gatherer and presenter of evidence. Your outcomes report will be your final input into the matter. Going to court or a formal hearing is part of that.
- If your suspect does have a case to answer for fraud please set out your report as per the later guidance in this chapter.
- Another underrunning advantage or benefit of following lateral and cognitive thinking qualities is that this will also serve to ensure you have kept the chain of custody of the evidence.

- Summary Points: Lateral and Cognitive Thinking. We all think differently. Some people are 'strategic thinkers'. Others are inquisitive by nature. What *investigations thinking* needs is a combination of the two. This is a similar analogy in that if you were an entrepreneur, you will have your business plan in your head. You will have facts, figures, standards, legalities at your conscious level of thinking because a trained mind has placed them there. Figures and financial frameworks should be second nature, even if you are not a 'numbers person'. You will also have the ability to research and analyse as well.
- The same goes for fraud skills. You should be able to explain the basic law and definitions and distinctions of fraud from sharp practice, the difference between fraud and corruption and money laundering, key points of evidence, in clear and simple terms in a brisk manner with no hesitation or doubts. A fraud investigator who cannot do this will struggle in one way or another.
- The reverse logic of working backwards from a result of fraud will in some cases instinctively string together the train of events and metrics of the crime without consciously trying to find 'clues' and red flags. This certainly works in corruption investigations. The assimilation of the information and extraction of the evidence follows.
- Hence, an investigator needs a *trained* mind. Investigations thinking and work is a precise science. It is not, or better put, ought not to be a mundane output of corporate anti-fraud policy or an incidental role that only occasionally materialises from enforcement policy in some police forces and other enforcement organisations.
- You will know your own strengths and weaknesses better than anyone else (and those of your team if you are a manager) and the point is that you will need to clearly apply yourself to dimensions of thinking as put in this section.

An enthusiast trains until he gets it right, but a professional trains until he can't get it wrong!

Here are two brief but useful exercises in lateral thinking. Please attempt the questions first.

Lateral Thinking Exercise (1)

1. Name an ancient invention still in use in most parts of the world today that allows people to see through walls.
2. A black man dressed all in black, wearing a black mask, stands at a crossroads in a totally black painted town. All the streetlights in town are broken. There is no moon. A black painted car without headlights drives straight toward him, but turns in time and doesn't hit him. How did the driver know to swerve?
3. A five-letter word becomes shorter when you add two letters to it. What is the word?
4. In what sport are the shoes made of metal?
5. George and Gracie are found dead on the floor. There are no marks on their bodies. There's a broken bowl near them. What happened?

Lateral Thinking Exercise (2). Fraud

Four men are suspected of fraud. These are the statements made by each of them.
  Bob: 'Dave did it.'
  Dave: 'Tom did it.'
  Gerrard: 'I didn't do it.'
  Tom: 'Dave lied when he said I did it.'
  ■ Which ONE statement is true?
  ■ What kind of evidence will be in effect to prove the case against the guilty man?

Answers - Lateral Thinking Exercise (1)

1. A window.
2. It was day time.
3. Short.
4. Horse racing.
5. George and Gracie are goldfish. Their tank broke.

Answers - Lateral Thinking Exercise (2). Fraud

Hearsay evidence from Bob, Dave and Tom. Comments about Dave lying, Bob accusing Dave and Dave accusing Tom are not said in the presence and hearing of each other.

Then, the statements of accusation from Bob and Dave indicate direct evidence, but are not direct evidence until they are substantiated. Until then the statements are not evidence but information only.

The only true statement is from Gerrard, with his open denial. As yet, no fraud is actually established, merely suspected, so no crime is confirmed. The wording is exact.

If the fraud is then established, it will be circumstantial evidence against all of them which now comes into effect. They all will be suspects of the same crime.

Memory. The better half of intelligence

A key weapon in your investigative armoury is your memory.

> You may want to read this section with cross reference to the investigative interviewing section in this chapter, especially regarding the 'SE3R' model.
>
> Make cross-referral notes in your learning log.

What is very important to state however is that you do not need to worry about approaching every facet as a necessity of remembering things professionally in the same way. Memory is *not* like a computer. More like a 'story' that changes each time. (To bear in mind when dealing with 'eye-witnesses', or non-procedural evidence).

For example the investigator will be selective about these crucial points: What to commit to memory?

▪ How much of it?

▪ Why?

▪ How? How you remember it, to inform future recollection and in what situations.

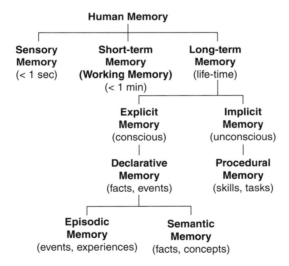

Memory training

This book is not going to venture into extensive memory exercises, but I think its inclusion at least as a topic is important because police officers and most professionals do not receive actual memory training and, as likely as not, neither do you.

For example, if you are studying for an exam you will adapt a form of memory use that is best for you. Educational theorists present learning styles in educational and training contexts. (In Chapter 5, we will engage with some effective exam preparation approaches.)

Filling your memory 'vault' with junk is no good to you or anyone else. Treat the aspect of memory as being the 'better half of intelligence' because it is the intelligent selectivity of memory dimensions and their application that develops you professionally.

If we fit the skill set of the investigator across the elements of human memory you can identify which element aids you best and why.

There are, of course, combinations of the elements that make up your memory.

For example, my dialogues with Umberto Aguilar (Chapter 1) a lawyer at the top of his profession. He displayed all the indicators of a procedural memory (both at work and in crime) and a semantic memory. A man with a massive intellect.

For my part, I can still remember definitions from when I first went to police training school over 30 years ago. Equally, I can remember the latest developments and issues, for example, the latest money laundering directives and their key points. This is not because I am better than anyone else, but because I choose to remember and think about how I remember.

The investigator of fraud, in line with the lateral and cognitive thinking approaches, uses memory effectively.

'Integrity is not a conditional word. It doesn't blow in the wind or change with the weather. It is your inner image of yourself, and if you look in there and see a man who won't cheat, then you know he never will.'

—*John D. MacDonald*

Observing ethical behaviour – not a rule, but a way of life!

A cornerstone of your work is ethical behaviour. You can be the most highly skilled investigator in the world, but if your ethical strand is missing then your professional situation and the implications of that need little explanation.

First some ground rules:

— Ethical Behaviour.

— Do <u>not</u> embellish evidence.

— Do <u>not</u> try to influence the outcomes.

— Do <u>not</u> be personal with your actions.

— Integrity.

— Data Integrity – observe this!

Individual and team dynamics of ethical behaviour are part of your approach to investigations. The worst possible thing in any form of investigations is not to follow your own rules.

Fundamentally, knowing your definitions of fraud is where it starts. As obvious as that may seem, the lesser motivated or ethically-challenged amongst us invariably have a problem with knowing the basic law. The pathway then followed is of guesswork, conjecture, and the more extreme colleagues follow a high-risk existence. Then there are the ones that give up too easily when the fraud or money laundering reporting allegedly gets too complicated or too data-orientated.

There is no shame in getting training or even asking for advice. Cheapening the case by cheating does the fraud victim no good and adds insult to injury when the investigator indulges in unethical practices.

Making the case easier is one, smaller, issue of ethical problems, but making a conscious choice to indulge in full-on investigative malpractice is something else. It is unacceptable, and mostly illegal at the same time.

Reference has been made to some examples of misconduct, but here are the more definitive ones:

- Lying to a client.
- Fabricating evidence.
- Any means of investigative malpractice.
- Failing to conduct due diligence to ensure that the identity of a client is verified and that the client has a lawful purpose to retain and instruct the investigator.
- Accepting bribes.
- Misleading a court, and perjury.
- Failing to ensure adequate security for personal information collected in the course of an investigation, and with that, not taking all reasonable steps to protect against inadvertent or negligent disclosure.
- Using information obtained during an investigation for separate personal gain.

There are many codes of conduct around, which are organisationally specific. You must know yours as well as anything else that matters to you, because a breakdown in ethics does become personal somewhere along the line.

Keeping an investigations log – a must!

This has different names, sometimes called a 'decisions log' but investigations log is a better title because it covers all aspects to support yourself first and foremost, serves as an audit trail and should, along with all other such logs, be analysed with their related outcomes reports and be fed into the future risk and governance policy of the company.

■ **Many investigations fall flat because of poor record keeping and file management. Therefore a log is a crucial underpinning need in any investigation.**

These forms are also used to record evidence and show the procedure followed. For example if an audit was carried out as part of the investigation.

 ## 4.4 'HANDS-ON'

'The worst enemy of the strategist is the clock. Time trouble … Reduces us all to pure reflex and reaction, tactical play. Emotion and instinct cloud our strategic vision when there is no time for proper evaluation.'

—*Garry Kasparov. Russian Chess Grandmaster*

'Respond' – do not 'react'

The great chess players use this maxim. It should also be yours as an investigator. Two basic points are:

■ Do not confuse urgency with panic.
■ Speed is needed sometimes.

Impressions given by some enforcement authorities are so standardised as to give little or no reassurance to anyone who reports fraud. The automated response 'in due course' to a report of fraud usually means little or nothing is getting done about it.

Hence, cyclic investigation response policies and practices usually entail an online or telephone service that merely cattle-herds and treats every case as the same.

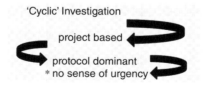

'Cyclic' Investigation

project based

protocol dominant
* no sense of urgency

We discussed earlier about investigation goals. Hence cyclic responses are merely automated and a glorified screening out process.

> The aim after establishing the presence of fraud is to ensure the person committing is accountable for it.

When it gets to actually investigating, this section I hope will guide productivity.

> **'Respond' - Do Not 'React'**
> ■ A general approach is **not** to bring in expert witnesses too early.
> ■ Do not confuse urgency with panic.
> ■ 'Measure' the scale of the problem and turn the issue around in a business-like manner.
> ■ *See the Behaviour – Not the type.*

■ **Speed is needed sometimes in an investigation.**

Aleksandr V. Suvorov, 1729–1800

Arguably the most successful and greatest military commander in history.

The Soviet Army under Suvorov fought 63 battles with 63 victories.

Among those defeated by Suvorov were some of Napoleon's future marshals. Moreover, there is also documentary evidence that Suvorov was feared by Napoleon.

The key to his success focuses on three informing points that are commonly used in business today:

1. Organisational development.
2. Training.
3. Empowerment.

Taking Suvorov's approach a step further, his tactic of 'speed' can be very useful guidance to investigators of fraud when speed (not overreaction) is needed.

Marshal Suvorov's campaign strategies and battle tactics relied on *extremely rapid movement* and *decisive shock*. The enemy (ideally) never knew what hit him.

> 'Money is dear; human life is still dearer; but time is dearest of all. … One minute decides the outcome of a battle, one hour the success of a campaign, one day the fate of *empires*'
>
> 'The enemy doesn't expect us, reckons us 100 versts away …suddenly we're on him, like snow on the head; his head spins. Attack with what comes up, with what God sends; the cavalry to begin, smash, strike, cut off, don't let slip, hurra!'
>
> —*Aleksandr Suvorov, The Art of Victory*

A scenario to start this off is from a standard incoming report of possible fraud and corruption:

Your company has a policy of recording all gifts.

A high value contract has recently been awarded by your company.

▪ **What could be done if the Corporate Hospitality and Gifts Register ('bribes book') was empty even though it was believed that some procurement executives have been lavishly entertained by someone in your company?**

What will be your first response be to this?

Wrong Answer

'I would focus on proving the alleged lavish entertainment took place and then look at whether the procurement policy was followed when the supplier was appointed (tender process not followed, other suppliers not considered, etc.). If you can prove the lavish entertainment took place and that the procurement policy wasn't followed, then I think you can say the evidence indicates bribery. This would then be something the company would have to take very seriously and would highlight the importance of complying with the gifts and hospitality register.'

How on earth will he prove *the* 'lavish' entertainment took place? He doesn't even know what he is looking for. Chasing ill-judged interpretation and evidential problems will waste time.

This response assumes too much. It just states the obvious really.

Another Wrong Answer

'The first thing I would do is to go and check these procurement guys' expenses and phone calls. Check if they were frequently visiting any suppliers.'

The classic default reaction of 'let's jump on the procurement guys'. 'Examining their expenses' and of course, 'see if they were frequently visiting any suppliers'. Not the senior people of course, they wouldn't do such a thing would they? Yes, it's those 'procurement people', it must be them because it says so in the text book that procurement is a 'vulnerable part' of the business operation, so let's wade into them and possibly wreck the investigation, destroy staff morale and alert the offenders – and if it is discovered the offender is someone other than from the procurement team, then under the carpet it goes.

It is also stereotyping and the following of labels and types of fraud – a major mistake. And briskness should not be confused and taken to mean investigative convenience and corner-cutting.

Victorian heuristics at its best – dealing in stereotypes and a clear case of 'confirmation bias' from the outset that will quickly unhinge any investigation.

- *Speed was needed, to strike at the likeliest spots first, but according to the case facts as they are – not jumping at those vulnerabilities which are theorised externally.*

Better Answer

This is more than just checking procurement procedures. There is possibility that someone or some people at senior level are driving or at least indulging or have knowledge of this corruption. On the information we have here, the indicators are clear, i.e. the lack of any recording of gifts in the 'gifts book'. In this scenario the message of the culture of this place sounds pretty much the same, i.e. who has management of the records? Who is accountable for maintaining the 'hospitality and gifts' record? There is clearly no senior oversight of this, a point established by the total absence of entries in it in the face of 'belief' (whatever that is supposed to mean – what form does this 'belief' consist of?).

Going into an investigation like this for me would entail eliminating the senior people first. The most thorough and robust background checking would take place for all senior managers and directors in situ, or those in a position to be influential in the case (not some flimsy due diligence). Establish outside business interests, associations, relationships. Expose conflicts of interest.

Then cross reference against the information stated, i.e. 'it was believed that some procurement executives have been lavishly entertained'. What does this consist of? Does it show a line of communication and substance to connect with a major dodgy deal of some kind? Or an 'apparently' bona fide contract? Eliminating the innocent from the scenario, leaving the information and evidence to show that your wrongdoer (briber) is being selective and particular – and with whom on the 'outside'.

If there is no such evidence present to implicate senior people then fine, but the investigation really should include this if the culture of the organisation warrants it. And even more so, if the culture is not an overarching one of dodgy dealing, the 'rogue' director needs to be weeded out. Eliminate the senior people first.

If there is evidence, then we are looking for the actual existence of some external evidence of a 'result' of the lavish gift or payment: photographs of them together, brief situational surveillance, phone, email interception – establish both the corruption link and its actual, operative existence. If the contract or benefit is in place it needs to be re-analysed for its express terms and how these are 'shaped'. Working back will expose the behaviour that constitutes the bribery and corruption to win that business, by whoever is behind it and whoever is involved with it.

This is not making allegations, this is investigation.

Then, go back to the in-house records and processes, presenting evidence and work backwards to the procurement processes and bids (not being followed) which is primary evidence in its own right, supported by clearly established evidence you have gathered and presented. This will leave a prima facie case to answer.

If the senior person concerned then tried to pass the buck to a middle manager, who was involved in the 'facilitation' or claims to be acting under instructions, investigate those named as robustly as the first ones (and it will be a smaller task but just as important). Then you have ALL the offenders and deal with them. Not just the fall guy who failed to keep a record.

Knowing where to start

▫ **The biggest hurdle most investigators have**

As mentioned, too many overlook the act and art of investigation itself. The dialogue tends to swirl around above in the realm of controls and policy. Indeed, the last scenario above is a classic example of a case which is either simply tossed aside as rumour, with 'no evidence' or simply discarded because of not knowing where to start. Serious fraud could be taking place, but a dappled first response will simply make a mockery of the case. As it stands you will have no idea of the extent of possible procurement fraud and the levels involved.

Naturally, regarding the last answer to the scenario, you could expect some hostile responses, but I would also wager (and have experienced first-hand) that, if done ethically and professionally, the genuine (ethical) and reasonable senior management would support the added value or better put, deeper approach of the investigation – the more thorough and brisk you are, the more respect you get (and yes, I have experienced that) instead of bowling in with conspicuously selective 'leap of faith' investigation approaches.

Here are two simple fraud situations with a suggested investigation starting point:

Insurance fraud.

Hugely inflated claim for car repairs after minor accident.

Start point:
▫ Scene visit to repairer's premises.
▫ Examine garage report of car condition when received.
▫ Compare with claim from customer. Compare any values from both forms also.

Procurement fraud.

Fraud in the post-contract award phase.

Collusion between staff with suppliers to raise and process false invoices, receiving bribes or 'kickbacks' in return.

Start point:
▫ Get hold of invoices (primary evidence) first. A clear objective.
▫ IT audit of procurement process and payments.
▫ Comparing of preferred supplier lists (have these been by-passed?)

The above are simply suggested first steps in possibly a longer investigation.

The 'capability list'

We follow our 'lavish entertainment' scenario with this tactic to *internal* fraud:

Capability List		Fraud present

1 *Intellectual* level of Fraud Offender needed for this case (not 'educational')
....
....
....

Consequences

2 **Experience level in this busines?**
....
....
....

3 *Responsibility level, informing the practical capabilities?*
i.e. can override controls
   Management only access to accounts
....
....

4 **Precise nature of behaviour and value of fraud**
....
....
....
....

The 'capability list' explained   As we know, some rare fraud cases cannot be foreseen, and for a single case, whereby you need to root out the individual (or more than one) offender, having obviously established fraud is present in the case, you can first use the **'capability list'.**

You are compiling a list of names (yes), which builds or shortens as you reach each category.

The concept of the capability list is to make an analysis of who is capable of such fraud behaviour internally. In terms of these two points:

1. Who is or could have been physically present, and 2. Who can carry out *that* fraud?

1 is to bring in some brief profiling skills. IT skills? High literacy levels?
   Add names into your (confidential) list.

2 is to pitch the level of experience, rank, position in the main business.
   Add names into your (confidential) list.

3 is to establish the *business capability* of the offender: Times, dates when happening, work shifts, off sick (if one suspect appears in the above categories but now you find he was off sick during the 'activity times', remove from list).
   Add names into your (confidential) list.

4 is to establish that your thief is being selective. 'Value' means where the offender strikes and which departments in the organisation are the first points of the offender's target. For example, credit office, finance? Other?
   Add names into your (confidential) list.

NOTE:
- **The 'capability list' does not apply in all fraud investigation scenarios.**
- **The 'capability list' does not replace associate analysis and mapping.**
- **The 'capability list' is not accusing anyone. It is to create inroads to the offender.**

- If you have a case of continuing internal fraud which is going on across a range of departments and operations then you need to reappraise your entire fraud prevention policy and investigative capability.

Investigative interviewing

The PEACE Model

- The PEACE Model.
- SE3R.
- Interview, not interrogation.

Interviewing is one of the most critical areas of investigation. Shied away from by those who consider that 'solutions' and data churning are the answer to curing global fraud.

Interviewing: an entity mostly avoided altogether by many who are meant to investigate fraud.

Interviewing: an entity that, if more of it was done more often, would enable us to detect more fraud.

The PEACE Model was developed in the early 1990s as a collaborative effort between law enforcement and psychologists in England and Wales. The model is now used by police forces and all manner of authorities in many countries.

Professor Eric Shepherd (Chartered Forensic Psychologist, Chartered Counselling Psychologist, Chartered Scientist, AFBPsS, FCMI, FCIPD) pioneered a new era in developing skills that were to bridge the gap from traditional policing approaches to interviewing in criminal cases to an iconic and vocationally driven model of excellence. The PEACE Model was conceived as a way to stem the proliferation of false confessions that were resulting from the incessant accusatory style of interviewing, compounded by what can only be termed as legal and professional gamesmanship and trickery and amateur psychological tactics.

The PEACE model holds that a relaxed subject with whom the interviewer has rapport, is more likely to co-operate. It is also far more pleasant for both parties if the atmosphere is not charged with aggression and intimidation. As a non-accusatory model, the PEACE model is considered to be best practice and is suitable for any type of interviewee, victim, witness or suspect.

In his text, *'Conversation Management'*, Professor Shepherd provides the leading authority on investigative interviewing, translated into numerous languages. Of course, the PEACE Model applies to all criminal cases, and for this chapter, I will set out some key benchmarks of the model and then move to fraud-specific issues. The 'SE3R' model to follow is a skill-based resource. Interviewing in person is the major fact finding tool we have to obtain information, reliably establish the facts and ascertain the veracity of statements.

P	**– Planning and Preparation**
E	**– Engage and Explain**
A	**– Account, Clarification and Challenge**
C	**– Closure**
E	**– Evaluate**

Practicalities When entering into investigative interview awareness and training, it is useful to set yourself objectives:

Objectives: you are aiming towards and will be able to:
- Demonstrate new skills in how to appraise information quickly and accurately to prepare and prioritise evidence and information for a subsequent interview.
- Demonstrate competence in obtaining co-operation and putting witnesses and all parties in the case at ease, giving them confidence in you.
- Identify and apply new composite skills in this essential area.
- Overcome some common problems and enhance positive outcomes in an investigation.
- Confidently deal with complex investigations or inquiries that necessitate interviewing.

In a resource book or training approach, it is as equally important to set out the pitfalls of bad interviewing practice, both outside and inside the interview room.

Outside of the interview room, these pitfalls include:
(I have personally witnessed all of these examples that follow, in a range of jurisdictions)

- Lying to suspects about the strength of your case, before the interview even starts.
- Lying to lawyers and representatives of suspects about the strength of your case. Examples being inventing fictitious witnesses or telling them you have evidence which you have not yet obtained.

- Insulting or 'put-downs' of lawyers and such representatives, such as accusing them of 'defending criminals'.
- Refusal to disclose evidence. If you have evidence there is no problem disclosing evidence. What you do not disclose is sensitive information. There is a difference. Furthermore, if you do not have the skill as an investigator and as an interviewer to obtain unique knowledge of the crime from the suspect, you will achieve nothing by being arrogant with the suspect's representative. Please be aware also that there is a legal requirement in many jurisdictions in an enforcement context that you give disclosure of your case before interview (not a list of your intended questions). Likewise in HR, a pre-disclosure letter.
- Bypassing lawyers and representatives of suspects and going directly to suspects and holding interviews which are invalidated. Often, the falsehood of the representative not being available is put forward to further this malpractice.
- In internal cases, managers calling suspects to interviews as supposed meetings under the guise that the meeting is about something different. Then starting questioning the suspect about an issue with no legal or professional basis to it.
- Conversely, HR managers treating witnesses as 'whistleblowers' and circumventing formal HR policies when it is a senior level executive who is the suspected fraud offender (a sure indicator of a Narcissist company culture).
- Selective breaches of data protection laws and unprofessional disclosures of someone being investigated.

Inside of the interview room, these pitfalls include:
(Again, I have personally witnessed all the examples which follow.)

- Comments by interviewers, such as:
  'I have interviewed in many cases, including murder cases, so I know a thief when I see one.'
  'If you don't tell us the truth, you will be dismissed here and now.'
  'Your name has come up.'
  'We know you're guilty, this is your opportunity to tell us your side of the story.'
  'I hereby order you to answer my questions.'
  'I know it's normal behaviour where you come from, but it is unacceptable here.' (Remember stereotyping?)
- **'Closed' legal questions by interviewers, such as:**
  'So what you are saying is that you stole the money.'

Nonverbal communication accounts for 55% of your communication:
- Glaring, finger pointing. Square-on physical intimidation.

Tone is 38% of your communication:
- Shouting, heckling. Threats. Hostile and aggressive questioning.

Your choice of words is 7% of your communication:

▪ 'You are a liar.'
▪ In one case the interviewer, a police officer, was just shaking her head saying, 'lies, lies, lies' whenever the interviewee spoke. A perverse combination of the above problematic approaches.

All the above lead to unreliable confessions.

The Conversation Management Model. PEACE

↙ One useful approach for you is the self-appraisal of skill development as an interviewer. Whenever I conduct a training course on investigative interviewing, I assess and give feedback to candidates on each of the following.

Planning and Preparation	This assesses closely students' application of the PEACE Model and the concepts behind the Management of Conversation Model, including effective questioning techniques, which will expose any deceit or concealment.
Engage and Explain	Did the candidate clearly explain the reasons for the interview and explain the routines to be followed during the interview?
Account	How effectively are ludicrous accounts challenged?
Closure and Evaluation	After each interview is complete, the interviewer will then give a 2-minute explanation to the assessor to place the interview in the context of the whole investigation and review the information obtained along with that already available, giving due consideration to any points required to prove the offence and setting out the next course of action.

The PEACE Model in Action – Suspects

Interviewing: Suspect who answers questions
Interviewing: Suspect who produces a written statement

Benchmarks for you to research further and contained in conversation management are:

Remembering and forgetting offence related experience Telling and listening. Making sense of disclosed detail RESPONSE. Mindful of behaviours for relationship building Managing information Active listening, observing and assessing	Right person, right place, right time questions The right manner of questioning Assisting remembering (cognitive) offence-related detail Responding to inappropriate behaviour Interviewing Witnesses Interviewing the developmentally disadvantaged suspect or witness

From the above list of benchmarks, how would you respond, for example, if a suspect tried to bribe you in the middle of an interview?

▩ Or if you received these responses? (I have received all of these responses in interviews.)
'I had only borrowed the money, I would pay it back.'
'This is in return for my efforts for the business.'
'Nobody has suffered as a result of this.'
'I have taken the money for a good purpose.'
'I did not know that this was a crime.'
'The business had deserved this.'
'Since the business evades tax, I have taken something which was already mine.'
'Insurance is a form of gambling. They know the score.'

Do you sit back and say to yourself that you have a confession and that is enough?
The answer to that should be no. There is an absolute duty to find out why as well as what happened. Certainly at the macro-level, in order to overcome these justifying excuses, businesses should explain ethics rules to employees, inform them that fraudsters would definitely be penalised, establish moral codes in the organisation, and provide training on them.

Likewise, not to act appropriately after this unique knowledge of guilt arrives with you could leave a danger of affecting morale in the company, with a vicious circle of suspicion.

Denial-based responses I have received include:

'You are reading something into this that isn't there.' ...... (a classic)
'The rules are not clear.' ...... (another classic)

Other pitfalls to avoid are:
- Entering an interview with a lengthy list of pre-set questions.
- Leading or 'loaded' questions.
- 'Shoehorning' of facts to fit a particular offence.
- Thinking through the PEACE model will help you 'think out' the pitfalls that are there if you are careless or even reckless with your interviewing approach.

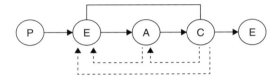

Planning. Would you have a prepared list of questions? If so, what if the suspect simply produces a written statement from his pocket? The point is about appraising the evidence logically, as opposed to being focused on producing questions.

Engage. Which point of the evidence history are you first engaging with and why?

Account. Does the account given make sense according to the evidence, not your own version?

Closure. Does the closure of the interview lead to the need for more enquiries? Or is this the 'cut-off' point?

Evaluation. Not to jump to judgement. The interview needs to be appraised against the other evidence, especially against any testimony that informed the interview. Verbal definitives for one.

Equally, take a determined and structured plan of study and training in interviewing practices.

SE3R – a tool of interviewing excellence

SE3R was also devised by Professor Eric Shepherd. It is a technique that gives the practitioner a sound grasp of, and immediately stores in memory without any conscious effort, the fine-grain detail contained within documents – such as statements – and in verbal exchanges – typically interviews – conducted face-to-face or on the telephone, or recorded electronically.

Because SE3R enables the rapid, comprehensive capture and analysis of fine-grain detail it reveals what really was disclosed, what was disclosed in a vague or odd manner, or not disclosed at all. Using SE3R the practitioner can make a timely response to identified issues and anomalies; for example, through immediate probing, engaging in additional lines of enquiry, and planning and preparing for a subsequent interview.

The use of SE3R has grown steadily within the UK police service and in police forces in other countries. People in all professions can benefit from its use:

- Officers attending basic, intermediate and advanced/specialist. investigative interviewing courses.
- Interview advisers.
- Senior investigating officers.
- Intelligence analysts.
- Officers in major incident teams, those engaged in reviews of unsolved cases, and those investigating specialist areas of crime.
- Call-centre based claims advisers and handlers.
- Members of specialist fraud and investigation units.
- Claims assessors and investigators operating 'in the field'.

SE3R is also used in the banking sector, e.g. to assist in screening for and investigating fraud across the product and service range, and in internal investigations. SE3R is increasingly being used in many countries by staff in multinationals fulfilling a number of key roles.

- Investigators.
- Security specialists.
- Compliance and anti-corruption personnel.
- Control function staff (e.g. conducting audits).

The practice of any professional or institution working with narrative detail and making critical decisions based upon fine-grain analysis benefits from using SE3R.

- Lawyers, legal staff and others – including expert witnesses – working in criminal, civil, and tribunal systems.
- Those engaged with vetting applications and staff.
- Project managers and researchers.
- Healthcare professionals – counsellors and psychotherapists – and academics.

SE3R Main Elements

Key Information and Processing Skills

- Imaging.
- 'Mental echoing'.
- Consciously registering key ideas.
- Regulating the information flow.

Mentioned in Chapter 1 were the following:

■ KNOWLEDGE DETAIL	■ EVENT DETAIL	■ EPISODES AND CONTINUOUS STATES
- Identities	- Actions	- Simple everyday episodes
- Locations	- Interactions	
- Objects	- Reactions or Responses	
- Relationships		
- Routines	- Utterances	
- Rituals	- Verbal Exchanges	
- Plans & Intentions		

COMMENTARY   Feelings, attitudes, disposition, emotion (i.e. 'it's difficult for me to say this') excuse or justification, qualifying (i.e. to modify, to make something less absolute, or to communicate inability, e.g. 'I have done this about 6 times').

- **Irrelevant Detail - WEAVING A TEXT – SUMMARY**
  - People drift or digress onto matters unrelated to the narrative. In spoken text there is a great risk of the teller doing this and weaving in irrelevant detail.
- **Spoken Text - SPONTANEITY AND ITS EFFECTS**

In everyday conversation, a long pause before speaking is a cause for concern. Why the delay? Why does this person have to pick the words carefully before saying them?

The demand for spontaneity, to say something without undue pausing means there is little time to consider in working memory what to say before saying something.

AREAS REQUIRING PROBING   Probing = investigation/questioning to obtain further detail, expansion and/or explanation.

You remember detail without consciously trying to do this.

Basic Tools for creating an SE3R for fraud cases.

- Black Pen.
- Coloured Pens. For example when creating an SE3R or report from a recorded interview.
- Blue = probed detail, red = checking back/final probing.
- Green = information provided by an external source.

SE3R Format Sheets – can be created on a simple note pad.

Event Line				
Knowledge Bin	Knowledge Bin	Knowledge Bin	Knowledge Bin	Knowledge Bin

Applying SE3R to an Interview   One line of thought in helping prepare for interviews is in the institutional context whereby the mind of a fraud offender (it could be argued), is in a permanent state of denial, because what the person has done is not an organisational norm, whether that is against an organisation or, stealing from the employer.

You will of course gain an impression of someone being interviewed, but you need to *objectively review* motivations and methods of the offender.

First, is the generic PEACE Model plan.

Planning & Preparation	Engage & Explain	Account Clarification & Challenge	Closure	Evaluation
Plot events on a timeline for information retention	? Engage in a conversation	Uninterrupted Account	Summarise account for mutual understanding	Evaluate information obtained
	First impressions	? High use of open questions, summaries		? Aims and objectives reached
What is known about interviewee and what needs to be established	? Explain purpose of the interview	? Expanding and Clarifying the Account	? All areas sufficiently covered	
		? Question Loop...	? Explain future activities	? Re-evaluate evidence in investigation
Points to prove, facts in issue	? Reason, routines, outline, expectations	Open, Probe, Summarise as appropriate, Link	? Facilitate positive attitude of	? Evaluate own performance
Identify possible defences	Assess needs of interviewee		accurate and reliable information	? Evaluated by supervisor/ advisor

(Continued)

Planning & Preparation	Engage & Explain	Account Clarification & Challenge	Closure	Evaluation
Practical issues (e.g. where, when, how.....) *Aims and objectives*		*? Done chronologically, methodically* *? Locks person down into their account* *......Clarification & Challenge* *? Challenging the inconsistencies & contradictions* *? Use the words of the interviewee, words of others and contradictory information/ evidence* *? Non accusatorial* *? Ask interviewee to explain the differences between their account and the accounts of others*	*? Review needs of interviewee* *? Maintain professional style*	*? Needed for personal development*

You then use an SE3R sheet to fill in the detail specific to the interview. The closer detail is used in the SE3R framework.

Overview – the SE3R framework

- ■ **S – Survey**
- ■ **E – Extract**
- ■ **R – Read**
- ■ **R – Review**
- ■ **R – Respond**

The SURVEY Stage

- ■ Apply key processing skills.
- ■ Engage in straight through processing of information, i.e. reading the text, or listening to a suspect, witness or victim, or observing the event from beginning to end.

- In a 'real time' interview, getting an uninterrupted first account from the individual.
- If you are receiving a briefing – when there will be only one account – it may or may not be followed by the invitation to ask questions.

Never skip the Survey Stage.

The EXTRACT Stage It is good practice at the Extract stage to tell the victim that you will first listen to his or her account without interruption from beginning to end. Then you will ask them to go through this again, but this time you will make notes (using an SE3R sheet).

- If we refer back to this invoice as an example, and interview the witness *Jane Smith – Accounts Manager, Rorton International*:

You need to

- Disentangle and locate knowledge detail, narrative detail and commentary in the appropriate area of your SE3R sheets

- Respond actively to the detail – annotating as you go along

- Emerge with a sound grasp and memory of what you have captured and annotated.

Event Line				
First contact was made by fraudster to victim on 24 Oct 2009 false invoice	JS suspicious of invoice (red flags) notified accounts director -phone call at first AD calls meeting with JS	checks made -fictitious entries found- examined by forensic expert - no such service supplied	employee suspended on 22 Oct 09	
Knowledge Bin *Victim name* *Rorton International* *-Nature of fraud personally* *Value involved*	Knowledge Bin *witness Jane Smith (JS)* *accounts manager,* *false invoice submitted by the offender–*	Knowledge Bin *how far if at all the* *victim unknowingly assisted offender?* *-not at all* *no interaction*	Knowledge Bin *other issues suspicious only, i.e. mobile phone, dates, needs to be clarified in interview*	Knowledge Bin *suspect is employed by company- probably unaware of discovery yet, but must keep this confidential*

From the above you can be in a clear position to interview the suspect, knowing what is of evidential value and what needs further probing. There is much said and practised concerning 'liars' and 'truth-tellers' and their giveaway signs, but remember that it only matters what you are in a position to prove. Do not always rely on these signs to underpin your case against a suspect. Train yourself to avoid 'relevance filtering' in an interview.

You must **read** any written statement you take from the witness/victim arising from the interview. If the written statement has been taken by another investigator you must accurately assess it against your SE3R notes (and the tape, if it was recorded) as it is crucial for a possible court case that the statement reflects the witness account exactly.

You then **review** - you systematically assess and analyse with a view to instituting action planning.

Action Planning – investigate actions you and others need to take.Who will decide what further action will take place. Be prepared for a court case (civil or criminal, or civil tribunal) – observe ethics policy and professional conduct issues (confidentiality, disclosure, expert witnesses).

▪ **For a more involved fraud case we could use the following scenario:**

CASE **SCENARIO:**

An offender launders the proceeds of organised crime and transfers millions of dollars overseas, transferring the funds over 10 months through his business, a Money Service Bureau (MSB) trading as MSB Helmkunt Forex.

A, part of an organised crime gang, used false documents to claim $90,000 that had been banked by fellow gang member, N. A provided money laundering services for other gangs involved in serious crimes including drug dealing. Investigations revealed A had transferred cash to organisations in Afghanistan, Pakistan, China, India and the United Arab Emirates.

How would you interview 'A'?

IN THIS CASE - EVENTS EPISODES CONTINUOUS STATES
- ■ **Actions.**
- ■ **Reactions.**
- ■ **Responses.**
- ■ **Utterances.**
- ■ **Thoughts.**
- ■ **Reasoning.**

Extended activity, financial transactions, engagement with 'organised' criminals, circumstances, condition or state of affairs.

> Interviewing is **not** easy. It takes training and practice and a discipline to stick to the PEACE Model elements, otherwise an interview can be a very telling and uncomfortable event for all concerned.
>
> The approach *must* be constructive. Otherwise there are serious implications.

'PEACE,' 'SE3R' and identifying unique knowledge

A revisit to the case study from Chapter 2 is used to present an end-to-end investigation plan. In this example an interview component is built into it.

> Miss X held various positions at the apparel company including Administrative Assistant to the President and Director of Human Resources. Her duties and responsibilities included sales and marketing, accounting, human resources, merchandising; and she had authority to approve and sign purchase orders, invoices, and cheques in amounts of less than $75,000, if these matters were in the normal course of business.
>
> For approximately nine years, between 1999 and June 2008, Miss X generated fictitious invoices and submitted those invoices to her employer for payment. Since her duties gave Miss X authority to approve and sign purchase orders and cheques for amounts up to $75,000, she would approve those fake services invoices and ultimately transfer those funds into her personal bank accounts. According to court records, in August 1999, Miss X created a fictitious business entity to facilitate the fraudulent scheme.
>
> The money was used to pay for her son's college tuition and to finance trips to Disney World, the Bahamas, Europe, and Australia. She also installed a $20,000 home theatre system with these proceeds.

Investigation Pathway

The 3 Cs	Capability List	Suspect	Unique Knowledge
Fraud established Results and indicators established, holidays, new TVs, etc. Misreps by forgeries – and at point of submission of fake invoices	Background enquiries to match any other staff who have equal company financial authority Eliminating the impossible – other participants	PEACE Interview. Prepare with direct focus on the potential unique knowledge points If fraud denied, unique knowledge is established but evaluation of interview means more enquiries	Tie in lavish purchases EXACTLY with evidence of fraudulent conduct at work. **It can be established even without the holidays etc.** that fraud occurred if the financial irregularities cannot be accounted for – baseline to open-ended proof **Case established.**

Resourcing

Once you have grasp of the scenario, please do not shoot yourself in the foot by poor resourcing, either by over-resourcing or under-resourcing.

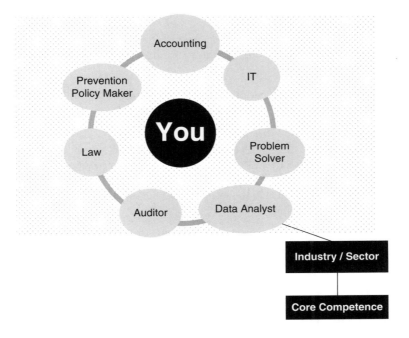

In this fraud scenario, who from the above skill and competence and specialist areas would you bring into the investigation and why? I am purposely using quite an open scenario.

Mr S was an officer and member of multiple business entities that operated and leased gasoline stations in the area.

Mr F was an officer of JSC Corporation, a business operated by S, and also served as a bookkeeper and office manager for several of S's businesses. From 2008 through 2011, F arranged for third parties to negotiate cheques from Sunset Incorporated made payable to JSC Corporation.

The cheques from S, which totalled $845,000, were not properly reported to the accountant and, as a result, were not included as income on JSC's corporate tax returns filed with the IRS. In addition, S and F participated in the sale of a gasoline station owned by one of S's businesses, MTK & KLC Partnership.

They advised the accountant for MTK & KLC that the gas station sold for $175,000 less than its actual sale price, thus resulting in an understatement of income on the MTK & KLC partnership income tax return.

The key to successful resourcing is foreseeing where protocols will be needed (such as court orders), and then analysing how much time, for example, a forensic accountant will need in this case. Guided hours of each response will help prioritise and design out down-time.

Here is the scenario again. But this time, apply fraud concepts *and* time management skills.

Mr S was an officer and member of multiple business entities that operated and leased gasoline stations in the area.

Mr F was an officer of JSC Corporation, a business operated by S, and also served as a bookkeeper and office manager for several of S's businesses. From 2008 through 2011, F arranged for third parties to negotiate cheques from Sunset Incorporated made payable to JSC Corporation.

The cheques from S, which totalled $845,000, were not properly reported to the accountant and as a result, were not included as income on JSC's corporate tax returns filed with the IRS. In addition, S and F participated in the sale of a gasoline station owned by one of S's businesses, MTK & KLC Partnership.

They advised the accountant for MTK & KLC that the gas station sold for $175,000 less than its actual sale price, thus resulting in an understatement of income on the MTK & KLC partnership income tax return.

✓ Certainly in this case, an *independent* forensic accountant will be needed. You may well have essential accounting skills but if you are going into higher levels then you really need to have a specific skill-level expert. It cannot be the same accountant whom the offenders misrepresented to. Instead, the first accountant will be a witness giving both direct and primary evidence.

- Taxation issues can be addressed by the accountant for liabilities and compliance.
- A commercial lawyer will also be needed, but not unless it gets to the point of company documentation being clarified regarding names and trading names, to whittle away any doubts about the companies involved in the scenario (many people in-house do not even know the names of their own companies properly, and the issues of trading names etc.). Some offenders will do this to muddy the waters in regard to the base of the allegations. Remove all doubts at the baseline.
- You as problem solver could then engage in applicable due diligence to establish the officers of each company named. If the above offenders' names are missing this will give further evidence of this case of fraud. The point being that the simple task will be to establish the fraud of the monies, not spending too much time on establishing where the offenders other business interests are. The elimination of all other possibilities will leave the truth of the case.

Scenarios

Definitions: a timely reminder

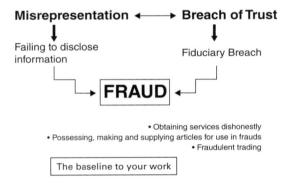

This template could help to put some structure to your fraud case scenario:

3 Cs evaluation:	No Action – endorse case record		
Fraud Not Present			
Fraud Present	Continue below ↓		
Response			
Resourcing Plan Time Lines:			
Investigation steps			

Internal Fraud: Now use the template with this case scenario.

> Miss J wrote 500 cheques amounting to $8.7 million on her employer's bank account to cover personal credit card payments and cash advances between 2011 and 2014, and also used a company credit card to cover approximately $1.3 million in personal expenses.
>
> Miss J hid her theft by forging accounting spreadsheets and destroying bank records.

External fraud attack: Now use the template with this case scenario.

3 -Cs evaluation:	Fraud Present Continue below ↓.		
Response	*Obtain company bank statements – authenticate if necessary*	*Audit of cheque records and cash disbursements* *No further analysis needed at this stage. Retain main records* *Banking cheque clearance procedure needed. Obtain most recent cheques*	*Make capability list* *Eliminate any possible involvement from temporary staff, interns, consultants, previous staff, as far as possible at this stage* *(it is common for offenders to blame outsiders)*
Resourcing Plan Time Lines:	*Forensic auditor (case has already brought out fraud, hence expert needed)*	*Locate handwriting expert (do not involve unless eventual suspect denies writing the cheques)* *Data recovery specialist*	*IT audit* *Need capability of checking spreadsheet document properties and editing of them.* *IP addresses in case any of this was emailed to private email addresses*
Investigation steps *Closure on capability list* *Who has specific authority?*	*Analyse and compare the information from the records as above* *Circumstantial case against one offender.* *Suspend suspect*	*Ask bank's credit card investigator to notify if the suspect was making any payments to personal credit card balances using company cheques*	*Interview suspect* *Ask suspect to account for the editing of the documents* *Account for records that are missing but substantiated by audit* *Establish unique knowledge of the crime.*

Two offenders are targeting law firms.

Offender (1) creates an identical fake website of one law firm. He hacks into the database of the same firm, steals client details from ongoing litigation cases and accesses notes.

Offender (2) makes phone calls to selected clients, saying he is new to the company and their case needs some advance payments to cover disbursements. He tells customers he is not taking payments by phone for 'security purposes'. Telling customers he was new would discourage them checking up.

Offender (2) told customers they would get 'email conformation' and to make a payment transfer to the company client account (which would be on the email sent by Offender (1) in the (fake name) of Offender (2) who called the victims).

Victims paid into offenders' bank account. 5 of the law firm's customers were 'hit' with fabricated legal charges to the amount of $500,000.

Offenders close down the fake website.

3 - C's evaluation:	Continue below ↓		
Fraud Present			
Response	*Meeting with company* *Probe politely into possible collusion*	*Meeting victims – peculiarities of phone call*	*Establish if this is one of many firms*
Resourcing Plan Time Lines:	*IT specialist to take over practicalities*	*Obtain emails from customers – to check sender IP address in subject header*	
Investigation steps			

Unfamiliar cases

Here is an account of a previous case of mine.

Take the case of the crooked field agent who sells bank loans on behalf of banks and does home visits to customers to facilitate a bank loan and also to save the customer going into a branch. The offending agent then uses a customer's name, but uses a fake national ID (knowing very well that the due diligence process back at the bank is, to all intents and purposes, fictional) to get the loan paid to himself. The bank loan is released to the fraudster agent who used a customer's name.

There is no 'scene of crime', there are no 'red flags', so where is the 'trigger point' to ring out to you, the investigator, that fraud has and is possibly still taking place?

1. The agents or 'consultants' are engaged by 'business heads' not by HR or personnel orientated departments, moreover without any kind of process between them (no personnel files for example – just a list of agents' names in a data base, and not kept up-to-date very well).

2. Hence, they are taken on with no due diligence taking place. They are taken on to expedite business development and enhance customer service/convenience. Fine in principle, but the silos in which they work effectively alienate the agent(s) from the bank loan facilitation process. The target-chasing business development functionaries of the bank are not 'thinking fraud'.
3. Consequently, the risk aspect widens, and widens so much that it cannot even be read or assessed how much fraud is actually happening in a simple scenario like this.
4. When loans are not repaid, there is little or no investigation of the reasons why. There could be occasional standard follow up ('arrears' civil actions etc.) but, in the main, the failure to repay any of the bank loans is not normally seen as a 'red flag' for fraud.
5. There are of course, records of which agents handled which loans, but again a cold recording system and who is to say that there is not systemic fraud going on, with agents out there using each other's names and so on? They know the banks and they know that if they keep it vague enough and away from the systems, no one will challenge it.

We are still pursing 'solutions' through either IT systems or suddenly assuming for some reason that it's all about cybercrime and hacking phone apps nowadays.

One bank alone can have over 100 field agents.

Such fraud activity is rampant in some geographical regions, such as in the United Arab Emirates (whereby banks in Dubai commonly use this service, and also in Malaysia). So our straitjacketed thinking in investigating fraud leaves a situation whereby fraud against banks and customers is swirling around but nobody is investigating it. Unlike a scene of crime there are facts to work with, and data, leading to evidence of it. Here in this case, the evidence is there, the 'scheme' is simple, but because the trigger point isn't visibly there like a typical crime 'scene', the case rarely gets investigated, if at all, (because many investigators don't know where to start).

First steps are to visit the customers, the victims (of course the bank is a victim but it is probably fair to say that the customer will have losses passed on to them in some form or another). In any case the most logical starting point for the investigation will be with the customers.

▪ Simple measures like taking any business cards left by the agent.
▪ Description.
▪ Contact local police. This case is of high public interest. You will likely as not get resistance from the banks to this, but it needs to be argued that it is necessary. The police may also have data about 'fake agents' enrolling with banks for this scheme and then disappearing. It is important that some kind of liaison with the local police is made.
▪ Interview bank staff who manage the agent databases. Compare with names of those at customers' houses (if any) to database. Search of due diligence process of applications.
▪ Screening investigations on staff managing databases, associates and possible collusions and kickbacks.

Remember:

- Most criminal cases, including frauds, usually get decided on a small number of key facts. Evidence to support those facts is provided as a consequence of human activity.
- Do not confuse the number of offenders with the number of facts. Capturing the offenders is part of the investigation. The evidence is what it is.

Catching the co-accomplices as well!

There are three main barriers when it comes to identifying – or better put, not even trying to identify – any offenders other than the one that has been caught. Even worse, the scenario when a fraud is reported but there is no heed given to even how many offenders could be involved.

- **Reporting Centres**. Because their processes are so automated, organisations only take reports which fit the process. Hence, narrow reporting and recording parameters are set up so as to suit the organisation as opposed to supporting the fraud victim.
- **Poor police investigation policies.** The insistence of having monetary limits on the reporting of fraud cases inhibits the investigation by reason of policy. Likewise, with the insistence on individual reporting of cases.
- **Poor police investigation practices.** Many police officers have poor investigation skills. I have experienced cases whereby there is clearly more than one offender involved (such as our real estate agent case) and it was a case of saying to the principal offender, 'Did you do it?' 'Yes.' 'Ok, thanks.' The problem is, that that particular case could not have been possible if it were not for another person being involved and balancing the act. Even if the so-called accomplice did not know that his involvement was actual fraud activity, this person should be at least investigated.
- What is made worse is when it is *known* that there is more than one offender involved.

CASE **STUDY:**

The offender, whilst employed at a bank as an Investment Manager, accepted a bribe from a criminal customer to authorise the opening of a new investment account for the criminal who was depositing monies which were proceeds from the sales of drugs.

The offender had full knowledge that the opening balance ($10,000) was proceeds of crime. The offender falsified internal bank records to make the account seem legitimate.

This case involves 'all three' crimes (fraud, money laundering and corruption). The money laundering offence would lead this case, but the internal fraud of the bank records needs investigating.

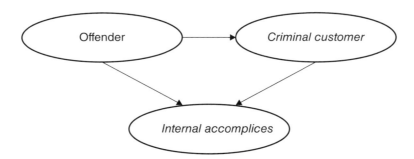

The danger is that this one offender could be one of several targeted in the bank to open accounts or invest in some way. The larger banks have a huge portfolio of business.

First steps will be to suspend the manager and then audit all new accounts and any continuing client relationship accounts being managed. This will be a start to catching accomplices, which is what this case study is designed for.

Then, please be mindful of the fact that there is nothing to be learned or gained by dwelling on the facts you know. If the evidence is continuing, a piece of evidence is not going to change, and going over the same will mean opportunity is lost to investigate the larger scenario.

Interviewing provides a key way into this. Moreover, associations' connections and mapping sometimes entail that some of the offenders are not known personally to each other. Hence the need for skilled IT staff to use advanced IT resources effectively. (See next section.)

Using IT to inform fraud investigations effectively

- @'E-Discovery'
- Data Recovery

'E-discovery' is an IT version of investigating and finding evidence in data format. This refers to the *process* in which electronic data is sought, located, secured, and searched for with the objective of using it as evidence in a civil, criminal or in-house case.

E-discovery can be done offline on a particular computer or in a network. A court order or government sanctioned hacking for the purpose of obtaining critical evidence is also a type of e-discovery.

Data Recovery tends to support 'E-discovery.' Data recovery is usually applied as a technical service in the following instances:

- Deleting files.
- A computer virus.
- A corrupt file system.
- A power outage.
- A forgotten password or data encryption.
- Disk problems, accidental formatting.
- Deleted or inaccessible partition.
- Fire or water damage.
- Short circuit or mechanical problems.

Just as forensic investigators recover evidence from scenes of crime, the data recovery capability will be a valuable physical support from which evidence can be extracted or 'discovered'.

There is also the matter of security. Once a data recovery expert or company becomes involved in a case they will be a witness, providing primary evidence should any of the data they recover be submitted as evidence.

Data analytics: fraud

If you are familiar with identity resolution (i.e. Identity Resolution Engine [IRE]) technology, its strengths address these barriers directly:

1. Volume – IRE can process millions upon millions of transactions daily in the largest and most demanding application environments.
2. Complexity – Non Obvious Relationship Analysis finds hidden relationships, or neural networks, across multiple disparate and remote data sources, including both internal and external data.
3. Eliminating 'clean' transactions and prioritising potential 'dirty' ones.

Data mining

With larger and larger sets of data available to businesses, understanding what is really going on behind a data set and the ability to spot trends and make predictions has become crucial, not only in business but against fraud also. Mathematical and statistical models and associated software are used to analyse big data.

Data analytics in investigations

There are of course excellent texts available on this subject alone. Here are key headings in this context.

Even Amounts A digital analysis technique to identify even monetary amounts, numbers that have been rounded up or rounded down. This is a clear red flag of fraud and should be examined. In practice this could be, example, where financial receipts do not justify the amounts.

Ratio Analysis The calculation of ratios for key numeric fields. This analysis gives pointers of the status of a company, data analysis ratios point to possible symptoms of fraud.

Trend Analysis An analysis of trends across years, or across departments or divisions. These can be useful, not so much in detecting frauds, but as a preventative measure, as this is about *possible* frauds.

Example: in terms of corporate fraud trends and patterns, evidence is used as inferential data and statistics, to infer a fuller picture from sample data.

If you remove everyone with a CEO title that might be the equivalent of a 'middle' or at the very best upper middle management level in a company of any substance, history unfortunately suggests that there is a problem at the CEO level in larger companies. Are there good people at that level? Of course! But let us not kid ourselves that the road to success and virtue don't quite often diverge.

- **Skilful trend analysis does serve a strong purpose in informing investigation.**

Associates and mapping

There are many companies and their technical products that help law enforcement and commercial organisations investigate and combat fraud, money laundering and other criminal and terrorist funding activity.

Good output in this context is whereby clinical fraud research examines the relationship between demographic, social network, and criminal history variables, and the distance between the home and locations of individuals (associates) involved in organised fraud. Specialists from environmental criminology can clinically identify routine activities theories, journey to crime research, and social network analysis in order to explore the geographic and social space of criminal associates. Often, the distance between individuals in a fraud activity network and their associates vary systematically, with network characteristics (centrality measures) but not with demographics or criminal history variables.

Highly technical use of nodes and algorithms accelerates many hours of manual sifting.

 ## 4.5 MANAGEMENT OF INVESTIGATIONS

Baselines of investigation planning

One basic team dynamic that should be settled is that all involved should be speaking the same language. By this I do not mean English or Arabic, I mean the terminology used.

We referred earlier to jargon, such as 'up-coding' and 'unbundling', in healthcare fraud and, if you speak in a language that no outsider understands, then you have a problem. Broken down further there is nothing worse than members of a team all speaking in different terminology. The 'downtime' created is one problem because it wastes time in constant repetition or confusion. But even worse is that it can be possibly damaging to the investigation.

Managers and supervisors really must keep this at the forefront of dialogue and exchange. Fraud cases have enough anomalies within the case as it is, without it being compounded by one or two mavericks who like to indulge in a 'who can talk the most jargon' contest. Likewise speaking to victims of fraud in jargonised language does nothing more than to irritate.

Technical issues need to be explained, as do operational terms. We are not robots, and it is not the suggestion that everyone just quotes definitions. The idea is to have an objective listener understand your meaning. Dialogue must be clear and brisk. Never hesitate to ask for clarification if you need to.

An added danger of course is the case evidence being shaped to such an extent it makes the facts fit. If the case goes to court the term 'procrustean' appears (which is an attempt to force these facts into the language of an Act or policy not designed to fit them), and produces grave difficulties for both judge and jury, which they would not wish to see repeated. Resourcing an investigation at first means human resourcing.

Please remember also that your strengths in your skill set are not always readily shared by others. If you have a good memory for faces and or figures, you need the supporting evidence.

The keeping of that investigations log is a must.

Receiving a case from someone else, or handing a case on

Be clinical, be structured and be methodical at this stage of the case (as you would be in all other stages).

As much as you like, or have worked with, a colleague for so long, the handing on of fraud cases for investigation takeover is a key danger area for more reasons than one.

Taking for granted that the case is sound may be a convenient presumption from an investigation view point, but it can be a costly mistake.

You may say you do not have the time for one-to-one meetings, and the file is just tossed over to you as the colleague is getting out of the door to go on holiday, but you really ought to find the time. It need not take long, merely a brisk handover: looking at the main facts, the evidence obtained, and the evidence still to be obtained. A review of the investigations log will be important.

If, in the unfortunate situation that you take over a case because of illness for your colleague, then you really should conduct first of all a Three Cs can of the case, as though it is brand new and has never been looked at before. There is little point in talking to colleagues going into a sterile discussion of the case, as this will be a form of 'office hearsay'. You need to review the case as it is. This is, if you think about it, a positive team dynamic.

Another good practice (if taking over the case) is to contact the victim(s) and witnesses to introduce yourself. There is nothing worse than a victim of fraud trying to email or telephone the previous investigator and getting no replies. It can lead to relationship problems, an immediate poor impression of your commitment and more time wasted. Take the time to review any statements briefly with them because, with due respect, you may well hear something new, or not quite in line with what is in the case file. Your respect for and familiarity with your absent colleague does not clinically cover previous poor investigation at certain points. It happens. You need to address it, if need be, or, if all is in order in the case, keep up the momentum.

> Be clinical, be structured and be methodical at this stage of the case (as you would be in all other stages).

'The road to hell is paved with good intentions'

—Karl Marx

Managing a fraud investigation's caseload

Even with the most advanced risk management systems there are, this does not always address caseload, and these are not to be confused with each other.

One unfortunate example I can relate to is when training with a police force and I asked the honest question about how many cases a team member carries on average. I won't divulge the number here, suffice to say what I heard was a management issue, whereby every team member can be engaged or 'tied-up' on one single case, and in the team it was a concern that, having gone and arrested fraud and money laundering suspects and seized assets, no other cases were being attended to. That kind of nosedive from busyness to nothingness still amounts to the same state of non-productivity.

- ↗ The above 'sanitised' or coded information is to help you avoid collateral professional pitfalls that can dent your skills and talents.

Equally, if you at least believe that you are so swamped with cases you fall into the 'cyclic investigations' trap and syndrome, this is not so much about not being a good investigator, but not quantifying the case evidence in line with your workload.

In particular in fraud cases, it is always good practice to pin in your schedule your own deadlines just before the formal deadlines, to allow for a final review before the set cut-off point. It looks quite appalling when a member of the public, or worse still, a victim of fraud is told to ring an investigator back to get an update on a case. Failing to plan is planning to fail.

Later in this chapter the 'Assessing your skill set' section, will, I firmly believe, help you with this task here. Please do get involved in this, as it will give you a sense of proportion of time as well as weighing the strength and significance of the different items of evidence and testimony.

Here are some general but useful main tips for avoiding stress in your workload.

1. Plan your time properly.
2. Complete at least one 'quick thing' first thing.
3. Use lists – use that log. It is your friend!
4. Prioritise.
5. Tackle difficult tasks early in the day if possible. Keep to a 15-minute rule for tasks you know can be done in that time (but do not rush appraising case evidence).
6. Talk to colleagues.
7. Utilise supervision.
8. Do not suffer in silence. You are not alone!
9. Never panic.
10. Ask yourself if it is safe not to intervene.

Setting simple and clear team or organisational counter-fraud efficiency

This section is about management oversight of teams as opposed to managing an individual case.

Visual representation to teams works well, to support meetings and briefings. Because policy is an entity that is produced or reviewed periodically, management of investigation teams sometimes can benefit from the so-called 'Discretion Line' approach (as introduced by Lyer, Morino and Frang, 2002).

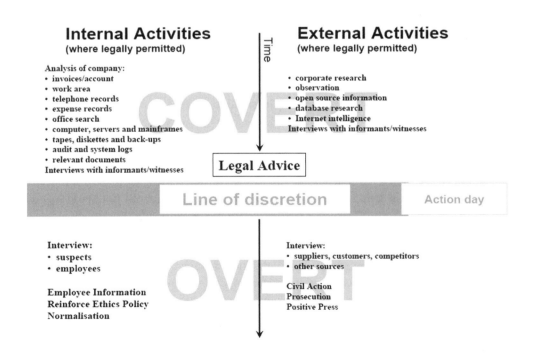

On the left of the model, the accepted usual activities are listed. According to the rationale, a company or enforcement authority should not cross the 'line of discretion' until it is professionally and legally safe to do so.

Another reason why your team must know their definitions as well as they know their own life stories.

Team building skills are crucial to ensure effective investigations

Even if you are not management, an understanding of teamwork best practices is highly useful.

Being part of an investigations team is being part of something larger than yourself and having an understanding of goals.

Team objectives of fraud investigation and prevention

In all, we *must* avoid this ...

The blind leading the blind ...
There are two team-oriented objectives:

1. Company mission, compliance statements and objectives (wider perspective).
2. Task objectives (narrow perspective).

Key Tasks
Setting up a Fraud Response Plan:
To ensure that fraud incidents are investigated in a systematic (not robotic) way.
Responsibilities Clearly Defined

Establish Key Points in an Investigation
But be aware of pressurising. This can lead to corner cutting.

Evaluate Your Resources
Have protocol to meet if, for example, you need to bring in an expert witness.

Know How Far to Go
Instill team consistency in this context.

4.6 ASSESSING YOUR SKILL SET

At this point in Chapter 4 we engage with exercises and activities to assess and develop points of your skill set:

1. **Appraising information.**
2. **Ability to identify, extract and weigh evidence from information.**
3. **Classifying and prioritising evidence in fraud scenarios.**

The exercises to follow are set in order, to correspond with the above.

1 Appraising information

The Three C's model is a basic approach to appraising a case to establish if fraud is present.

Taking a step higher now, we examine how to appraise information when fraud is established.

The analytical mind – preparing yourself

- Learn about problem-oriented analysis.
- How to 'Scan for problems'.
- Defining a problem or reference point.
- Know what kind of problem you have.

> ▪ I have also included a self-check template to enable you to gain a measurement of where you are with certain skills and competence levels.
> ▪ I use these in my training courses and provide feedback on these.

This exercise is to give you practice at the lateral and cognitive approaches.

You have a set of six items of paperwork, which will be typical in a fraud case scenario. You will be required to do the following:

∎ Prioritise the items in a short report and briefly explain why you have prioritised them in the way you have.
∎ Find points of misrepresentation in the items.
∎ Create action points to correct other more involved issues you find in your assessment.
∎ Find the links between certain items.

PRIORITISING THE ITEMS You may, for example, place item number 3 at priority 1, or item number 1 at priority 6, etc. depending on your appraisal of the information and what is required.

THE ITEMS The items will include:

∎ Witness statement.
∎ Data Analysis information.
∎ Phishing Email.
∎ Invoice.
∎ Letter of Complaint.

Items are selected from the above and other, similar items in a variety of fraud contexts.

⊱ **Good technique will use the following structure:**
ISSUES: Identify and note the issues, errors, concerns.
LINKS: Any links with other items?
ACTIONS: What action is necessary and why? Who will carry out the task? Delegation? Report?
PRIORITY: Explain why you have prioritised this item where you have.

⊱ To help you measure and record your response and competence level, I have provided a template below. The items follow the template.
⊱ Take a sheet of paper or your *learning log* to complete this exercise.
⊱ **Complete the ISSUES, LINKS, ACTIONS for each item.**
⊱ If you are in a team, you could assess each other's exercise.
⊱ Following the above, I have set out sample responses to each, and a sample of a feedback report to a student on my training programmes.

Assessment Criteria

POSITIVE		NEGATIVE	
Prioritised the items well.		Showed a poor sense of priority.	
Spotted even minor errors with good attention to detail.		Accepted items without properly checking them.	
Identified the links between the items.		No, or far too few links identified.	
Handled crucial information well.		Little competence shown in this area.	
Identified issues in the items which needed urgent corrective action.		Failed to clearly identify what the issues were.	
Created sound action points to correct the issue.		No sense of urgency shown when needed.	
Takes responsibility for a task when necessary.		Positively avoids responsibility.	
Communicated well when needed.		Communicated with the wrong people.	
Good knowledge of the law of fraud.		Poor knowledge of the law of fraud.	
Appraised the information well.		Was inconsistent or too simplistic with appraising the information overall.	
Other Comments			
Pass		Ref √	Fail

Item: Invoice

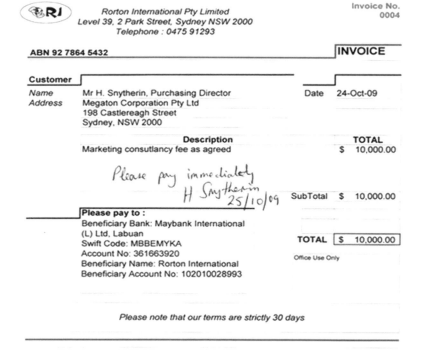

ISSUES:
LINKS:
ACTIONS:

Item: *Witness Statement*

> My name is Mr. Y. I am an internal auditor at XYZ Financial Services LLC.
>
> Last week, I think it was Thursday, I went to our branch office in town to carry out our monthly audit. I parked in the staff car park as usual and as I entered the building, I saw Miss K leaving the building in hurry. She saw me, and suddenly changed direction so as to go away from me in the opposite direction. She was carrying a large office folder; I recognized the XYZ format on it. I thought nothing of it as Miss K was obviously in a hurry.
>
> I went into the office and found that the full audit file for the client expenditure was missing. It contained all the paper invoices for the procurement of regular items of expenditure to support certain clients. I informed the CFO straightaway.

LINKS:
ISSUES:
ACTIONS:

Item: *Letter of Complaint*

> Dear Sir
>
> I wish to make a complaint about a letter I have received from your bank. It states I am in arrears with my bank loan. Account Number: ABC1234-101. I am confused and concerned because I have never taken a loan from your bank. Surely this is a mistake, but please can this be looked into, because I have received a bill for arrears owed, which cannot be right.
>
> Regards,
> A. Customer

ISSUES:
LINKS:
ACTIONS:

ITEM – Phishing Email

Original Message—— From: ATM UNIT-CBN [mailto:cuz550@aim.com]

Sent: Sunday, January 25, 2015 7:28

AM Subject: NOTIFICATION OF YOUR ATM CARD!! ATM Visa/Debit Card Unit, Website: www.cenbank.org Address: P.M.B 0187, Garki Abuja Nigeria. Date: 26/01/2015.

Attn: Fund Beneficiary, The Federal Republic of Nigeria in conjunction of the United Nations have released your Contract/Inheritance/Compensation Fund of $10.5 Million United States Dollars deposited with the Central Bank of Nigeria (CBN) as your Compensation of your recent scam victim by the Nigerian and African fraudsters. Sequel to the meeting held on 1st January 2015 concerning your fund; The President, Dr. Goodluck Jonathan and the UN Secretary General Ban Kin-Moon has ordered for immediate payment of your Contract/Inheritance/Compensation Fund of $10.5 Million United States Dollars through the Central Bank of Nigeria (CBN) without further delay since the fund belongs to you unaccompanied.

On the method of payment; Government of Nigeria and the United Nations has ordered the Central Bank of Nigeria (CBN) to pay your Fund of $10.5 Million United States Dollars through ATM Visa Card which shall deliver to your doorstep by Courier Delivery Company while you cash your fund at any ATM Machine near your location.

How to receive the ATM VISA CARD; you should provide your personal details as follows; Your Full Name; Your Full Address (where you wish to receive your ATM Debit Card); Your Occupation; Your Country; Your Phone Number; Sex/Age; Your Passport or National ID Number; Warning; Due to high rate of internet scam, you are not allowed to pay any upfront fees or advance charges online or to any group or individual because the fund belongs to you. Also, the Central Bank of Nigeria (CBN) will release the PIN NUMBER (secret numbers) of your card upon the reception of your card at your doorstep and the maximum withdrawal of your fund is $10,000USD per day whereas your card will valid till June 2017.

Warning; Due to high rate of internet scam, you are not allowed to pay any upfront fees or advance charges online or to any group or individual because the fund belongs to you. Also, the Central Bank of Nigeria (CBN) will release the PIN NUMBER(secret numbers) of your card upon the reception of your card at your doorstep and the maximum withdrawal of your fund is $10,000USD per day whereas your card will valid till June 2017.

Regards, Dr. Ahmed Ali Director; ATM Unit, CBN

ISSUES:
LINKS:
ACTIONS:

ITEM - Data Set - Fraud Patterns
Node Data Set (ccnodes.sas7bdat)

	7	NODE_ID	CATEGORY	SUBCATEGORY	TYPE	FRAUDULENT_TRANS_NUM	TOTAL_TRANS_NUM	GROUP
75	■	Customer075	Customer	25to34	c	3	15	4
76	■	Customer076	Customer	25to34	c	1	16	4
77	■	Customer077	Customer	Under25	c	2	11	4
78	■	Customer078	Customer	45to54	c	4	17	4
79	■	Customer079	Customer	65andOver	c	2	9	4
80	■	Customer080	Customer	25to34	c	4	13	4
81	■	Merchant0001	Retail	DrugStores	m	0	1	1
82	■	Merchant0002	Retail	FoodStore	m	0	1	1
83	■	Merchant0003	Services	Restaurants	m	1	1	1
84	■	Merchant0004	Services	Restaurants	m	0	1	1
85	■	Merchant0005	Services	OtherServices	m	0	1	1
86	■	Merchant0006	Services	OtherServices	m	0	1	1
87	■	Merchant0007	Retail	General	m	1	1	1
88	■	Merchant0008	Services	OtherServices	m	0	1	1
89	■	Merchant0009	Retail	GasStation	m	1	1	1

ISSUES:
LINKS:
ACTIONS:

> **Below is a sample feedback report issued to a student on my training programme when this exercise was undertaken under examination conditions.**

POSITIVE		NEGATIVE	
Prioritised the items well.	√	Showed a poor sense of priority.	
Spotted even minor errors with good attention to detail.		Accepted items without properly checking them.	√
Identified the links between the items.		No, or far too few links identified.	√
Handled crucial information well	√	Little competence shown in this area.	
Identified issues in the items which needed urgent corrective action.		Failed to clearly identify what the issues were.	√
Created sound action points to correct the issue.		No sense of urgency shown when needed.	√
Takes responsibility for a task when necessary.		Positively avoids responsibility.	√
Communicated well when needed.	√	Communicated with the wrong people.	
Good knowledge of the law of fraud.	√	Poor knowledge of the law of fraud.	
Appraised the information well.		Was inconsistent or too simplistic with appraising the information overall.	√

(Continued)

Other Comments

This exercise is designed to assess both the ability to prioritise and act accordingly in a given situation in fraud investigation and detection.

Student B – performance in this assessment has been 'protocol dominant' which unfortunately has left a number of gaps in terms of lateral thinking.

Priority of the items was sound and logical, but the response is mostly an overview of the items as opposed to a proper examination of them. Comments such as 'this will be done in due course' were put when really, urgent action was needed.

Student B demonstrated a sound grasp of the essential law, but the response falls short when the requirement to discover faults, omissions or red flags was presented. Therefore a lack of willingness to investigate in some skill areas is present. Also avoiding responsibility for a task – even contacting a witness. For example, another entry in the response report states 'I would pass this to my manager' – with no further comment.

The student must engage more confidently with these lateral issues. Also, scrutinise evidence more carefully and be more perceptive of the implications of not acting when necessary.

Pass		Ref √	Fail	

Appendix A: sample response to Skill Assessment

Item: Invoice

ISSUES: Numerous 'red flags'. The hand written request of payment for example contradicts the statement at the bottom of the invoice where it states payments are due within 30 days. No tax details. Bank account number does not tally with beneficiary. Only 4 invoices issued? No details of consultancy work. ABN number does not tally with main bank details (personal account?)

LINKS: Links with statement of witness (Finance Manager)

ACTIONS: Interview Finance Manager urgently. Submit formal data protection request to HR. Confirm 'red flags' and clearly define the presence of fraud. Check invoice process. Check authenticity of billing client. Interview employee. Up-date records.

Item: Witness Statement

ISSUES: Statement contains hearsay, needs clarifying. Good amount of information.

LINKS: Links with invoice and email from Finance Department.

ACTIONS: Interview Finance Manager. Establish actual evidence from statement. (New statement needed?) Suspend employee (does not mean employee is guilty).

If fraud is definitely present be sure to identify the actual offender. Beware of possible malicious allegation (probe previous history between Miss D and employee).

Check loans records – have these audited if necessary to provide informed evidence of opinion. Check payment ledger of admin fees paid for each transaction in period concerned.

Item: Letter of Complaint

ISSUES: Potentially serious and widespread internal fraud going on. Any due diligence taking place of agents? They are taken on to expedite business development and enhance customer service/convenience. Alienated the agent(s) from the bank facilitation loan process. Using ID theft, names of customers to take out bank loans and keep money.

LINKS: None.

ACTIONS: Check policy of engaging agents. Call complainant. Liaise with head of investigations for investigation plan as a priority. Discuss urgently with colleagues.

Item: Data Set – Fraud Patterns

ISSUES: fraudulent transactions. Clear data showing levels in our main customer-driven businesses.

LINKS: Item 3 – Agents using ID theft, names of customers to take out bank loans and keep money.

ACTIONS: create new subject field. Engage IT to assist with internal investigation into bank agents committing widespread fraud – using ID theft. Needs new data capture to establish extent of problem, canvassing customers?

Build into investigation action plan. Can be useful tool for future fraud prevention risk policy.

Item: Phishing Email

ISSUES: Of course you have to provide all of your data and ID to get a new ATM card, the cash of course gets 'couriered to your door' and then you get a new ATM card from that bank with whom you have never even opened an account to withdraw it – 10 million!

LINKS: He may as well have put, 'Dear Sir, I am a money launderer. I also commit ID theft using banks as a cover.'

ACTIONS: Retain item in unused material file. As a precaution, ensure with key contacts that no one has responded to this. Build into investigation action plan. Inform future fraud prevention risk policy. Forward email to IT auditor or forensic data recovery expert if anyone has fallen for this.

Forward email to intelligence handling personnel (circulate to key contacts if independent investigator).

The reports of my death have been greatly exaggerated'

—Mark Twain

4.7 INVESTIGATION OUTCOMES

Report writing

This chapter is rounded by an advisory element with some examples and indicators of reading beyond your investigation and findings in your case, and pre-empting how someone will read and defend the case – and try to undermine it.

Having worked through some approaches and exercises of fraud investigation, we reach the crucial point of communicating. There are many excellent programmes and resources available about effective outcomes reports.

A fraud investigator who cannot report or communicate in writing generally will fail!

Main points of note

This section is to bring out some supporting pertinent points:

(Again, and like the issues in investigative interviewing, at this point I will offer you some personal experience of things to look out for as well as reporting itself. I have seen examples of the issues to follow.)

- Your outcome report will represent your handling of a case. As obvious as that seems, so many investigators overlook this and venture off into a wayward journey of romanticised writing and self-promotion.
- Following on from the above, of course external investigators, auditors, etc. use their letterhead forms, but some venture into inserting sales pitches into their reports. Some even put sales websites in them, which is ridiculous.
- In the outcomes report, if there is no case to answer then say so clearly. The worst thing you can do is to try to colour a report using sniping comments to make it look like someone got away with it. In a formal report, avoid comments like 'he got the benefit of the doubt'. If you were unable to establish fraud in the case then you cannot force liability or guilt into it or tinge the report with personal malice or disapproval. You could also be sued.
- Please avoid childlike posturing in a report, as one I read: *'little did she know that I was on the case'.*
- Equally, refrain totally from using insults and derogatory comments. The fact you are writing about an emotive victim crime does not warrant extraneous loutish additives in a report. Cite words that are applicable or cited by the offenders themselves.
- If you do your enquiries well, you can write in the emotive impacts of financial losses it had, for example. One poor lady in one of my cases had a heart attack because of the stress. Ensure you include such an aggravating feature. Broaden the content to get the full extent of the seriousness of the fraud across at *applicable points* in the construct of the report.

- Likewise, it may well be appropriate to insert what the motivations of the offender were, such as to feed drugs habits or substance abuse.
- Use clear language. Do not use jargon or a technical word unless it is *precisely relevant*.

Avoiding 'bad duplicity'

Bad duplicity is like charging someone with murder and manslaughter at the same time, or back in our context, charging an offender with fraud and corruption at the same time. Unless it is exactly appropriate to include fraud and corruption in one indictment, the main case is led by the most appropriate case evidence, thereby forming the charges. Money laundering is a separate indictment. It is often the case, of course, that a money laundering case will contain a fraud, but the fraud behaviour and evidence derived from it form part and parcel of the overriding money laundering case.

In a similar context to the case referred to in Chapter 1, that of the UK politician jailed for fraud. This was a good (or bad) example of bad duplicity. This term usually applies in an enforcement context when an offender is charged to appear in court. It is really embarrassing that it has reached the stage whereby the defence need to make a submission to the court on the ground that charges have been brought erroneously. In that case, the defence were right and this was endorsed by the judge who ruled accordingly. The case should not have arrived in court from the prosecution in that state.

Hence it is no use talking about 'leaving the law to the lawyers' as I have heard said by senior police officers, because lawyers rely heavily on being instructed correctly by investigators and officers in their reports.

You should apply the above principles in-house also. Bad duplicity causes problems at a crucial stage.

Structures and formats

'Content not form'

1. Compiling a report at the beginning stage. A forward thinking report. How to pull out the best information and structure it. This involves pointing the ways forward and recommending who and what is a priority to be investigated and why.
2. An interim investigation report (mid-way through an investigation as an update).
3. The Outcomes report.
4. Governance and Policy. Compiling a report following a fraud risk or AML assessment or review of procedures. Demonstrating the issues and excellent written presentation of ways forward to improve protection for your organisation.

How are reports read?

Research on how managers read reports discovered that they were most likely to read (in order): the abstract or summary; then the introduction; then the conclusions; then the findings; then the appendices.

This is not to suggest that you should spend less time on writing up your findings. But it does show that the sections you may think of as less important (like the abstract or introduction) are actually often the places a reader gets their first impressions.

Checklist for good reports
- Does it answer the purpose stated (or implied)?
- Does it answer the needs of the projected reader?
- Has the material been placed in the appropriate sections?
- Has all the material been checked for accuracy?
- Are graphs and tables (if used) carefully labelled?
- Is data in graphs or tables also explained in words and analysed?
- Do the discussion and conclusion show how the results relate to objectives set out in the introduction?
- Has all irrelevant material been removed?
- Is it written throughout in appropriate style (i.e. no colloquialisms or contractions, using an objective tone, specific rather than vague)?
- Is it jargon-free and clearly written?
- Has the format and construct inspired been acknowledged with a reference?
- Have all illustrations and figures taken from someone else's work been cited correctly?
- Has it been carefully proofread to eliminate careless mistakes?

Sample report structure

To ensure a high calibre report, the following structure should be followed:

Executive or Background Summary
1. Items of List (Primary evidence, documents).
2. Witnesses.
3. Name of Offender.
4. Facts of case.
5. Victim Impact.
6. Findings.

Good examples of fraud outcomes reports may be found at the Association of Certified Fraud Examiners (ACFE) resources.

CHAPTER FIVE

Training and Education

'Training is light, and lack of training is darkness. The problem fears the expert.
If a peasant doesn't know how to plow, he can't grow bread. A trained man is
worth three untrained: that's too little – say six – six is too little – say ten to one.'

—*Marshal Aleksandr V. Suvorov (1729–1800), 'The Science of Victory'*

 ## 5.1 TRAINING: WHAT DOES IT MEAN TO YOU?

Introduction

Training and some key points:
The above question posed means exactly what it says about what counter-fraud training actually means to all people in all places.

This chapter is about the lifeblood of the investigation capability, but unfortunately the topic of training is as fragmented as the approaches to the topic itself.

Moreover, how far is e-learning effective?

The importance of professional accreditations (supported by continuing development) is included. To help, there is included some pointed guidance in both study skills and approaches to and taking of exams in different formats.

Overall, this crucial chapter urges readers to identify and to pull out the maximum benefit for themselves in finding the right training. I encourage that the investigator *insists* on this at whatever stage in her/his career.

Academic qualifications

If your interest lies partly or wholly in the area of academic study, you are highly encouraged to follow the best possible programme. The emergence of new undergraduate and postgraduate study programmes in cybercrime demonstrate new connections with the counter fraud challenges in hand. Fraud-specific centres of learning and study have helped the academic world make a quantum leap in contributing new emphasis to addressing victims issues (which were either downtrodden or dismissed, not only by the judiciary) and new connections with practitioners. At all levels, this has really gone far in closing that particular divide.

In-house training

Not to be underestimated. As a leading in-house and corporate trainer, I have had more than one 'healthy discussion' with professionals who argue that e-learning has overtaken the need for in-house classroom or personal delivery for two or three-day programmes. My response to that is that such a claim is total nonsense.

Masterclasses are gap-fillers for many professionals and, when delivered well, can bring an intense and focused short programme, which produces high-calibre learning outcomes. It takes a highly motivational trainer to create maximum value. E-learning is effective, but the more cynical suggest that it is good for herding numbers of staff in banks through a programme, to pass an audit for example, in order to get them compliant in as quick a time frame as possible.

In over 20 years of delivering professional training, assessing and lecturing (in universities and colleges) in over twenty countries across five continents, I have had the chance to reinvest massive amounts of learning from colleagues and attendees from all manner of organisations back into operational competencies. It is by only engaging well with local people on localised issues that you can claim to bring something they do not have already, in terms of expertise. Hence, this is the point: there is a balance to be found, in that if you had nothing new or innovative to offer, recipients and professionals in other countries would not invite you to go and train them. At the same time, the biggest mistake you can make is to go with a dogmatic or nationalistic training agenda. I know some superb trainers who make every training delivery fully worthwhile and of value to participants.

Finally at this point, before I am misunderstood to be against e-learning, I am not. In fact I helped design a programme for a large business development team. It is simply that e-learning is as proportionate as any other aspect of training. Theorists introduce concepts such as 'crystallised learning' which are more aligned to realisation as opposed to recital as e-learning promulgates.

Professional accreditations: fraud specific and collateral qualifications

There are now many of these around. Organisations like the ACFE and ACAMS have their own accreditations. You need to first qualify for their accreditation by passing an online multi-choice examination (see below for my study advice).

Also, and referring back to the 'know your business' element in Chapter 2, if you work in a specialised sector or industry, it is well worth supplementing your CFE accreditation, for example, with an accounting qualification, or one specialising in finance.

5.2 PREPARING YOURSELF FOR EXAMS

Multi-choice exams

Unlike the essay style questions, this is not about discussion or evaluation. This format of examination question is to test your problem solving ability, and to vamp up your communication skills. The format is subjective and is designed for you to apply short accurate answers to sudden or brief questions posed.

Hence: PROBLEM = ANSWER in a quick and accurate turnaround fashion.

Multi-choice questions – specific guidance

Focus on accuracy as opposed to volume. The ACFE syllabus for example is comprehensive, so don't try to commit the entire course content to memory.

The aim is to attain an excellent and accurate 'workaday' professional knowledge of this part of anti-fraud work.

- **Separate the topics and your way of thinking with it.**

- Deal with each topic so that you are able to explain it on its own relevance and merits clearly and simply in a few seconds, with no doubts or grey areas.
- Question what you read. Why a particular rule exists for example. What principles are set by it? Does the rule or law you are learning prohibit, compel, or guide? Is it compliance based? Know the differences. You will then remember them.
- With definitions, 'ring-fence' these. Learn definitions until you cannot forget them. Key words will help you.
- For other chapters – 'skills' for investigation: 'pull out' the skills from the content and mentally 'rehearse' these to ensure your new skills are used to the maximum (but kept in legal check). The learning will blend and your knowledge of the strict ethical rules will be accurate and confident.
- Following on from that, clearly identifying types of fraud will come instantly if you have problem solving ability, which you can develop if you study effectively in

dealing with different fraud scenarios or some involved case studies as side-study or practice. This actually saves time in the long run, as opposed to going for endless repetition-reading of the content.

▪ Be careful not to 'skip' or do what we call 'relevance filtering' – memory and understanding are not always the same thing (i.e. don't just *think* that you know it – *know* that you know it).

▪ For the procedural elements such as the law, divide this into the procedural law (which is mostly rule-based) and the substantive law (the Act that creates the offence, for example, which helps you identify fraudulent behaviour in different situations). You can use labelling or mental 'signposting', i.e. question what each point 'triggers' – is it a legal protocol or deadline of some kind for admissibility in court? Is it regulatory? If you are an auditor for example, your procedural capability will be strong on this. Apply it to the exam.

▪ Don't see the study manual as just words on paper: use visualisation and comparatives, and discussion – seeking out and indulging accurate dialogue – keeping accuracy and rationale in mind.

▪ You need both thoroughness and brevity as a study balance. Do not dwell on complicated topics. Identify the elements which will provide understanding and link them in your study. (You will find that this will create understanding for the points you had difficulty with.) Do this and you will build in excellent sharp knowledge as a rounded skill-set into your 'subconscious'. You can then 'recollect and apply' at will.

▪ In regard to the exam itself, in this type of multi-choice exam, some of the option answers are very 'close' or subtle in difference, so it is accuracy that matters.

▪ The manual is set out in a clear and procedural/vocational format which is a big help – but there is a lot of it naturally, so you need to be smart with your study approach. If you read the materials perceptively, with a purpose, and pull out the main points and link phrases, you will deal with the exam more effectively than letting the content simply wash over you. Handle it in small manageable study segments.

When you sit the exam you will know why the answer you chose is right, but also be doubly confident and instinctively know why the other answers are wrong!

▪ **Test yourself with these 3 questions.**

Focus and Accuracy!

1. **Which ONE of these situations will be corruption and not fraud?**
   a. Contract terms 'shaped' to favour a particular bidder.
   b. Misrepresentation of contract terms.
   c. Formal bidding process not followed for the award of a contact.
   d. An external act of bribery to award a genuine contract.

2. **Examine this short scenario.**

T is the Director of a company. He secures government funding for training of his staff (which is over 2,000 personnel). T, instead of using the funding for training, uses the money for other purposes in the business. The company accounts show the funding to be recorded as 'liquid assets' (assets which can be easily converted to cash).

Which ONE of these is the correct answer to this scenario?
a. This is not fraud because the funding is actually accounted for.
b. This is theft of the funding and bad accounting practice, but not fraud.
c. T commits fraud, even though there is no victim.
d. T commits fraud. There is misrepresentation for gain, even though the funding is accounted for.

3. **Which of the following statements, if any, are correct?**
(i) In insurance fraud, evidence of dishonesty in one claim may not necessarily mean dishonesty in another, even if it is a similar type of claim to the previous one.
(ii) It is legal to share information about offenders who commit insurance fraud cases.
   a. (i) Only.
   b. (ii) Only.
   c. Both.
   d. Neither.
(Answers at end of chapter.)

Essays

These are still a standard mode of assessment on academic programmes in universities. Essay questions are in two types, evaluation format, or 'problem question' format.

Typical essay questions – evaluation format

'Definitions of fraud are at odds with each other.'

Provide contrasting examples of fraud cases to support your answer.
(2,000 words)

Examine and explain why social networking creates more opportunity for fraud and thus the creation of more fraudsters.
(2,000 words)

'Information about internal fraud received from a whistle-blower needs to be assessed so as to balance the needs of all involved.'

Discuss.
(2,000 words)

The detection of fraud demands management skills as well as investigation skills.
Discuss
(2,000 words)

'The massive rise in contract management and the outsourcing of goods and services has created an equal increase in procurement fraud.'

—(ACFE Report)

Discuss the above statement and evaluate the effectiveness of measures to prevent and control procurement fraud.
(2,000 words)

The Introduction

- Arouse the reader's interest.
- Set the scene.
- Explain how you interpret the question set.
- Define or explain key terms if necessary.
- Identify the issues that you are going to explore.
- Give a brief outline of how you will deal with each issue, and in which order.

Argument/Main Body

Contains the points outlined in your introduction, divided into paragraphs:
- Paragraph 1 – cover the first thing you said you will address.

The Conclusion

- Draw everything together.
- Summarise the main themes.
- State your general conclusions.
- Make it clear why those conclusions are important or significant.
- Do not introduce new material.
- In the last sentence, sum up your argument very briefly, linking it to the title.
- Set the issues in a broader perspective/wider context.
- Discuss what you've failed to do – answers not clear, space limited.

Final Editing of Your Draft Essay for Structure and Content

Re-read your draft, checking for structure and meaning:
- Does the main body do what the introduction says it will do?
- Is it clear what each paragraph is about?

- Is everything in the paragraph relevant to the main 'topic'?
- Is there enough in each paragraph to support the 'topic'?
- Is anything superfluous?
- Have you cited references correctly and listed them at the end?

'Problem' or scenario questions. The 'IDEA' method

Examinations in law and professional scenarios are still set in 'problem format' as opposed to essay format.

You need to apply your *professional* knowledge to the facts of a scenario and translate the scenario into a *professional* solution.

✦ **An example of a scenario question is as follows:**

X holds a home insurance policy and decides to make a claim based on a fake burglary at his house. X contacts the insurance company to obtain the necessary claim form. X completes the forms, stating that the intruders had broken into the house by forcing the back door, and then listing numerous items as stolen which he does not even own. But X retains the claim form until Y, a builder, visits the house to assess the damage to the door.

Y visits the house and suddenly produces an estimate for repairs from his folder and says jokingly 'here is one I prepared earlier'. Y makes no attempt to examine the back door, and when X checks the estimate, the estimate for costs quoted by Y is five times above the usual price for such repairs.

X now submits the insurance claim form. After the claim is processed, the insurance underwriters insist on having a cheaper and 'more realistic' quotation for the repairs.

Y provides another quotation, this time in a different trading name, and at a lower price quote. The insurance underwriters are suspicious of the new quotation but allow the claim.

X eventually receives payment on the false insurance claim and payment for the fictitious repairs as well. Y makes no money from this situation and says it is a 'customer service support policy' from him.

Discuss and explain the liability for fraud of the parties in the above scenario.

Before going any further, simply jot down your first response to the above scenario:

....

....

....

....

....

A weak answer to the scenario above would be:

> 'X is guilty of fraud, but just for the house items, because the insurance company paid out for the damage but they knew it was an incorrect claim so this can't be fraud .... legally Y hasn't done anything wrong because he didn't make any money out of it, it is just unethical behaviour for a builder...'
>
> A wayward and vague opening that quickly runs out of steam and is on a downward spiral in terms of content and quality.

  .... **Now we can refer to the 'IDEA' method.**

I **Identify:** First, *Identify* the actual presence of fraud and why this is, and by whom.

D **Define:** *Define* the law governing the behaviour and any applicable fraud definitions.

E **Explain:** *Explain* in detail why the parties involved have committed fraud, (or not).

A **Apply:** *Apply* clear conclusions. These should flow clearly from your explanation.

*For the same scenario a response using the IDEA method.

> *Focus on the facts of the behaviour of the parties involved discloses liability for fraud, capable, it will be argued, of being sufficient to prove the case to the required criminal legal standard. There is blatant misrepresentation coupled with dishonesty, which is the principal motivation, practised and acted out by both parties in this case. Suitable tests will be appropriately applied to support.*
>
> *Both parties independently commit fraud by misrepresentation, but also Y knowingly abets X to facilitate his fraudulent claim. To support this answer also, there is clear supporting evidence provided by the presence and use of articles to commit fraud – such as the pre-prepared quotation from Y and the clear mode of planning undertaken by X additional to the actual forgery of the claim form to facilitate the fraud.*
>
> *The insurance company is the victim, albeit there was suspicion of the insurance claim. This will be endorsed by reference to a suitable examination of liability in fraud, whether the 'victim focus' test of fraud is sufficient to prove the offender's liability, as opposed to a commonly perceived standard of the victim having to be deceived. The dialogue that took place between the parties will also add impact to the evidence of fraud (this evidence could be obtained by interviewing them both – based on the documentation). Second-tier or supporting issues such as Forgery (the insurance claim and the two estimates by Y) will be determined if the use of the forged documentation forms part of the fraud case evidence. The application of the correct offence depends on the weight and significance of the evidence of the use of the items concerned. This will be explained and clarified below.*

In this case therefore, it will be argued why X is liable for fraud along with Y, with specific reference to decided cases and authorities, to chart and reference the behaviour of the parties. **(IDENTIFIED)**

Defined legal standards which will establish liability in this scenario are set out in:

[define the applicable law in your own jurisdiction]

Example: Section 34. The Prevention and Combating of Corrupt Activities. (South Africa)

Fraud: It is the unlawful and intentional making of a misrepresentation which causes actual prejudice or which is potentially prejudicial to another. **(DEFINED)**

(Other legal jurisdictions will differ, but the emphasis will be on misrepresentation.)

The two parties involved in the case come to meet in a situation which has been created by X. Their conduct consists of an interplay, which is common to the case scenario. X made the choice to commit insurance fraud and moreover has demonstrated a willingness to engage with and include more activity 'along the way' to reach his goal of fraud, explained by the fact that X delayed the submission of the fraudulent insurance claim until Y came up with the second quote for the repairs. The creation of the second quotation (under a false trading name this time also) reinforces the evidence of intention to commit fraud and 'naturally occurring' evidence that is present.

Simultaneously Y clearly demonstrates an approach and an intention to commit fraud on impulse if the opportunity presents itself. This is demonstrated by the evidence of Y having pre-prepared and highly inflated quotations, which he carries around with him. In situ, Y did not even examine the alleged damage to the door of X's house and simply handed over his fake estimate. It does not matter and is of no legal consequence if Y either knew or did not know that X was himself in the process of committing insurance fraud as far as Y's liability is concerned.

Hence the misrepresentation to the insurance company by Y via X is more than 'potentially prejudicial' and at this point it aligns 'naturally' with X's plans. But on this basis alone however it is argued that Y commits fraud on his own. The fact that Y does not make any financial gain does not negate liability in his case.

X has a case to answer for fraud by misrepresentation and by failing to disclose information material to a claim, which is classified as dishonesty in fraud in itself. The continuing steps X takes to reach the intended result of getting insurance money by fraud outweigh and overreach the lesser effective offences (in this case) of forgery, for example, as it is clear that the documentation is to further the fraud and not simply to mislead on its own, or create some other kind of benefit aside from fraud. The key reference points of X's behaviour to establish his liability are:

The submission of the fraudulent application (the acts of preparation of completing it are passed). Also, the incidence of Y's involvement consolidates the evidence against X yet more.

The standard of legal and industry tests in insurance cases is also satisfied in that the insurance company needs to prove previous dishonesty, not just suspicion, and sets the high standard that dishonesty in one claim does not provide evidence of fraud in another - and has a duty of care to abide by this rule in cases where they suspect wrongdoing (such as the second estimate). Insurance companies can take out subrogation proceedings in such a case, but are unlikely to succeed: HSBC Rail (UK) v Network Rail Infrastructure [2006] 1 WLR 643. Therefore, the insurance company must take an informed risk-based decision. This would explain why they paid the claim.

Likewise the test of 'immaterial' fraud in insurance cases is withstood here, borne out by this expla-nation: 'Immaterial' fraud occurs, where a policyholder acts fraudulently simply to obtain payment of a genuine insured loss. For example, where the policyholder has lost the receipt for a stolen item but, facing pressure from the insurer, produces a forged receipt to make the claim. In X's case, this can be completely negated as false anyway. **(EXPLAINED)**

In conclusion it will not be necessary to prove 'joint enterprise' between X and Y.

A court may infer both direct and primary evidence in this case and convict X and Y on separate counts. The prosecution will be at liberty to adduce and present evidence from the scenario as a whole. If the case is disposed of outside of a criminal justice process, the insurance company can refuse the claim and apply local policy, even if fraud is confirmed. **(APPLIED)**

Scenario Questions / IDEA – Summary

- The key to answering a question of this format is to re-state the question, *but in the legal and professional facts it poses.*
- Avoid using terms such as '*X is guilty*' – guilt is decided in a court, but not all fraud cases reach the courts. Many cases are disposed of by policy or in-house HR procedures.
- Be clinical and objective. Skill must complement process and the law. **Deal with the scenario on the law as it is – not as you think it ought to be!**
- Do not make the classic mistake of dismissing or leaving out a decided case or authority or definition just because you do not agree with it. In fact, you should quote this in your answer, to demonstrate both your knowledge and your ability to apply reasoning and weigh an argument to reach your conclusions in a slick, constructive and business-like manner.
- Therefore 'signpost' the answer, by inserting cases/references and extracts of defi-nitions and applying the strength of their applicability in the case. Cite why one reference is stronger than another to add strength and underpinning content to your answer (keep this brief).
- This an important point because in the event of civil legal actions (aside from breaches of contract) the criminal law standards are referred to in order to establish and define fraud, and the applicable tests are applied – albeit different policies exist in different industries.
- **Know** where to summarise and **know** where to explain and develop. Too much sum-marising will mean brevity at the cost of content and will cost you in marks. On the other hand, too much or over-explanation will swamp the answer (and leave an underlying resentment for the assessor, who has to wade through a pile of amorphous information whilst having numerous scripts to mark – assessors are only human).
- Therefore relevant omission is as crucial as relevant inclusion!
- Be clear in the language you use. Do not write in some poetic or cryptic style which can barely be deciphered by another reader, just as an endearment to scholarship.
- Use technical or uncommon words but only when they are *precisely relevant*. Even then ensure, if necessary, to explain its meaning in the surrounding text.

Answers to Practice Multi-choice questions

1 - d This is a blatant act of corruption with no fraud present. (The other options may contain an element of fraud also.)

2 - d T is liable for fraud. Just because an item is present in the accounts and finance records and documented, it does not disbar possible fraud behind it. T has misappropriated government funding for unsanctioned purposes. Can likely talk his way around an internal audit, but a forensic investigation will expose fraud. If it could also be established that the use of funding and it being accounted has been to cover other debts or credit monetary processes and liabilities, then this will be 'fraudulent conveyance' also.

3 - c Both statements are correct.

Final Summary

*F*raud remains one of *the* most challenging concepts to deal with as a crime. Behind this, many influences spur and invoke thoughts, opinions and reasoning of what 'dishonesty' is in a crime which is all about imputing dishonesty, whether those influences are social (the abhorrence of having such a criminal around in the community), the religious, the loss to your business, legal reasoning, or your own standards of behaviour.

Incidentally, but importantly, not to apply your skills is as pointless as being a concert pianist and never playing the piano. Unless you have personal reasons for not applying your talents and skills, it is an unfortunate discarding of them, both to you and to those who can benefit from you. The world needs competent and committed fraud investigators more than ever.

'Train hard, Fight Easy'

Marshal Aleksandr V. Suvorov, (1729–1800), 'The Science of Victory'

Bibliography

Accounting Principles: Generally Accepted Accounting Principles (GAAP).

Anderson, J. M. (2003) Why we need a new definition of information security, *Computers & Security*, 22 (4): 308–313.

Association of Certified Fraud Examiners, *Report to the Nation on Occupational Fraud and Abuse*. ACFE. 2014.

Association of Certified Fraud Examiners. *Managing Business Risk*. ACFE, 2008.

Audit Commission (1998) *Ghost in the Machine: An Analysis of IT Fraud & Abuse*, England, UK.

Auditing (International Standards on). International Auditing and Assurance Standards Board (IAASB).

Bank Secrecy Act 1970.

Basel III Framework: The Net Stable Funding Ratio. The Basel Committee on Banking Supervision (the 'Basel Committee') published final standards relating to the Liquidity Capital Ratio. January 2013.

Berger, P. L., and Luckmann, T. (1967) *The social construction of reality: a treatise in the sociology of knowledge*, Harmondsworth: Penguin.

Bribery Act 2010 (UK).

Bureau of Justice Statistics (BJS), 2011 /2014.

Burke, R. H. (1998) *Zero tolerance policing*, Leicester: Perpetuity Press.

Canter, D. and Alison, L., (1997) *Criminal Detection and the Psychology of Crime*. Ashgate Publishing Co. ISBN-13: 978-1855214545

Chartered Institute of Professional Development (CIPD). *The Psychological Contract*. CIPD Journal. 2014

City of London Police Insurance Fraud Enforcement Department (IFED) and Association of British Insurers (ABI) *Annual Review* (2012).

Compliance X. Bitcoin Money laundering scheme. http://compliancex.com/two-bitcoin-exchange-operators-charged-in-money-laundering-scheme.

Dark matter: the hidden capital flows that drive G10 exchange rates. Deutsche Bank Market Research Report, 2015.

De Board, R. (1978) *The psychoanalysis of organizations: a psychoanalytic approach to behavior in groups and organizations*, London: Tavistock Publications.

Demetis, D. S. and Angell, I. O. (2006) AML-related Technologies: A Systemic Risk, *Journal of Money Laundering Control*, 9 (2): 157–172.

Dodd–Frank Wall Street Reform and Consumer Protection Act. 2010.

Duperouzel, A. (2003) Anti-Corruption Resource Guide. United Nations Office on Drugs and Crime http://www.unodc.org/pdf/9dec04/resourceguide_e.pdf

Economic Espionage Act 1831.

Esoimeme, E. (2014) *A Comparative Study of the Money Laundering Laws/Regulations in Nigeria, the United States and the United Kingdom.* Eric Press. ISBN-10: 1502784963

Esoimeme, E. (2015) *The Risk-Based Approach to Combating Money Laundering and Terrorist Financing.* Eric Press. ISBN-10: 9789486030

EU Directive on Money Laundering (the 4th Directive, 2014).

EU Directive: Procurement. EU public procurement directive, 2013.

Farrel, S., Yeo, N., and Ladenburg, G. (2007) *Blackstone's Guide to the Fraud Act 2006.* Oxford University Press. ISBN: 978 - 0 - 19 – 929624 - 8

False Claims Act ('FCA'), 31 U.S.C. §§ 3729, et seq. (USA).

Feldman, R. (2009) *The Liar in Your Life: How Lies Work and What They Tell Us About Ourselves.* Virgin Books (Aug. 2009). ISBN-10: 1905264585

Financial Services Authority (UK). Banks guilty of mis-selling. PPI scandal and Barclays Banking Group. http://www.independent.co.uk/news/uk/politics/exclusive-new-bank-interest-rate-protection-scandal-as-big-as-ppi-9558029.html

Financial Action Task Force (FATF). Money Laundering. http://www.fatf gafi.org/pages/faq/moneylaundering/

FireEye, Inc. *Spear Phishing Attacks – Why they are Successful and How to Stop Them. Why Automated Analysis Tools are not Created Equal.* (Whitepaper) 2014.

Fitzgerald, D., and Dutton, T. (2013) Arrest First, Ask Questions Later? *Criminal Law and Justice Weekly.* (Case of Tchenguiz).

Foreign Account Tax Compliance Act (FATCA) 2010. (USA)

Foreign Corrupt Practices Act 1977 (FCPA).

Fraud Act 2006 (UK).

Freedom of Information Report re: City of London Police and Action Fraud (UK). 2014.

[Prepaid] Fraud Mitigation: Leveraging the Processing Relationship to Prevent Fraud Throughout the Prepaid Lifecycle. Conducted by Javelin Strategy & Research. October 2009

Goldstraw-White J. (2011) White-Collar Crime: Accounts of Offending Behaviour. Basingstoke: Palgrave Macmillan, 2011. ISBN: 9780230355521

Gudjonsson, G., and Copson, C. (1997), *Criminal Profiling: Is it useful?* Psychology Research.

Hopkins, B. (2013) *The Patterns of Big Data.* Forrester Research, 2013.

Handy, C. B. (1993) *Understanding organizations,* London: Penguin.

Hurtt, K. (2001) Auditing: Development of an instrument to measure professional skepticism.

Ioannou, M., and Hammond, L. (2015) The Detection of Deception Within Investigative Contexts: Key Challenges and Core Issues. *Journal of Investigative Psychology and Offender Profiling.* Volume 12, Issue 2, pp. 107–118.

Jewkes, J., and Mayid, Y. (eds) (2010) *Handbook of Internet Crime.* Willan Publishing. ISBN: 978-84392-524-8

Katz, N. (2012) *Detecting and Reducing Supply Chain Fraud.* Farnham: Ashgate Publishing Ltd, 2012. ISBN: 9781409407331

Kaupthing Bank Hf. Iceland. Tchenguiz criminal trial. Serious Fraud Office. http://www.bloomberg.com/news/articles/2012-04-04/sfo-refused-trial-delay-as-it-probes-tchenguiz-arrest-errors

Kets de Vries, M. F. R. and Miller, D. (1984) *The neurotic organization: diagnosing counter-productive styles of management.* San Francisco: Jossey-Bass.

Ketz, E. (2003) *Hidden Financial Risks: Understanding Off-Balance Sheet Accounting.* Wiley. 2003.

Knetzger, M., and Muraski, J. (2008) *Investigating High-Tech Crime.* ISBN-13: 978-0131886834

Konrad Adenauer and Stiftung. Media Training Programme for sub-Saharan Africa. 2014.

KPMG – Global Anti-Money Laundering Survey 2014.

Krix, A. C., Sauerland, M., Lorei, C., and Rispens, I. (2015). Consistency across repeated eyewitness interviews: Contrasting police detectives' beliefs with actual eyewitness performance. *PLoS ONE*, 10, e0118641. doi:10.1371/journal.pone.0118641

LaFree, G., Miller, L. and Dugan, M. (2014) *Putting Terrorism in Context. Lessons from the Global Terrorism Database.* Routledge.

Law of Money Laundering promulgated by Royal Decree No.34/2002. Sultanate of Oman. 2013.

Leedom, L. (2014) A criteria for antisocial personality disorder. *American Psychiatric Association's Diagnostic and Statistical Manual of Mental Disorders, Fourth Edition (DSM-IV).*

Leslie, Ian. (2011) *Born Liars,* Quercus publishers (May 2011) ISBN-10: 184916424X

Levi, M. and Rueter, P. (2006) *Money Laundering.* Copyright 2006 by The University of Chicago. 0192-3234/2006/0034-0004$10.00

Longworth, P. (1965) *The Art of Victory: The Life and Achievements of Field-Marshal Suvorov, 1729–1800.* Holt, Rinehart and Winston.

MAYBO Training Organization, specialists in Conflict Management and originators and copyright owners of the MAYBO 'SAFER' model of dynamic risk assessment for risks of violence in the work-place.

Menning, B. W. (1986) 'Train Hard, Fight Easy': The Legacy of Field Marshall A. V. Suvorov. *Air University Review*, December 1986, pp. 79–88.

Murphy, P. (2007) *Murphy on Evidence.* Oxford University Press. 12th edition (2011) ISBN-10: 0199594678.

Newburn, T. (2007) (ed) (2013) *Criminology*, Abingdon: Routledge, UK. ISBN 9780415628938

(House of Commons). Norfolk and Norwich University Hospitals Trust. Andrew Breeze. www.edp24.co.uk, 17 June 2009.

Norris, F. (2013) In China, Detecting Fraud Riskier Than Doing It. *New York Times.* nytimes.com/2014/08/29

Oeberst, A. (2012) If anything else comes to mind . . . better keep it to yourself? Delayed recall is discrediting: Unjustifiably. *Law and Human Behavior*, 36, 266–274. doi:10.1037/h0093966

Ormerod, D. (2011) *Smith & Hogan's Criminal Law*. Oxford University Press; 13 edition (28 July 2011) ISBN-10: 0199586497

Police and Criminal Evidence Act 1984.

Proceeds of Crime Act 2002.

Prosecution of Offences Act 1985.

Racketeer Influenced and Corrupt Organizations Act (RICO) 1970. (USA).

Regulation of Investigatory Powers Act 2000 (UK).

Ross, I. (2012) The complexities of online fraud: beyond mere prevention. *e-Finance, Law and Policy Journal*, issue 10. October, 2012.

Ross, I. (2015) *Intellectual Property Theft: 'The Hidden Business Crime.'* DSC Publications Ltd. 2015.

Ross, I. (2015) *Social Media and Fraud: 'The Bigger Picture'*. DSC Publications Ltd. 2015.

Ross, I. (2015) *Narcissist Leadership and Inevitable Fraud*. DSC Publications Ltd. 2015.

Saleh, A. (2011) The Choice of Law and Dispute Settlement Resolution in Islamic Cross Border Finance Transactions. *Islamic Financial News*, May 25, 2011 volume 8, issue 20. 2011.

Samonas, S. and Angell, I. (2009) The Risk of Computerised Bureaucracy. *Journal of Information System Security*. Volume 5, Number 2 (2009) pp. 3–25. ISSN 1551-0123. Publisher: Information Institute Publishing, Washington DC, USA.

Sarbanes-Oxley Act 2002 (USA).

Serious Crime Act 2015.

Serious Fraud Office (UK). SFO make Public apology to Robert and Vincent Tchenguiz. http://uk.reuters.com/article/2014/07/31/uk-britain-settlement-tchenguiz-idUKKBN0G00SD20140731

Serious Fraud Office (UK). SFO ordered to the Old Bailey to explain bungled Tchenguiz investigation. Report, *The Telegraph*, May 2012.

Shepherd, E. (2007). *Investigative Interviewing: The Conversation Management Approach*. Oxford University Press. ISBN 0199214093, 9780199214099

Shepherd, E. (2001). 'SE3R': *A resource book* (4th ed. 2008). Forensic Solutions Ltd

Sullivan, B., Freilich, A. and Chermak. M. (2014) *Financial Crimes Perpetrated by Far-Right Extremists in the United States:* 1990–2013. The National Consortium for the Study of Terrorism and Responses to Terrorism (START). Science and Technology Directorate of the U.S. Department of Homeland Security. University of Maryland.

Sutherland, E. H. and Cressey, Donald. (1992) *Principles of Criminology*. 11th edition. Lanham, Md.: AltaMira Press, 1992. ISBN 0-930390-69-5

Suvorov, A.V. *The Science of Victory* (*Nauka Pobezhadt*).

Transparency International, Corruption Perception Index. 2014.

Tsirin, A. (2014) *'The Fight Against Corruption Being Waged Only On Paper.'* Cited in the International Program for Monitoring Corruption project (MONKOR), http://www.rferl.org/content/corruption-russian-monitoring-eurasia/26972282.html

Tsouras, P. G. (1992) *Warriors' Words – A Dictionary of Military Quotations*. London: Cassell Arms and Armor Press

United Arab Emirates, UAE Law No. 24/2006. Consumer Fraud. 2006.

U.S. Securities and Exchange Commission (SEC).

Walden, I. (2010) *Computer Forensics and the presentation of evidence in criminal cases.* (Cited in Jewkes and Yar) Willan Publishing. ISBN: 978-84392-524-8

Wrightsman, L. S. (2001) *Forensic Psychology*, London: Thompson Learning.

Zur, O. (2012) Rethinking "Don't Blame the Victim": Psychology of Victimhood. *Journal of Couple Therapy*, 4 (3/4), 15–36. Haworth Press, Inc.

TABLE OF CASES

Hayward v. Zurich [2015] EWCA Civ 327 Neutral Citation Number: [2015]. Court of Appeal. Case No: B3/2013/2789

Miller v. Minister of Pensions [1947] 2 All ER 372

R v Da Silva [2006] EWCA Crim 1654, 11/7/06. Court of Appeal

R v IK [2007] EWCA Crim 491, 8/3/07

Stoll v. King, 8 How. Prac. (N. Y.) 299) (USA)

Svanoe v. Jurgens, 144 111.507, 33 N. E. 955; (USA)

Tchenguiz v Serious Fraud Office. High Court of Justice (Queen's Bench Division) Divisional Court. 31/07/2012. Neutral Citation Number: [2012] EWHC 2254 (Admin) Case No: (I) CO/4236/2011 (II) CO/4468/2011. Royal Courts of Justice Strand, London, WC2A 2LL.

Tchenguiz and others v Grant Thornton UK LLP and others (Proctor, third party). Neutral Citation Number: [2015] EWHC 1864 (Comm) XCN2015-1131

Index

Compiled by INDEXING SPECIALISTS (UK) Ltd., Indexing House, 306A Portland Road, Hove, East Sussex BN3 5LP United Kingdom.